New Mexico 2050

NEW MEXICO

2
0
5
0

EDITED BY
FRED HARRIS

University of New Mexico Press | Albuquerque

20   19   18   17   16   15   1   2   3   4   5   6

LIBRARY OF CONGRESS CATALOGING-IN-PUBLICATION DATA

New Mexico 2050 / edited by Fred Harris.
pages cm
Includes bibliographical references and index.
ISBN 978-0-8263-5555-3 (pbk. : alk. paper) — ISBN 978-0-8263-5556-0 (electronic)
1. New Mexico—Economic conditions. 2. New Mexico—Social conditions.
3. Education—New Mexico. 4. New Mexico—Environmental policy.
5. Indians of North America—New Mexico. I. Harris, Fred R., 1930–
HC107.N6N415 2015
330.9789001'12—dc23
2014042899

COVER CLIP ART © 1990–1992 RT Computer Graphics
COVER PHOTOGRAPH BY Lila Sanchez
AUTHOR PHOTOGRAPH COURTESY OF Shauna Bearman
DESIGNED BY Lila Sanchez
COMPOSED IN Optima and Adobe Garamond

CONTENTS

New Mexico 2050?

A Prefatory Poem

Hakim Bellamy

New Mexico has been called
lots of things
by the Upper 48.

My favorite
is "recession proof."
Like some sort of backhanded condiment,
like vinegar, when I ordered chile,
like drought, instead of "desert,"
like climate change for dinner
instead of rain for breakfast.

But "mean"
is not what they mean.
When poor is the new normal,
you can't feel the economy flatline.
Just like you couldn't feel it
when it was booming.
Just like the bottom of the ocean
unmoved by the waves.

What they meant
is "irrelevant,"
even "insignificant."
Because we take everything
as a compliment.
Because at 2050,
with the oldest state capital in the country,
we look damn good for our age.

Compared to their Dow Jones Average
we are finally exceptional,
breaking the curve
one border at a time.

36 years from here,
New Mexico will still be exotic to others
and enchanting to us.

We'll still be inventing
new names to call ourselves.
Still be creating new races
every monsoon season of love.

New Mexico will still be magic,
Like a horizon-taut canvas
making something out of nothing.
Pulling a rabbit out of the mesa
waiting a sign, with both ears
to the sky.

Nothing under its sleeve
but sacred heart ink.
Acequia Sangre underneath
its adobe-flavored skin.
Hungry for the snowpack
to finally shed a tear.

As the highways grow
wider and western than the Rio.
As the river banks
collapse like a recession
in vein.

As the scales of justice
elevate us out of poverty
instead of shackling us to it.

As the education system
weights opportunity
over place of worth.

As the sites
become more sacred,
and the sacred
becomes more scarce.

New Mexico will endure,
evolve and enchant,
as it has always done.
Under many different names . . .

But what about
the *Nuevomexicanos*?

Preface

What Can We Be? What Will We Be?

FRED HARRIS

THE *PAST* IS PROLOGUE. TRUE. AND SO IS THE *PRESENT*. BUT in New Mexico, neither of these is necessarily destiny.

A local announcer once opened the great annual Montana Crow Indian Fair Rodeo with the words, "Ladies and Gentlemen and all you white people, we have cowboys here tonight from all over the world—and many other places!"

Well, I'm not a cowboy exactly, not an Indian either, but I've been nearly all over the world, and many other places, and I've never found any place I like as much as New Mexico. That's the truth.

We've got our problems. Everybody knows that.

And maybe people say that we've made our own bed. But we don't have to lie in it. The problems we have here in this wonderful state were by and large made by people. And they can be solved by people, too. That's what this book is about.

A blueprint for New Mexico's future.

A handbook for New Mexico's leaders and public officials, present and potential.

A textbook for New Mexico's students.

A sourcebook for New Mexico's teachers and researchers.

A hymnbook for proud New Mexicans who want our beloved Land of Enchantment also to become the Land of Opportunity, fully and for all.

■ ■ ■ ■

That, I am sure, is what John Byram, the dedicated and farsighted director of
the University of New Mexico Press, had in mind when he asked me to organize, produce, and edit this book, *New Mexico 2050*. And that's what I, too, had
in mind when I agreed to take on the task, after adding in my own mind a
theoretical subtitle for the book: What Can We Be? What Will We Be?

With a grant (for which we're most grateful) from the McCune Foundation to assist with project expenses, I set out to find recognized New Mexico
experts in each subject field.

And I found them: our contributors. All of us went to work. And it has
been a labor of love.

This is an honest book. I asked the contributors for each chapter, first, to be
descriptive—to say frankly and plainly what the present situation in New
Mexico is—about the economy, for example, or the environment. And they
have done that. They tell what our liabilities are, of course. But they also tell
what our assets are.

This is a courageous book. I asked the contributors for each chapter,
next, to be *prescriptive*—to say fearlessly what we need to do in New Mexico
to make things better. They have done that, too.

And this is a hopeful book. I asked the contributors for each chapter,
finally, to be *predictive*—to say optimistically what the well-informed and
wise people of New Mexico, and their leaders, can and will bring about in
our state's future. And the contributors have also done this.

Here in New Nexico, our ability to do what needs to be done is, of course, very
much dependent upon our state's economy. That's why we've placed first in this
book the solidly researched and excellently stated work of two outstanding
economists—Lee Reynis of the University of New Mexico and Jim Peach of
New Mexico State University—their chapter, "New Mexico Economy."

The highly damaging and growing income inequality in our nation and
in New Mexico is a problem that necessarily threads through virtually every
chapter of this book, but chapter 1 deals with it first and quite centrally—

setting forth the alarming dimensions and terrible effects of income inequality as well as how it can and must be ameliorated.

Chapter 1 is enriched by the addition of two sort of "guest essays," one by Henry Rael on tradition-based, culture-based economic development, which he knows so well, and the other by Chuck Wellborn, who knows as much about fostering and nurturing homegrown industry as anyone going.

Quite obviously, the most fundamental thing we must do in New Mexico—for ourselves and our state, for our kids, and for their kids—is to improve and invest more generously in education outcomes, to invest in our own people. No New Mexican, nobody anywhere, knows this subject better than Veronica C. García, a lifelong educator, an education policy expert, and a passionate education advocate—the author of chapter 2, "New Mexico Education."

Health is as important to New Mexicans as education, maybe more so. That's why we got the most knowledgeable person we could find to write chapter 3, "New Mexico Health and Health Care"—Nandini Pillai Kuehn, a committed and richly experienced New Mexican. And she deals with this complex subject with great understanding and unusual clarity.

Demographics may be as determinant for New Mexico as our DNA, and politics is the way we can do something, not just stand there. We were so pleased, then, when New Mexican Gabriel R. Sánchez, a first-rate and nationally recognized political scientist, aided by Shannon Sánchez-Youngman, an outstanding political science doctoral student, took on the vitally important task of researching and producing chapter 4, "New Mexico Demographics and Politics."

Chapter 4 is enhanced by an accompanying essay on African Americans and other minorities in New Mexico, written so convincingly by the popular attorney and activist Pamelya Herndon.

New Mexico is mostly called the Land of Enchantment because of our precious land, water, and environment. Noted environmental journalist Laura Paskus and Adrian Oglesby, a water law and water management expert, tell us, expertly and well, how, in the face of dire threats and harsh challenges, we can keep New Mexico a Land of Enchantment and make it even better—in chapter 5, "New Mexico Environment and Water."

We knew that if we were going to put first things first in this book, we had to spotlight first Americans, first New Mexicans—as we do in chapter 6, "New Mexico Indian Tribes and Communities." And we turned to the one person who could best produce that chapter, Veronica E. Tiller, a tradition-grounded and superbly educated Jicarilla Apache who is the editor and publisher of the renowned and award-winning reference guide to 362 American Indian tribes, *Tiller's Guide to Indian Country*. She expertly tells us all we may hope to know, ought to know, about New Mexico's Native Americans, and she shows us how they can lead us all into a more satisfying and rewarding shared future.

V. B. Price is more than an authority and an advocate in the field of New Mexican cultural affairs and the arts. He is an icon himself, a New Mexican work of art and a treasure. In chapter 7, "New Mexico Cultural Affairs and the Arts," he focuses our attention on how much the "creative workers," those working in the arts and culture of our state, are a central part of what makes New Mexico New Mexico—what makes us want to live here, what makes people want to come here, what valuable contributions these creative workers make to our economy, and how much more they can contribute if we will but more fully support and encourage them and fund what they do.

A professional planner by trade and recognized for being brilliant at it, New Mexican Aaron Sussman not only makes chapter 8, "New Mexico Transportation and Planning," required authoritative reading for anyone who wants to know all about New Mexico and New Mexicans right now—where we live, where we go and how, who we are, and what we can and should be in the future—but he also puts it all down in a such a marvelously cogent way that he causes us to really enjoy ourselves while we're learning.

And finally—and I should have, in fact, put this first—Hakim Bellamy, the great Albuquerque poet laureate (2012–2014) has, in his wonderful and challenging prefatory poem, "New Mexico 2050?," put a serious query to us that we undertake in this book to respond to in a sound and inspirational way.

Read on.

Chapter 1

New Mexico Economy

LEE REYNIS AND JIM PEACH

NEW MEXICANS DESERVE BETTER. NEW MEXICO CAN DO BETTER.
This is a state with abundant natural resources, including oil, natural gas, coal, copper, uranium, and potash. New Mexico has been a major contributor to technological change, especially since World War II. Two of the most important inventions of the twentieth century, the atomic bomb and the personal computer, originated in New Mexico. The state is home to two national laboratories (Los Alamos and Sandia), three major research universities, and hundreds of private firms involved in high-technology activities. New Mexico exports a variety of products and services to the rest of the nation and around the world. The people of New Mexico are hardworking, energetic, and innovative. Individually and in combination, these economic development assets should be indicators of an extraordinary economic development success story.

The New Mexico economy has grown considerably since the end of World War II. Except during the 1960s, New Mexico's population and employment growth rates have been higher than the comparable national figures. Yet New Mexico has not realized its full economic potential. In 2012 New Mexico ranked forty-third among the fifty states in terms of per capita income.[1] New Mexico's per capita income in 2012 ($35,079) was 82 percent of the national average. Around fifty years ago (1962), New Mexico's per capita income ranked thirty-ninth among the fifty states and was also 82 percent of the national average. For the last five decades New Mexico's per capita income has ranged from 75 to 82 percent of the national average.

New Mexico has also been slow to recover from the severe national recession that began in December 2007. While New Mexico was not as severely affected as many other states, as of December 2013 the state had 38,700 fewer jobs than it had in December 2007 and had experienced no growth in employment since the official end of the Great Recession in June 2009. Unless New Mexico employment growth accelerates, it may be 2017 or 2018 before New Mexico has as many jobs as it did in December 2007—that is, it may experience a decade with no job growth. It will have been lost in the dust by its fast-trotting neighbors and virtually every other state in the country.

New Mexico's economy lacks one or more leading sectors that can bring dollars into the state and generate growth in other sectors. The state depends heavily on federal government expenditures and primary commodity exports, such as energy, minerals, and agriculture. The national political environment suggests that the state can no longer depend on federal government expenditures as an engine of economic growth. A history of repeated cycles of boom and bust should make us cautious about hitching the state's future to oil or other commodities. Rather, we should use the revenues generated wisely and invest in the future but not plan on a continued bonanza. New Mexico, like other states, has a rapidly growing health- and educational-services sector, but this sector can be an engine of growth only so long as it brings in resources from outside.

New Mexico's economy can perform better than it has. New Mexico must prepare itself to compete for jobs and income in a twenty-first-century economy—an economy that is increasingly dominated by technological change and international trade. A prosperous New Mexico economy—one that provides the opportunity for jobs and adequate income for all New Mexicans—requires, among other things, substantial investment in its physical and human resources, the development of a leading sector or sectors, major changes in state and local policies, significant efforts to reduce income inequality and regional disparities, and a systematic and comprehensive long-term economic development strategy.

New Mexico can create the conditions needed for long-term economic growth and development. Other states and nations have done so. If New Mexico is to become an economic success story, the required investments and other actions will be the result of deliberate (public and private sector) policy decisions within the state. We must do it ourselves while recognizing the limitations of state and local efforts. Individual states do not conduct fiscal and monetary policy. Individual states do not control the demand (or prices) of their export commodities. But individual states, including New Mexico, can have a profound influence on economic development policies that matter.

Now we want to address: (1) the current state of the New Mexico economy, including the history and structure of major industries; (2) obstacles to economic development, including inequality, poverty, and rural-urban disparities; and (3) policies to promote a healthy New Mexico economy in 2050.

The Structure of the New Mexico Economy: An Overview

The industrial structure of the New Mexico economy and the national economy differ greatly. As measured by employment in 2012, New Mexico depends more heavily on public sector employment (23.2 percent) than does the nation (16.0 percent).[2] The mining sector accounts for 3.1 percent of total New Mexico employment but only 0.6 percent of employment at the national level. Conversely, manufacturing employment in New Mexico accounts for 3.8 percent of total employment, while the comparable figure for the nation is 9.0 percent. Differences in industrial structure help explain differences in growth rates between the state and the nation as well as state and national differences in income per person. If New Mexico had the same industrial structure as the nation, the state's growth rate would be very similar to the national growth rate. An analysis of selected major industries in New Mexico follows.

Agriculture

The historical importance of the agricultural sector is illustrated by the trend in farm earnings as a percentage of total New Mexico earnings from 1929 to the present (figure 1.1). In 1929 farm earnings accounted for almost one-third of total New Mexico earnings, including compensation and self-employment income. Farm earnings were sometimes as high as 20–25 percent of state earnings in the 1930s and 1940s, but in the early 1950s they plummeted to between 5 and 10 percent. Since the mid-1960s, however, farm earnings have been consistently below 5 percent of state earnings on an annual basis, and since the 1980s they have rarely averaged above 2.5 percent.

Figure 1.1. New Mexico farm earnings as a percentage of total earnings, 1929–2012

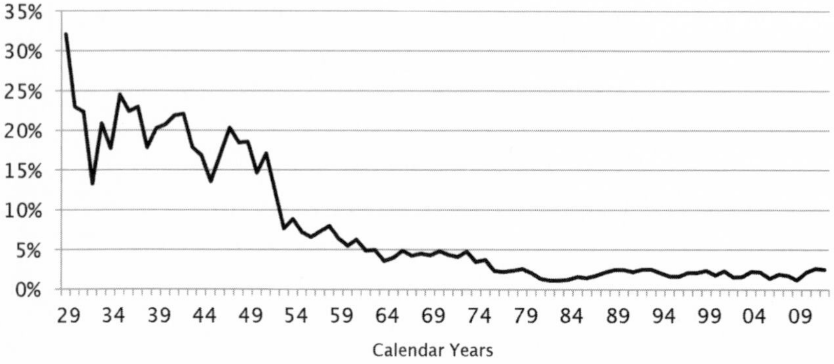

Source: U.S. Bureau of Economic Analysis

This is the case despite the emergence of the dairy industry in the late 1980s. New Mexico made a deliberate attempt to develop an industrial cluster that would support an emerging dairy- and cheese- product industry as well as produce a market for New Mexico alfalfa. The growth of the dairy industry explains about 80 percent of the growth in alfalfa production.

A 2005 report from New Mexico State University noted that New Mexico "has been one of the fastest growing dairy states."[3] According to the most recent data from the Dairy Producers of New Mexico, the state has "approximately 150 dairies and the largest average herd size (2088) in the nation."[4] In 2014 the state was ranked ninth in the nation for milk production and fifth for cheese.

There is no question that the dairy industry has brought economic benefits to the state. The question is at what cost. Tight regulation might minimize the threats of groundwater contamination.[5] Unfortunately, production of milk and cheese based on alfalfa takes an enormous amount of water. In its milk and cheese exports, New Mexico is effectively exporting water.

Energy and Minerals

New Mexico is a state rich in natural resources, including timber, agricultural resources, oil, natural gas, coal, uranium, copper, and potash. In 2011 New Mexico ranked sixth in the nation in the production of crude oil, produced 5.3 percent of the nation's natural gas, and ranked fourth in installed photovoltaic capacity.[6] In 2012 New Mexico ranked first in the nation in potash, perlite, and zeolite production and third in copper production.[7] The extraction and use of these resources provides important economic benefits, including employment, income, and tax revenues for New Mexicans.

The New Mexico oil and gas industry is one of the most important sectors of the state economy. In 2013 the value of oil and gas production in the state exceeded $15 billion; directly and indirectly, the oil and gas industry accounted for more than 30 percent of state revenue, and it directly employed more than 18,500 workers.[8]

OIL

Oil production in New Mexico began in the early 1900s. Data on the production of crude oil in New Mexico goes back to 1924, when the state produced 98,000 barrels.[9] New Mexico oil production peaked in 1969 at 129.3 million barrels.[10]

Beginning in 1970, New Mexico oil production began a long decline, falling to only 60.1 million barrels in 2008. Many observers of the New Mexico oil industry in the 1990s and early 2000s assumed that the decrease in production was an irreversible long-term trend. Peak oil was upon us. The only question was how long it would be before we "ran out of oil." But by 2013, New Mexico oil production went up again, reaching 97.6 million barrels—nearly a 60 percent increase since 2009. In 2014 New Mexico oil production exceeded 100 million barrels—a figure not reached in forty years.

Nearly all (95 percent) of the increase in oil production in New Mexico in recent years has occurred in Eddy and Lea Counties. The boom in production is the result of relatively high and stable prices and several advances in oil exploration and extraction technology. The best known of the technological advances are hydraulic fracturing—fracking—and horizontal drilling, but many other technological changes also contribute to increased production, including advances in seismic testing, digital mapping, more efficient drill bits, and dozens of others. The technological changes are not limited to New Mexico. The combination of new technology and relatively high prices has resulted in a dramatic increase in oil production in many areas in the United States and in other nations, a phenomenon called a "hydrocarbon revolution."

Whether the increase in oil production in New Mexico (and elsewhere) can be sustained for many years is an unanswered question. In the New Mexico portion of the Permian Basin (Eddy and Lea Counties), proved reserves seem to increase each year despite increases in production. There are large untapped oil reserves in the San Juan Basin in a geologic formation known as Mancos Shale, which may be brought into production in the next few years. Some estimates suggest that the Mancos Shale may contain as many as six billion barrels of oil, enough to extend current New Mexico production levels for about sixty years. Current obstacles to increased production in San Juan County are a lack of refining capacity and transportation infrastructure.

Some observers are less optimistic and point to rapid decay rates (the rate at which production from a new well declines). This fear may be exaggerated. But there are other reasons for tempering optimism. Armed with technology, the United States has led the hydrocarbon revolution but the technology will spread. Shale oil is not unique to the United States, and worldwide competition will grow.

NATURAL GAS

The natural gas industry is closely associated with the oil industry, and the two are represented by the New Mexico Oil and Gas Association. While many wells produce both commodities, the two industries differ in several respects. Both oil and gas are hydrocarbons, but they are not perfect substitutes and they respond to different market forces. Frequently the term *natural gas* is a reference to dry natural gas, but natural gas liquids are growing in importance. In New Mexico most of the oil production is from Eddy and Lea Counties, but these two counties also produce substantial amounts of natural gas. San Juan County produces a lot of natural gas but, as yet, very little oil.

New Mexico produced 27.93 billion cubic feet of natural gas in 1935.[11] By the early 2000s, New Mexico was producing 1.6 trillion cubic feet of natural gas per year, and state revenue from natural gas greatly exceeded oil-based revenue.[12] New Mexico natural gas production has been declining since 2007 due to low natural gas prices.

COAL

New Mexico has been producing coal for more than a century, but more than half of all coal mined in the state has been produced since 1993. Between 1882 and 2012 New Mexico produced 1.05 billion short tons of coal.[13] In 2012 New Mexico's four active coal mines produced 22.5 million short tons of coal.

Most of the coal mined in New Mexico is used for electricity generation. In 2012, 68.2 percent of all electricity generated in the state was from coal-fired plants (24.994 gigawatt hours), but electricity production in the state, as in the nation, is relying more and more on other sources, particularly natural gas.[14] This trend results from environmental regulations and low prices for natural gas.

Employment in the state's coal-mining industry has been declining, reflecting the dual effects of changes in mining type and technology and of decreases in production. Today's coal miner in New Mexico produces about thirty-five times as much as a coal miner did in 1934. State revenue from the severance tax on coal production has been decreasing in recent years due to production declines, as well as to changes in coal severance tax rules.

URANIUM

New Mexico was the largest producer of uranium in the world from the 1940s to the early 1980s. New Mexico's uranium production peaked in 1978 at 17.1 million pounds of triuranium oxide (U308). Employment in New Mexico's uranium industry peaked in 1979 at nearly eight thousand employees.[15] Production and employment dropped rapidly in the 1980s as national demand for uranium declined after the Three Mile Island incident and with decreased demand from the Department of Defense. By 1992 mining operations had essentially ceased in New Mexico and only minor recovery operations continued.

New Mexico's uranium reserves are the second largest in the United States, after Wyoming.[16] As of 2014, several companies were exploring the possibility of opening new uranium mines and milling operations in New Mexico. The possibility of renewed uranium mining in the state has generated a great deal of opposition from Native American and environmental groups, understandably concerned about the uranium industry's legacy of environmental damage as well as deaths and long-term disabilities from mining in the 1950s and 1960s.

RENEWABLES: SOLAR, WIND, AND GEOTHERMAL

Generation of electricity from renewable energy sources in New Mexico grew rapidly from 2003 to 2013 and will continue to grow as a percentage of total generation. In 2003 New Mexico generated 88.0 percent of its electricity from coal and another 10.7 percent from natural gas.[17] There were no solar or geothermal generation plants, and the state's first wind-energy generation facility, the New Mexico Wind Energy Center in De Baca and Quay Counties, had just opened, with a tiny capacity of only 204 megawatts.

By 2013 coal accounted for 67.1 percent of electricity generation in the state and natural gas accounted for another 25.1 percent. Wind generation increased from less than 0.1 percent to 6.1 percent of the total. Solar generation reached 1 percent, and the state's first geothermal electricity generation plant opened in Hidalgo County in late 2013.

In New Mexico as in many other states, the expansion of renewable electricity generation has been stimulated by state and federal subsidies, rapid decreases in capital costs for solar, and the development of renewable portfolio standards (RPS). An RPS is "a state policy that requires electricity providers to obtain a minimum percentage of their power from renewable energy resources by a certain date."[18] New Mexico, thirty other states, and the District of Columbia have adopted RPSs in one form or another.[19]

Under the provisions of the RPS today, New Mexico investor-owned utilities are required to generate 20 percent and rural electric cooperatives to generate 10 percent of their total retail sales from renewable energy resources by 2020. Sources can be solar and wind, at least 20 percent each, with geothermal, biomass, and other contributing at least 10 percent. The renewables industry in New Mexico won't generate a lot of operating jobs, but it appears to be on a strong expansion path, with new projects generating construction jobs. National pressure to reduce the proportion of electricity generated by hydrocarbons, particularly coal, is intense. Rapid technological advances are occurring in the renewables industry, and these developments should make renewables price competitive with traditional generation within a few years. In addition, it is likely that RPSs are a permanent feature of the electricity sector.

Manufacturing Industry

New Mexico's manufacturing industry has always been small by national standards. In 1940, the earliest date for which information is easily available, manufacturing employment in New Mexico accounted for over 5 percent of total nonagricultural employment, versus almost 35 percent nationally (figure 1.2).[20] Nationally, manufacturing peaked at over 41 percent of total employment in 1943, in the middle of World War II, and has declined as a share of total employment almost continually since then.

By 1973, manufacturing employment in New Mexico had increased as a share of total nonagricultural employment to 8.3 percent, but it gradually diminished in importance thereafter and was below 7 percent by 1992 and below 5 percent by 2003. Major cuts at Intel's Rio Rancho plant combined with the Great Recession took manufacturing down further, to below 4 percent by 2009, where it remains today.

As a direct employer, the manufacturing sector in New Mexico has always been tiny. Why care about this sector at all? First, most manufacturing businesses export the bulk of their product to people outside New Mexico, and this can bring in dollars from out-of-state customers that will support additional jobs and production activity in New Mexico.

Second, manufacturing jobs often pay better than jobs in other sectors and generally have better benefits. Manufacturing wages vary incredibly from one subindustry to another: an average worker in the textile products industry commanded less than $500 per week in 2012, while a worker in computer and electronics manufacturing averaged $1,725 and a worker in petroleum and coal products was pulling down $1,767 on average. Overall, the state's average weekly wage in manufacturing in 2012 was $1,068, compared with $783 across all workers in New Mexico. There are few other industries—only mining, utilities, professional and technical services, management of companies, and the federal government—where wages are, on average, higher than in manufacturing.

Third, this sector's contribution to New Mexico gross domestic product is more than twice its contribution to employment—10.3 percent in 2012.

Figure 1.2. Manufacturing employment as a percentage of total employment, 1940–2012

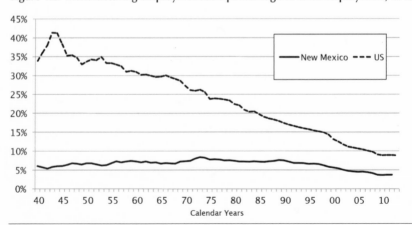

Source: U.S. Bureau of Labor Statistics, Current Employment Statistics

Fourth, the national laboratories located in New Mexico (Los Alamos and Sandia), the state's major research universities, and the concentration of scientific and engineering expertise (fourth-highest concentration of PhDs in the nation) help to create a culture and an environment that seem to foster creativity. New Mexico has a concentration of people working on the cutting edge to solve interesting problems. And beneath the behemoths like Sandia and Los Alamos, Intel and Honeywell, there are scores of tinkerers and small start-ups involved in trying to solve problems and developing new products to meet tomorrow's needs, often before the needs themselves are acknowledged. The New Mexico manufacturing sector has an incredibly dynamic substrata that should be recognized and appreciated, and nurtured. It is recognized by others. New Mexico businesses like Emcore and recently Titan have attracted outside capital and equity investments, and many have been targets for buyouts.

New Mexico has historically been great at spawning new businesses based on new technologies or new applications of technologies. It has not done so well in nurturing these start-ups into adulthood. Bill Gates was not the first nor the last high-tech entrepreneur to leave New Mexico and build a company elsewhere. But wouldn't New Mexico love to have Microsoft here today?

Tourism

New Mexico's well-deserved official nickname is the Land of Enchantment. Tourism has been a large business in New Mexico since before statehood, when railroads promoted the state as a tourist destination. New Mexico boasts great natural beauty, and its thirty-one state parks, seven state historic sites, thirteen national parks and monuments, and thousands of square miles of national forests and other public lands offer ample opportunities for hunting, fishing, hiking, and other outdoor activities. Other cultural amenities include dozens of museums and art galleries galore.

Assessing the economic effects of tourism is tricky business because it is difficult to separate tourists from outside the state from other travelers, such as business travelers or state residents who might only be visiting relatives.

Out-of-state visitors contribute to the economy. In-state visitors have little economic impact because if they were not traveling, they would be spending their money on some other sector of the state economy. On the other hand, better that they spend in New Mexico than elsewhere.

The New Mexico Tourism Department reports that there were 32 million overnight and day visitors to New Mexico in 2012 and that these visitors spent $5.9 billion in the state. Overnight-only visitors accounted for 14.5 million visits. In recent years, visits to state parks have averaged just over 4.0 million, with an additional 1.5 million visits to national parks and monuments. There is no breakdown of park visitors between in-state and out-of-state origins. According to the New Mexico Tourism Department, overnight visitors spend $215 per day, while day trip visitors spend about $70 per day.[21]

Separately, the National Park Service reported 1.5 million visitors to national parks and monuments in New Mexico in 2012. More than half (55 percent) of these visitors were to White Sands National Monument (447,000) and Carlsbad Caverns National Park (381,000). These national park visitors spent $81 million and created 1,100 jobs in the state, according to the National Park Service study.[22]

A rough idea of the overall size of the tourism industry in New Mexico can be gleaned from a 2011 economic impact study conducted by Tourism Economics.[23] According to that study, tourism generated $5.5 billion in direct sales, 64,057 direct jobs, and $1.2 billion in tax revenue. The study also estimated the indirect and induced effects of tourism. Indirect effects result when a sector that is directly affected by tourism purchases inputs into its production (e.g., a restaurant buys food and cleaning supplies). Induced effects occur when the employees in sectors directly or indirectly affected by tourism spend their incomes within the state. The total effects of tourism—including direct, indirect, and induced effects—were larger than the direct effects alone. The total effects were $7.8 billion in sales, eighty-six thousand jobs (more than 10 percent of total state employment), and $4.0 billion of state gross domestic product (about 5 percent of the state total).

While tourism is one of New Mexico's largest industries, it could be much larger; the state devotes few resources to attracting tourists from other states. New Mexico visitor centers and other facilities, as well as many state parks, need substantial improvements. Rest areas in New Mexico are few and far between, and many of them were constructed decades ago and are badly in need of modernization. The New Mexico Tourism Department and the New Mexico Department of Cultural Affairs have small budgets, and the state spends little on advertising for tourism. Expansion of the state tourism industry requires a healthier national economy and additional investment by the state.

Arts and Cultural Industries

Arts and culture have always been part of New Mexico's enchantment and have always been vigorously promoted. According to *New Mexico Art Tells New Mexico History*, an online exhibit from the New Mexico Museum of Art, "When the transcontinental train reached the territory of New Mexico in 1879, a 'culture rush' began, and European-American artists and anthropologists hurried to the region to collect artworks and document native lifestyles before everything was changed by the influx of outsiders. The drawings, photographs and paintings that artists made at this time were often used to advertise the exotic Southwestern landscape, and the native people who lived there."[24]

Arts and cultural industries continue to be important to New Mexico's economy. Narrowly defined, this industry employs over forty thousand people, including some six thousand who are employed primarily as independent professional artists, writers, and performers—the fourth-highest concentration in the United States. If one includes in addition those employed in cultural tourism, art and cultural education, and industries linked to the unique culture and heritage of the state, arts and cultural industries account for 10 percent of total New Mexico employment.[25] Access to new technologies, like broadband, have the potential of giving New Mexico, as well as New Mexico artists and cultural workers, wider exposure outside the state as well access to global markets. (See chapter 7 for more discussion on this topic.)

There are important synergies between the arts and cultural industries and tourism. Popular TV shows filmed in New Mexico (*Breaking Bad* and

In Plain Sight) made Albuquerque neighborhoods and New Mexico vistas characters of interest in themselves. Similar effects have come from many movie productions filmed on location in New Mexico, some of which may have received assistance from Albuquerque or other local film offices as well as incentives from the state. Just as the transcontinental railroad, the Harvey Girls, and publications by anthropologists and others did over a century ago, such broad market exposure today will continue New Mexico's aura of enchantment, bringing tourists to the state as well as new customers for its arts and cultural industries.

Health Care Services and Social Assistance

Health care and social assistance have continued to grow in New Mexico in good times and bad, and today the industry employs over 140,000 people, most of them working within the private sector and including doctors, nurses, and other health practitioners; health technologists and technicians (practical nurses, lab techs, dental hygienists); and home health aides and others in health care support occupations.[26] There are growing numbers of New Mexico jobs in community and social service assistance occupations and in related management occupations, as well as in office and administrative support and other nonhealth occupations in the industry.

According to the U.S. Census Bureau, New Mexico has had one of the highest rates of nonelderly uninsured in the country—24 percent in 2010–2011, second only to Texas, with 27 percent. Some of the nonelderly who are counted as having private health insurance are employees of federal contractors, like the national laboratories, Sandia and Los Alamos. Counting children, many of whom receive health care benefits under Medicaid, and the elderly, who receive coverage under Medicare, New Mexico is very heavily dependent on government, with as much as 75 percent of state health expenditures being paid by federal, state, and local governments. Among these government payers, the federal government, which pays for health care services through Medicaid, Medicare, the Indian Health Service, the Veterans Administration, and other programs, is by far the most important. This dependence of the health services industry on the federal government will increase under the new Affordable Care Act, in part as eligible New Mexicans sign up for the Medicaid expansion included in the act.

New Mexico's vast size and low population density have long posed a challenge to the health and well-being of New Mexicans. In the first half of the twentieth century, home visitation programs, which provided both health care services and health education, were critical to reducing New Mexico's infant and maternal mortality rates, then among the highest in the country, and to the prevention and control of infectious diseases, including tuberculosis, the leading cause of death in New Mexico until the early 1940s.[27] At that time the Work Projects Administration, set up as part of the New Deal, began to send public health nurses into rural and remote New Mexico communities

Infectious diseases such as tuberculosis, diarrhea and dysentery, whooping cough, and measles, which claimed the lives of so many New Mexicans in the first half of the twentieth century, are no longer the scourge they once were and are now greatly overshadowed by rising death tolls due to chronic conditions such as cancer, diabetes, and heart disease. But the provision of needed health care services outside the major medical centers of Albuquerque, Rio Rancho, and Las Cruces remains a huge challenge. All but one of New Mexico's counties are presently designated as underserved. Dr. Dan Derkson, formerly with UNM Health Sciences, has estimated that four hundred new primary-care physicians are now needed in New Mexico. Attracting and training more midlevel heath personnel will help but not solve that problem.

Small-town private doctors are a disappearing breed in New Mexico.[28] In some areas, they have been replaced or augmented by the opening of new health centers, many of them federally qualified health centers. At the same time, some rural hospitals in the state are shutting down services like labor and delivery, with some threatening to close their doors permanently as key funding sources disappear.[29]

New Mexico will benefit economically—through an increase in and an influx of federal money—from the implementation of the Affordable Care Act, including the Medicaid expansion. More importantly, New Mexicans individually will benefit, health-wise. And New Mexico and its residents would benefit further if Congress extended the coverage of the Affordable Care Act to undocumented immigrants as well.

The Federal Presence in New Mexico

The federal presence in New Mexico is enormous. Total federal employment (military and civilian) in New Mexico has fluctuated around fifty thousand, rising a bit above this level in the 1970s and 1980s then gradually contracting in the 1990s, reaching a low of forty-five thousand in 2008 and then sharply increasing in 2009 and 2010 to over fifty thousand. The 2010 increase in federal government employment was largely due to temporary employment associated with the decennial census. Federal civilian and military jobs, which accounted for almost 13 percent of total state employment in 1969, accounted for only 4 percent state of total employment in 2008 and 4.6 percent in 2012, after the recession and, as of this writing, the last year for which this data are available.

The data on federal employment capture employment on military bases and in federal agencies, like the Bureau of Land Management and the FBI, but they do not count employment at the two national laboratories, Sandia and Los Alamos, nor do they include jobs at the Waste Isolation Pilot Plant federal nuclear repository outside Carlsbad (currently closed as a result of a radiation leak). Indeed, they do not count any of the jobs supported by federal government contracts. A recent study of government-financed employment across the states estimated that federal contracts in New Mexico funded private sector jobs that in 2012 amounted to 7.7 percent of total employment in the state.[30] New Mexico was second only to Virginia in the percentage of total nonfarm employment supported by federal contracts.

Assessing the impact of the flow of federal dollars into the state has been made more difficult by a Census Bureau decision to end production of its *Consolidated Federal Funds Report*, which detailed federal spending to states by program and to counties and communities by program and by recipient agency or organization. The latest data from this source are for 2010. Federal expenditures in New Mexico for that year were $28 billion, or $13,578 per capita.[31] New Mexico ranked sixth among the states in the per capita flow of federal dollars and was once again number one in the nation for the ratio of federal expenditures to federal tax paid.

The U.S. government has had a military presence in New Mexico since at least the mid-1850s, when troops were deployed to control the Indian population and otherwise help open up the frontier to settlement as well as to mining, logging, and other commercial activities. But the federal presence increased dramatically during World War II as airfields were established around the state. New Mexico's four present major military bases—White Sands Missile Range and Holloman, Kirtland, and Cannon Air Force Bases—all date from this period, as did Walker Air Force Base in Roswell and other bases and airfields that have since been closed. During World War II the federal government also launched its highly secret effort to develop the atomic bomb—the Manhattan Project—at Los Alamos. The New Mexico Museum of Art has summed up the impact of the Manhattan Project in this way: "The test at Trinity Site signaled the entrance of New Mexico into a new era and marked the integration of the oldest settled portion of the United States with industrial and urban America, for the growth of industry and cities in New Mexico really began during World War II."[32]

Clearly, the choice of Los Alamos helped put New Mexico on the cutting edge in terms of technology, as did the addition of Sandia National Laboratory, which began as "the ordnance design, testing, and assembly arm of Los Alamos National Laboratory," and the Air Force Research Laboratory at Kirtland Air Force Base. These research institutions have large procurement budgets and have been sources of funding for many New Mexico suppliers and other businesses. And there is technology transfer from these powerhouse laboratories; patents are licensed and find commercial applications, private companies partner with the labs and develop new products, and lab scientists occasionally become entrepreneurs. But the promise of technology spin-offs has at best been only partially realized. The national laboratories, steeped from the beginning in secrecy, remain even today largely high-tech enclaves fenced off considerably from the rest of the New Mexico economy.

The federal presence in New Mexico extends far beyond the state's military bases and national laboratories. Other federal government programs have a major impact on many aspects of the state's economy, too, including health care, education, arts and culture, and national forests and national park lands, as well as income-support programs for the elderly and the poor. The federal government also has a major role in establishing and enforcing the rules of the game that govern banking and commercial activities and that protect workers and the environment. And the federal government has a unique ability to affect the overall economy through its conduct of monetary and fiscal policies.

Still, unfortunately, despite the huge federal presence in New Mexico, poverty and inequality remain major challenges here.

Poverty and Inequality

Of course, poverty and inequality are not the same thing. Economic historians remind us that for much of human history everyone was poor but there was very little inequality. Poverty is an important concern because it is morally repugnant and unnecessary. Poverty rates are also important because billions of dollars are distributed to states and localities through federal programs based on those rates. Poverty rates also have implications for the nation's economy. Children in families living below the official poverty line are less likely to complete high school or college and less likely to have the education and skills to fully participate in our modern economy.

The United States has had an official definition of poverty—the so-called poverty threshold—since the early 1960s. The poverty threshold was originally based on a multiple of the amount of money a family of four needed to purchase food for a minimally healthy diet. While there are now alternative measures of poverty, the basic concept remains in place. As of 2013, the official poverty threshold for a one-person household was $12,119, while the threshold for a family of four was $24,028.[33]

Poverty rates in New Mexico are high when compared to national or surrounding-state rates. In 2012, 20.8 percent of New Mexicans were living below the poverty level, a percentage exceeded only by Mississippi's 24.2 percent.

In New Mexico, as in the rest of the nation, the poverty rate among children under age eighteen (29.8 percent) is much higher than for the general population (20.8 percent), while the rate for those sixty-five years old and older (11.9 percent) is lower. The poverty rate among New Mexico men (19.4 percent) is lower than for women (22.2 percent). Non-Hispanic whites in New Mexico have a poverty rate of 13.9 percent. Among Hispanics the poverty rate is

25.6 percent. The poverty rates for African Americans (30.3 percent) and American Indians (36 percent) are much higher than for other groups.

Educational attainment is an important determinant of poverty levels in New Mexico. For the population twenty-five years old and older, the poverty rate is 16.4 percent. For those with less than a high school diploma or GED, the poverty rate (33.8 percent) is more than double the rate for all persons twenty-five years old and older. Only 5.6 percent of those with a bachelor's degree or higher fall below the poverty line. The highest poverty rate in New Mexico is for families with children under age eighteen, a female head of household, and no husband present (46.7 percent).[34]

Poverty rates vary considerably by county in New Mexico. Based on five-year averages, Los Alamos County had the lowest poverty rate (4.9 percent) while McKinley County had the highest (33.6 percent).[35]

A healthy New Mexico economy in 2050 will depend in large part on whether those who are poor can become full participants in a twenty-first-century economy. Poverty reduction in New Mexico is and will be a major policy issue for the foreseeable future. It will be addressed later in this chapter.

Income Inequality

Inequality is controversial because great extremes in incomes offend many people's sense of fairness or justice. Why should a sports star be paid hundreds of times more than a schoolteacher? What kind of society do we want?

Inequality is also controversial because of disagreements about the relationship between inequality and economic growth. Some suggest that high incomes for the rich are necessary incentives in a dynamic market economy. Yet the United States experienced high rates of economic growth from the late 1940s to the early 1970s, when there was also a dramatic *reduction* in income inequality. And the trend toward increasing inequality since the 1970s in the United States has been accompanied by a slowdown in economic growth.

The inequality debate is a central factor in the discussion of many contentious national, state, and local policy issues, including tax and expenditure policy, minimum wage legislation, and debates about food stamps, unemployment benefits, and programs such as Social Security and Medicare that provide income security for the elderly.

In 2012, the latest year for which data are available, New Mexico's distribution of income was in many respects similar to and as depressing as the distribution in the nation. The share of total income in the lowest 20 percent of households in New Mexico (3.1 percent) was almost the same as in the United States (3.2 percent).[36] The share of total income of the highest 20 percent of households in New Mexico (50.1 percent) was also similar to that in

Tradition-Based, Culture-Based Economic Development
Henry Rael

When you are raising money to fund a new enterprise, you invest a lot of time thinking through what your product is and how to best position it within a fast-growing market. If you do your homework properly, you can include in your business plan and PowerPoint presentations multiple diagrams with a line plotting sales growth over time, with the year along the horizontal axis and "units sold" or "projected revenue" along the vertical axis.

The line starts off with a gradual incline, beginning in the year your company starts selling its products. After a given period of time (two years? five years?), the angle takes a sharp turn upward and continues at this rate for five, maybe seven years into the future. It looks roughly like a hockey stick. In this context, the hockey stick is a special shape that implicitly transmits to the investor the assurance that this opportunity will yield a rich return.

What the hockey stick does not reveal, however, is the ultimate trajectory of that line when plotted out over a longer period of time. Like anything that appears to defy gravity, it eventually succumbs, levels out, and curves toward zero. Products have their life cycles. The secret of the hockey stick is to have a pipeline of products, each brought to market such that the new product begin ramping up in production as the last-generation product is leveling off. This creates the sense that the hockey stick extends onward and upward forever. But in fact the infinite growth of the hockey stick is an illusion created by strategically timing the overlap of more circular trajectories. The hockey stick paradigm lines up a bunch of curves in such a way that they look like a straight line.

The hockey stick as a paradigm for economic development can be effective in certain environments, particularly those rich in resources. For many communities in New Mexico, this approach is ineffective due to lack of resources and skills, but also because it lacks a cultural resonance with many traditional, land-based people in the state. Relative to their understanding of how the United States (50.9 percent). The share of income of the top 5 percent of households in New Mexico (20.7 percent) was somewhat smaller than in the nation. In New Mexico, the mean, or average, income of the highest quintile was sixteen times the mean income of the lowest quintile, about the same as in the United States. While the shares are similar, the total dollars in income per household are, of course, smaller in New Mexico.

Income inequality is also intertwined with race and ethnicity. In 2012 the per capita income of Hispanics in New Mexico ($16,145) was less than 50 percent of the per capita income of non-Hispanic whites ($33,239). The per capita

the world works, the shape that holds more meaning is the circle.

Traditional, land-based people in New Mexico have a historical and cultural connection to the annual cycle of the seasons, to the flows of the rivers in the summer and in the winter, to the birth, growth, and harvesting of plants and livestock. While most are now at least one generation removed from maintaining these cultural practices themselves, the recognition and honoring of such cycles continues to resonate with them and inform their values. Economic development initiatives that will resonate with our most challenged populations and consequently have an impact on poverty will be those that are defined more by the circle than the hockey stick.

In the past, economic development and opportunity have been somewhat narrowly focused on relatively few approaches, including such strategies as building and nurturing large government institutions that provide large numbers of jobs or offering tax cuts to large corporations to attract what are usually low-paying jobs. While these strategies have resulted in some job creation, they are based on hockey stick projections that deliver value to out-of-state entities and do little to affect the high levels of poverty that are pervasive in the state.

HISTORY, CULTURE, LANGUAGE

Key elements of economic development approaches that are more aligned with the circle and that play to our assets include strategies that create and capture value for the state; initiatives that leverage our cultures, history, and languages; structures that support alternative models of enterprise development; and approaches that make education directly relevant to our economic environment and what is happening in the world that our students inhabit. Projects and initiatives that find intersections among these elements will have the advantage of leveraging some of the most powerful—and often unrecognized—strengths that we have.

How can these various elements come together to inform a specific economic development initiative? First off, these initiatives should be inspired by a real, identified market opportunity. Next, the challenges and barriers to success for the initiative should be identified. Finally, we

continued on next page

should look to our strengths to find unique, innovative solutions to these challenges, to find value in our assets.

According to the New Mexico State Extension Service, for example, the market for fresh vegetables and fruit in the Albuquerque metropolitan area is approximately $170 million per year, with the vast majority of those dollars leaving New Mexico in favor of out-of-state producers. A successful initiative that increased the share of the Albuquerque produce market supplied by New Mexico farmers would create value and capture it in the state. Two key challenges to making this happen include a lack of adequate local farming capacity and a local supply environment that is too disorganized and inefficient to supply our food-based businesses. Solutions to these challenges can be found in the culture and history of New Mexico.

THE ACEQUIA SYSTEM AS AN EXAMPLE

Many communities around the state maintain a deep cultural connection with the acequia system that conveys water from river to farm. Among other things, the system is a traditional mechanism for

expanding capacity through a cooperative structure. In the operation of the system, each participant plays a role in making it work and each derives value from the well-being of the mechanism. Over hundreds of years, this system enabled abundance in a landscape of scarcity.

The Albuquerque produce market initiative, for example, could draw on the acequia concept to address its challenges through a cooperative enterprise owned by farmers and food-product entrepreneurs, which would coordinate planting, harvesting, and distribution across large numbers of small growers. The co-op could also provide other aggregated functions, such as marketing and sales, processing, delivery, billing, and receiving, to maximize efficiencies and the profitability of member farms. This enterprise could address both challenges mentioned above by (1) rationalizing the supply while (2) driving economies of scale that build the viability and capacity of new food and farm enterprises. Support structures such as processing and delivery infrastructure, "local first" requirements for supply contracts, and revolving loan funds or other financial instruments are key roles

income of American Indians in the state ($12,216) was only 36.7 percent of the figure for non-Hispanic whites.

In New Mexico, income inequality is also a geographic phenomenon. In 2012 Los Alamos County's per capita income was $63,768, or 145.8 percent of the nation's per capita income, while McKinley County's per capita income was $29,914, or 57.1 percent of the national figure.[37] Regional disparities in the state are also obvious in terms of population change. Seven of New Mexico's thirty-three counties had a smaller population in 2010 than in 1930, and fourteen counties lost population just between 2000 and 2010.

that city and county governments could play in rounding out the initiative. This example illustrates the value-creation opportunities that can be found when we leverage our strengths to drive initiative development.

GLOBAL OPPORTUNITIES

Although the agriculture example is highly localized in nature, economic development strategies can have global reach and still operate within the approach described above. For example, as Latin American economies continue to grow and develop as markets for technology from companies based in the United States, there will be an opportunity to help these U.S. companies engage and service enterprise clients in Mexico, Argentina, Brazil, and other countries south of the U.S. border. With many families descended from Spanish settlers and a robust community of more recent immigrants from Latin America, New Mexico has the cultural and language assets needed to help play this role. The more that New Mexico appreciates, develops, and supports its residents' language skills, the more appealing it will be as a partner for technology enterprises and other companies wanting to do business in Latin America.

More specifically, such a strategy could be focused on a particular technology sector. Looking at cybersecurity as an example, New Mexico could also leverage and further develop its existing postsecondary educational infrastructure, which is already training a workforce for this sector. Developing curricula that start the preparations even earlier (in high school or middle school) would ensure a highly skilled workforce pipeline that could support growth and success. Making commitments to these approaches would enable cities and the state to approach large corporate enterprises with the possibility of locating well-paying software development and technology support jobs in New Mexico.

NEW MEXICO 2050

Will New Mexico take advantage of its special attributes? I think so, because it is in the interest of all of us to do so. I believe New Mexico will build on our tradition, culture, and language for a more vibrant economy for our state and more and better jobs for our people.

In brief, common measures of household income distribution indicate that, first, inequality in New Mexico is not much different from inequality in the nation and, second, income inequality has been increasing in both the United States and New Mexico since the 1970s.

Labor Force and Education

For most people, economic opportunity is defined by the opportunity to participate in the labor market. Whether someone is employed or unemployed, the occupation and industry they might work in, and the wage and salary income they may receive largely determine their consumption patterns and lifestyles. Labor market opportunities depend on an individual's education and skills, as well as other factors that an individual has little or no control over: age, sex, race, and ethnicity.

The characteristics of the labor force powerfully influence economic growth and the future of an economy. Modern economies demand highly skilled and highly educated workers. There are very few state or regional economic success stories in the United States that do not depend on highly educated and highly trained workers.

Before we consider some basic characteristics of New Mexico's labor force and offer some speculation on future opportunities, we must cover some labor market definitions. As defined by the U.S. Bureau of Labor Statistics, the labor force includes those who are employed and unemployed. People are counted as employed if they are working for pay, regardless of how many jobs they have or hours they work, whether they work for someone else or are self-employed. To be counted as unemployed, one has to be able and willing to work and to have actively sought employment within the last four weeks. The labor force participation rate (LFPR) is the percentage of the civilian population—all those age sixteen and older who are not in the military and not institutionalized—who are counted as being in the labor force.

For decades, LFPRs in New Mexico have been lower than those in the nation, and they declined rapidly during the recent Great Recession. Among the reasons for New Mexico's relatively low LFPRs historically was the state's relatively younger population and lower educational attainment rates, although New Mexico's racial and ethnic composition was also important.[38] LFPRs are at their highest among people between the ages twenty-five and fifty-five, and in New Mexico about 80 percent of this cohort was in the labor force before the recession hit in 2008.[39] About 70 percent of a second group, those between the ages of twenty and twenty-four, was in the labor force until

Figure 1.3. New Mexico labor force participation rates by educational attainment, 2005–2013

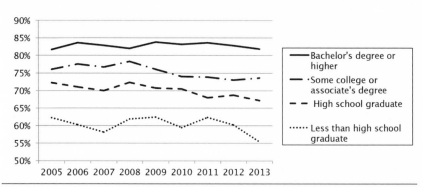

Source: U.S. Census Bureau, American Community Survey, table 1-Y S2301

around 2006, when the housing bubble burst. Close to 60 percent of those in the fifty-five-to-sixty-four age group were in the New Mexico labor force prior to the Great Recession, but only 40 percent of sixteen-to-nineteen-year-olds and only about 20 percent of those sixty-five and older were. The recession lowered LFPRs across all age groups, but the effects were most dramatic for teenagers, though imperceptible for those over age sixty-five.

Labor force participation varies by sex and by race and ethnicity. As is true nationally, New Mexico women have significantly lower rates of labor force participation than men, but there is variation depending upon race and ethnicity and related job prospects. Hispanic women have lower rates typically, but when women teachers and other public sector female employees were hit by funding reductions in 2011, the labor force participation of white women fell below that for Hispanic women. The LFPR for women heads of household, which was close to 70 percent in 2008, was down alarmingly, to under 60 percent, in 2011.

Labor force participation also depends on educational attainment. This is shown dramatically by figure 1.3. The LFPR of those with a bachelor's degree or higher stayed well above 80 percent throughout the nine-year period from 2005 to 2013, which included the years of the Great Recession, while the percentage for those with less than a high school degree hovered around 60 percent or less during this period, reflecting difficulty in finding jobs. Nationally, as James Applegate of the Lumina Foundation has pointed out, those without a high school degree lost 2.3 million jobs from the official start of the recession in December 2007 through February 2012, with basically no progress made after January 2010. By contrast, those with a bachelor's degree or better had gained 187,000 jobs by January 2010 and 2.0 million more jobs by February 2012.[40]

Finally, New Mexico's relatively low wage structure may also contribute to low LFPRs. A low wage means that the opportunity cost of not working is also low.

With bleak job prospects, many in New Mexico dropped out of the labor force during the Great Recession. They were ready and willing to work, but they became discouraged. They had looked for work in the previous twelve months but were not officially counted in the labor force; they were only marginally attached. By 2011 New Mexico had the second-highest percentage of people in the country who were marginally attached to the labor force, 2.3 percent. In 2012 New Mexico's unemployed, according to the same Current Population Survey series, numbered sixty-eight thousand, for an unemployment rate of 7.1 percent. Had all those who were discouraged or marginally attached been counted, the unemployment rate would have been 8.8 percent. If those who were involuntarily working part-time because that was the only work they could find were added into the calculation, the unemployment rate would have been more than 14 percent—roughly twice the official rate for New Mexico.

Unemployment rates in New Mexico and the United States are affected by similar demographics: highest for youth and those without education, higher for minorities than for non-Hispanic white males and females. In the Great Recession, unemployment rates were generally higher for men early in the cycle, as construction-related, manufacturing, and finance jobs were hit, with unemployment rising for women as declines in government revenues forced budget cutbacks leading to layoffs for teachers and other government employees.

The unemployment rate in New Mexico varies considerably by county. In December 2013 the lowest unemployment rates in New Mexico were in Eddy County (3.7 percent) and Lea County (3.8 percent), areas enjoying the benefits of an oil boom. The highest unemployment rates in New Mexico were found in Luna County (17.1 percent) and Mora County (15 percent).[41]

Employment growth in New Mexico depends heavily on what happens

Figure 1.4. Cumulative change in nonfarm employment, New Mexico and the United States, 2008–2014

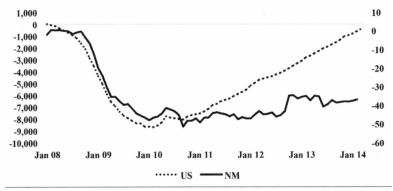

Source: U.S. Bureau of Labor Statistics

nationally. When the nation does well, generally speaking, New Mexico does well, and in many cases New Mexico's performance is superior. However, New Mexico has generally avoided employment declines even when national employment has shrunk as a result of recession. The state has been insulated by its very large government sector, which is typically less vulnerable to recessions. The Great Recession was the big exception. Government employment may have cushioned New Mexico's fall originally, but as the recession dragged on, all three levels of government felt forced by lower revenues to contract spending and reduce employment.

Indeed, there has been little nonfarm payroll employment growth in New Mexico since the onset of the Great Recession in December 2007. The cumulative change in employment in New Mexico and the nation are depicted in figure 1.4. While national employment will probably regain its prerecession levels in 2014, New Mexico appears to be several years away from doing so. From June 2009, when the National Bureau of Economic Research declared the national recession to be over, to December 2013, New Mexico was the only state without employment gains. New Mexico's neighboring states have all outperformed New Mexico since the end of the Great Recession.

The policy implications of New Mexico's slow employment recovery will be discussed later. But right now, we can't ignore another important aspect of New Mexico's labor market performance: earnings.

Earnings

New Mexico has ranked at the very bottom among the states in terms of job growth since 2010. It is perhaps difficult to believe that the state used to be one of the leaders in terms of job growth and indeed ranked among the top fifteen states in terms of average job growth in each of the four decades beginning in 1970. Yet even as New Mexico soared in terms of job growth, it underperformed in terms of earnings. This is part of the reason why New Mexico incomes are so low. Figure 1.5 looks at New Mexico's average wage as a percentage of that for the United States and also includes New Mexico personal income, presented as a percentage of U.S. personal income. Since 1990, New Mexico wages have fluctuated at around 85 percent of the U.S. average. Except in the mining industry and high-end manufacturing, New Mexico benefits, including health insurance, are generally inferior to what is offered elsewhere.

Figure 1.5. New Mexico average wage and per capita income as percentages of the United States, 1990–2012

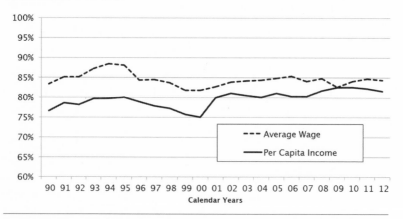

Source: U.S. Bureau of Economic Analysis

Education

Labor market outcomes and educational attainment are highly correlated. We've already discussed the relationships between education and labor force participation and between education and unemployment rates. Income and earnings in New Mexico are also highly correlated with educational attainment. Earnings include wages and salaries and proprietors' income but exclude other components of total income, such as transfer payments and dividends, interest, and rent.

In 2012 in New Mexico, the average earnings of a person with a bachelor's degree were 52 percent higher than those of a high school graduate and more than double the earnings of the average person without a high school diploma (see figure 1.6). The 2012 earnings of those with a professional degree were nearly three times as large as the earnings of a typical high school graduate. Despite recent speculation about whether a college education is worth the cost, the data suggest that education remains an important pathway to success.

Figure 1.6. Earnings of employed persons age twenty-five and older by educational attainment, New Mexico 2012

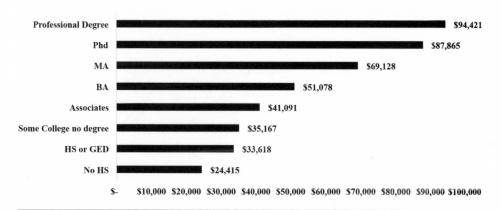

Source: U.S. Census Bureau, American Community Survey

New Mexico graduates about nineteen thousand students from high school each year. This figure is expected to rise modestly through 2024 and then begin falling.

Several indicators suggest future trouble for New Mexico high school education—and thus for New Mexico's economy. In 2012–2013, New Mexico had a high school graduation rate of only 70 percent.[42] In 2012–2013, 66 percent of New Mexico public school enrollees were eligible for free or reduced lunch programs, and 42 percent were so poor as to qualify for the Supplemental Nutrition Assistance Program (SNAP, also known as food stamps).[43] In New Mexico in 2012–2013, 13.6 percent of public school students were classified as habitual truants—students who accumulated ten or more unexcused absences within a school year. (Much more on education can be found in chapter 2.)

Consider the scores for New Mexico public school students in the fourth and eighth grades in the 2013 "Nation's Report Card" on reading and math, produced by the National Assessment of Educational Progress. Only 17 percent of New Mexico fourth graders were found to be proficient in reading, with a pathetic 3 percent rated as advanced—a performance below that of every other state, with Washington, D.C., alone having worse scores. Only 22 percent of New Mexico eighth graders were found to be proficient in math, New Mexico in that measure being ahead of only Washington, D.C., and Mississippi and tied with Louisiana.

Further, as reported in chapter 2, the 2013 national *KIDS COUNT* assessment issued by the Annie E. Casey Foundation ranked New Mexico at the very bottom—fiftieth among the states—in terms of child well-being, based on sixteen indicators, covering economic well-being, health, education, family, and community.[44]

New Mexico apparently fails many of its children long before they reach high school or even have a chance to think about going to college or vocational training. The literature on the benefits of intervening very early and before children's brains develop is compelling. The New Mexico Legislature is to be commended for recognizing this need and increasing, year by year, the programs available in the state for early childhood education and home visiting. But much more needs to be done in this area.

If New Mexico is having difficulty producing a sufficient number of well-educated high school graduates, then the production of the needed number of well-educated New Mexico college graduates is made a much more difficult task. But even though this is sadly true, it is also just as sadly true that New Mexico has not increased higher education funding in recent years; instead has actually *cut* such funding since 2008, by $4,588 per student, adjusted for inflation.[45] One bad result of this is that New Mexico's four-year universities have, during that same period, raised tuition by more than 25 percent on a per student, inflation-adjusted basis, thus pricing many lower- and middle-income students out of this known path to success, hampering amelioration of New Mexico's income inequality, and dampening hopes for economic development in the state.

State Revenues and Expenditures

New Mexico is one of the few states in the country in which funding for public schools comes largely from the state. In 2011 state sources accounted for 65.6 percent of all funding for New Mexico public elementary through secondary school system revenues, the fourth-highest percentage among the states. Per pupil spending in New Mexico is $9,070, a figure that puts it in thirty-seventh place among the states, a ranking that has changed little over the years.

Once, New Mexico public schools got a substantial percentage of their funds from local property taxes. But some years ago the state legislature changed that, setting up a statewide equalization system funded by state taxes while greatly reducing the ceiling on permitted school district property tax levies (from 8.925 mills down to only 0.5 mills) while raising the property tax levy limit for counties and municipalities. The potential state millage levy thereby lost to public schools and turned over to local governments could today generate over half a billion additional dollars for the schools, based on net taxable value in 2013, adding an increase of roughly 13 percent to their present funding.

The loss of the property tax as a robust funding source for school operations has also been followed by cuts in other taxes critical to funding the State Equalization Guarantee, specifically in personal and business taxes.

Personal Income Tax

In 2003 Governor Bill Richardson (2003–2011), then already known to have presidential aspirations, pushed through the state legislature a major cut in New Mexico's personal income tax rates, from 8.2 to 4.9 percent, phased in over five years, as well as a reduction in taxes to be paid on capital gains. The official fiscal impact report at the time indicated that by fiscal year 2007 these tax cuts would reduce state general fund revenues by $325 million, and the Legislative Finance Committee estimated that the impact over the five-year period beginning in fiscal 2004 would be a loss of $900 million.[46] It appeared that New Mexico was facing an impending fiscal train wreck, but then energy prices went way up and, with them, key school revenue sources, including severance taxes, federal mineral leases, and corporate income taxes. In July 2008 the West Texas Intermediate spot price for oil peaked at $145 per barrel (only later to fall precipitously, as did the price of natural gas).[47]

Business Taxes

Governor Susana Martinez, a Republican, took office in 2011, and she was able to get the 2012 and 2013 state legislatures to reduce the gross receipts tax burden from tax pyramiding (paying the same tax more than once) for construction and manufacturing; to reduce the corporate income tax rate, over five years, from 8.2 to 4.9 percent; and to give manufacturers the favorable option of phasing in over five years the use of a single-sales factor in apportioning their earnings to New Mexico. The official fiscal impact reports indicated the state could lose substantial revenues.

The argument for these tax cuts was that they were necessary to make New Mexico more competitive with other states. A 2012 study by Ernst and Young found that New Mexico had the highest business tax burden among the states—despite its substantial economic development incentives.

Economic Development Incentives

States compete with one another for business investment and job creation. It is often a race to the bottom, as states compete with one another in terms of tax burdens and whether they have imposed a "right to work" law. New Mexico offers an ever-expanding and somewhat bewildering array of economic development tax incentives, including a Technology Jobs Tax Credit, an Investment Tax Credit for Manufacturers, an R&D Small Business Tax Credit, an Advanced Energy Deduction, an Advanced Energy Tax Credit, and Tax Increment Development Districts (TIDDs), as well as the old standby, local authority to issue industrial revenue bonds and thereby give the business corporation involved an exemption from property taxes for the life of the bonds, as well as other tax benefits. New Mexico's once-broad-based gross receipts tax has so many special exemptions and deductions that it looks like "Swiss cheese" according to New Mexico Tax Research Institute director Richard Anklam.

States are frequently involved in bidding wars for industry, in terms of which state can offer the most lucrative incentive package—with inducements that may include cash grants, loans and loan guarantees, and services, as well as tax credits, rebates, and reductions. The *New York Times* not long ago conducted a nationwide investigation, examining thousands of such state and local incentive deals, and determined that, together, cities, counties, and states thereby give up annually more than $80 billion.[48] This survey showed that such New Mexico incentives cost at least $253 million per year, with $163 million of that going to oil, gas, and mining, and $47 million going to the film industry.

In New Mexico, after receiving state incentives, Phillips Semiconductor later closed its facility and moved elsewhere; Schott Solar, faced with tough competition from China, ceased production altogether; and Eclipse Aviation went bankrupt. For protection against these kinds of bad outcomes or the failure of a recipient corporation to live up to its promises—say, to hire a certain number of employees at certain levels of pay—the City of Albuquerque puts in place "clawback" provisions for investment recoupment. Think

New Mexico, a nonprofit think tank, has proposed state legislation to pro- vide for postperformance incentives like those adopted in Utah and some other states.

Unfortunately, the special tax deals and other incentives are aimed over-whelmingly at out-of-state businesses, which usually don't come and which, if they do come, frequently leave. Local businesses are frequently taken for granted. In this regard, it is interesting that a recent survey of New Mexico businesses by Research & Polling about what concerned them most found that the economy and access to a trained workforce were at the top of their list, with taxes near the bottom, a concern that points toward the need for adequate funding of New Mexico education.[49]

Policies for a Prosperous New Mexico

New Mexico faces serious economic challenges in both the short term and the long term. The immediate short-term challenge is the state's slow recovery from the Great Recession, which began to take its toll in 2008. The slow recovery of New Mexico's economy as of 2014 reflects, in part, several long-term structural problems.

New Mexico's economic problems are not insoluble. But the solutions require a new approach to economic development, a number of policy reforms, and substantial investment in both human capital and physical infrastructure. Without such changes, New Mexico's economy in 2050 is likely to have fallen further behind national norms for per capita income, employment, and population growth.

For several decades, New Mexico has relied on an economic development strategy based mainly on attracting firms from other states. This "steal a firm from somewhere else" strategy has received considerable state support in the form of specific worker-training programs, various tax incentives, industrial revenue bonds, loan programs, and infrastructure investments. The focus of this strategy is always on the next deal. The governor's office and the New Mexico State Economic Development Department regularly publicize and celebrate success stories under this program—and this is the case no matter which political party happens to be in power. These economic success stories should not be denigrated. They are important, but they have not resulted in a vibrant, dynamic economic environment, which is the key to New Mexico's future growth and development.

A new state economic development strategy is needed. This strategy should recognize that economic development is a long-term process.[50] The strategy needs to be long-term because New Mexico's serious long-term structural challenges, discussed throughout this chapter (e.g., education and workforce training, heavy reliance on federal government spending, racial and ethnic discrimination, inadequate infrastructure, the lack of a leading economic sector, and rural-urban disparities, among others), cannot be solved in a year or even five years.

Designing a long-term development strategy for New Mexico is not as difficult as it might appear. The strategy needs to be widely accepted and understood by the public. The logic of the strategy needs to be powerful enough to gain long-term support from the legislature and the governor. And obviously, the strategy needs to have a high probability of success.

Education and Technology

Two major themes with a high probability of success are education (broadly defined) and technology. The long-term strategy could be called the ET Strategy.

Education, broadly defined to include early childhood education through graduate or professional education, is an obvious area of focus. Twenty-first-century economies require highly educated and highly trained workers. Even in occupations and industries that are not generally thought of as high-tech, jobs are becoming increasingly complex. Educational needs in New Mexico are many, but two important needs for the twenty-first century are to dramatically reduce the portion of students who drop out of high school and to increase the portion of the population with a bachelor's degree or higher. In an increasingly international economic environment, all New Mexico high school graduates should be fluent in at least two languages. Bilingual workers are in great demand in nearly all occupations and industries. Scientific research is beginning to demonstrate the benefits of fluency in a second language throughout one's life. New Mexico, which already has a head start with its large percentage of Hispanics, could become the first state with a bilingual population. What a comparative advantage that would be. Other educational possibilities that would distinguish New Mexico from its competitors are easy to imagine.

Technology as a second theme in a long-term strategy is easily justified. New Mexico is a high-technology place. This is not something New Mexicans necessarily chose, although the care with which the structures at Chaco and other sites were built to align with the movements of the earth around the sun should convince anyone that close observation of the environment (science) and the incorporation of those findings into the design and construction of buildings (technology) have been very much a part of life here for centuries. And even if we did not choose technology, New Mexico was chosen as the place for the Manhattan Project, which gave birth to the state's two major national laboratories, Los Alamos and Sandia, which together with its research universities and an already vibrant, if small, high-tech sector can make it a technology powerhouse. This is the exciting vision behind Innovate ABQ (which Chuck Wellborn describes in the second insert in this chapter).

The development of new technologies is all about applying science to solve tough problems. And problem solving is aided by creativity—something for which New Mexico is also known. So emphasizing technology is a good fit for New Mexico. The presence of the national labs and major research universities, along with the Air Force Research Lab and the Santa Fe Institute, means New Mexico has many smart and creative people, both those who are homegrown and those who were attracted here, who can push ideas and find solutions. It has major corporations like Intel and has attracted interest if not always commitment from companies like the high-tech electric-car manufacturer Tesla, lately considering (but ultimately rejecting) New Mexico for a huge battery facility.

New Mexico has been at the forefront of development of many exciting and disruptive technologies, like the personal computer and, more recently, nanotechnology and MEMS technology. Frequently operating below the radar, vibrant high-tech clusters of businesses in aerospace, in lasers and optics, and in biotech work in New Mexico, as well as Miox and other companies working on water purification and many working in software development and digital applications.

Unfortunately, New Mexico is far better at giving birth to new technology businesses than it is to nurturing them into adulthood. Far too many of its promising high-tech start-ups leave the state. They attract investment from other companies, which may take them over in order to gain access to technology and then move the operation elsewhere. Or, in their effort to raise venture capital, they may be lured elsewhere. Or they simply may not find here the concentration of entrepreneurial talent nor the community that will set the creative juices flowing. New Mexico, isolated geographically and sparsely populated, has had a difficult time providing the critical mass so necessary to business success. The supply chains may not be here. There are limited options for raising capital. The state's labor markets are thin. Companies like Intel, under requirements to hire locally as a condition for an industrial revenue bond, have found it difficult to meet their labor force requirements locally. There simply are not enough people in New Mexico with the requisite skills.

This takes the discussion back to education. If New Mexico's economy is to move forward on this technology path, an educated, skilled workforce is absolutely essential. New Mexico schools need to excite, engage, and educate—the three Es that physics professor and former University of New Mexico vice president for research John McGraw sees as so essential. As New Mexico State University President Garrey Carruthers has said about his university, "It's all about discovery."

Given that technology is often disruptive, that the industries that lead today may be left on the curbside tomorrow while upstarts take off, New Mexico needs to provide its students with the core competencies that will enable them to be agile and prepared to go back to school or complete a training program if necessary in order to polish those skills that come to be in demand.

Innovate ABQ
Chuck Wellborn

Innovate ABQ describes a collaboration among the University of New Mexico, the City of Albuquerque, the County of Bernalillo, and private and public partners whose purpose is to create an "innovation district" near downtown Albuquerque.

INNOVATION DISTRICTS

An innovation district serves as a hub for interaction among people with various talents, skills, training, knowledge, and energy and a thirst for new ideas and solutions to business and societal needs. A primary goal, but only one, is to enhance opportunities for the creation and development of technology-based start-up companies.

STC AND THE RAINFOREST CONCEPT

Innovate ABQ originated in 2012 from University of New Mexico (UNM) president Robert Frank's desire for UNM to take a more prominent role in state and local economic development. He formed an economic development advisory group at UNM and asked Lisa Kuuttila, the CEO and chief economic development officer of STC.UNM (Society for Technical Communication, UNM chapter), to organize the effort.

Kuuttila was chosen because STC.UNM is the university organization responsible for identifying, protecting, and marketing commercially promising UNM faculty inventions. It also fosters the creation of start-ups based on UNM technology. I myself started STC.UNM and headed it for five years, beginning in 1995. Not long after I left that position, Kuuttila took over and, as the program has matured, she has made STC.UNM very successful, bringing in more than $15 million in licensing revenues in the last ten years (through fiscal year 2013) and spinning off sixty-three start-ups based on UNM technology. I continue to serve on the STC.UNM board.

Economic Development Projects

New Mexico also needs a systematic mechanism to evaluate economic development projects—something along the lines of the state-level planning agency proposed by Aaron Sussman in chapter 8.

State and local governments spend a lot of money and provide enormous tax incentives in the name of economic development. These economic development expenditures range from the construction of physical infrastructure (e.g., a spaceport) to job-training programs and industrial revenue bonds. The current practice is that each development project or deal is judged on its own merits. The question that is usually asked is whether each particular

After considering several alternatives, Kuuttila identified and recommended the Rainforest Concept as a model for developing an innovation district in Albuquerque. The Rainforest Concept originated with Victor Hwang and Gregg Horowitt, experienced venture capitalists who coauthored *The Rainforest: The Secret to Building the Next Silicon Valley*. The book presents an intriguing metaphor, arguing that Silicon Valley is a kind of rainforest, a unique innovation ecosystem in which talent, ideas, and capital are the nutrients.

An economic development summit hosted by UNM in September 2012 attracted leaders from the public and private sectors around the state. Victor Hwang was there to explain the Rainforest Concept, which drew significant interest. Ultimately, UNM, Albuquerque mayor Richard J. Berry, and other community leaders committed to creating an innovation district based on the Rainforest Concept, which would capitalize on New Mexico's outstanding scientific

research, strong entrepreneurial assets, and thriving creative community.

THE LOCATION

The next step was to select the central location for Innovate ABQ, as the district became known. President Frank led a group of UNM and community leaders on a visit to the University of Florida to visit its innovation district, Innovation Square. A community effort, Innovation Square consists of five million square feet of office space for the University of Florida's business incubator, start-ups, and research labs. It also includes residences, retail, and hotels. The group subsequently visited Arizona State University's similar and successful innovation district, SkySong.

UNM also engaged the international planning and design firm Perkins+Will to conduct a feasibility study to identify potential sites for Innovate ABQ. Perkins+Will has been involved worldwide in the planning and design of projects similar to Innovate ABQ. The firm completed

continued on next page

development deal is a good one. More important questions include, first, whether a particular development project will contribute to the long-term strategy of the state and second, whether the project represents the best expenditure of state funds.

The ongoing construction of Spaceport America in New Mexico's Sierra County provides a good example to consider. More than $200 million in New Mexico public funds has been devoted to this project, the hope of promoters of the spaceport being that, when finished, it would generate thousands of high-paying jobs and attract millions of dollars in tourist revenue to the area. It is probably too soon to evaluate whether the its study in March 2013 and the community ultimately accepted it, including the recommendation of a site at Broadway and Central in Albuquerque as the ideal headquarters location.

While the design concept was developed specifically for UNM and the City of Albuquerque, Perkins+Will also studied other innovation districts developed near research universities, including MIT's University Park, the University of California at San Francisco's Mission Bay, University of Pittsburgh/Carnegie Mellon University's Pittsburgh Technology Center, Georgia Tech's Technology Square, and the University of Florida's Innovation Square. Innovation Square has been most useful in providing a development framework for Innovate ABQ.

THE INITIAL DEVELOPMENT

The initial building to be constructed on the seven-acre Broadway site will contain a business incubator for technology-based companies, STC.UNM and other technology-transfer offices, technology

start-ups, and various support businesses. It will also contain laboratory space (with specialized equipment, fabricating capabilities, and clean rooms), learning spaces for education programs, coworking spaces, and meeting spaces for tenants and community entrepreneurial events. Twenty-six start-ups based on UNM technology are currently scattered around Albuquerque. Some of those start-ups, future UNM start-ups, and others start-ups will be located at the new facility.

Business incubators are highly regarded as cost-efficient job creators. One of the many benefits of business incubators is that they create a sense of community for the management and staff of start-up companies as they share challenges, ideas, and experiences, interactions that play significant roles in start-up company success. New Mexico already has several business incubators for more typical local businesses that have shown marked success.

The new technology incubator will also serve as a one-stop shop for outside companies, entrepreneurs, and investors

spaceport will eventually be an economic success. The more important issue is that no one involved in the process ever asked whether $200 million for this project was the best expenditure of public funds on economic development. In other words, would an investment of $200 million in state parks have a better chance of attracting tourists and generating jobs? Would a $200 million investment in water conservation research generate more jobs and income? Would the $200 million be better spent on early childhood programs? The answers are now simply unknown, because the questions were never asked.

seeking to evaluate technologies available for licensing from UNM and other research organizations located there. It will facilitate interactions between the incubator start-ups and investors and offer training and mentoring for the incubator tenants. Apprenticeships will be available for entrepreneurial students who wish to learn more about start-up companies; such students often serve as an important source of future start-up employees.

There are more components to the innovation district than just the Broadway and Central site. Other programs and activities will likely become a part of Innovate ABQ. For example:

- The founder of the BioScience Center, a successful privately operated biotechnology incubator in Albuquerque, recently announced that he will soon be opening a second incubator in the innovation district, specifically for information technology companies. It will be located directly across the street from the Broadway site.

- Largely on the basis of the Innovate ABQ project, the City of Albuquerque was designated one of five U.S. cities (the others being Seattle, San Francisco, New Orleans, and San Antonio) to receive significant grants and loans from a collaborative of twenty-two of the largest foundations and financial institutions in the country. This collaborative made a total of $80 million in grants and loans available to the five cities selected in its prior endeavor. The funds received in Albuquerque will support Innovate ABQ and other downtown revitalization and transportation projects.

- Central New Mexico Community College has announced that it will locate a satellite campus in the innovation district. The campus will be located in the First Plaza Galleria, very near the Broadway site.

The proximity of all of these groups and activities in the innovation district invites mutual support and collaboration, driving

continued on next page

Infrastructure

The need for additional investment in infrastructure in New Mexico is obvious. Much more than a book chapter could be written on this topic alone. A few of the many infrastructure needs for a modern economy include major improvements in roads, bridges, and highways and other transportation-related items. Economic growth could allow the state to invest in transportation infrastructure, but growth creates demand for additional infrastructure. Residents of oil-boom Eddy and Lea Counties know that the roads and highways in the region were not designed for the kind of efficiency and synergy greater than each could accomplish individually. Proximity has a multiplier effect in creating new ideas, programs, and businesses.

Various funding sources have enabled the purchase of the Broadway property in the first half of 2014. The City of Albuquerque has committed $2 million to the project and Bernalillo County $1 million, while the New Mexico Educators Federal Credit Union has made a very generous gift of $3 million. Additionally, a federal Economic Development Administration grant of $1.5 million has been received. Other donors have expressed interest as well.

NEW MEXICO 2050

My own experience and study tell me that Innovate ABQ will be a success: more opportunities for creative workers and for entrepreneurs, more start-up companies, and more good-paying jobs.

traffic generated by the increased oil operations. Those roads and highways are deteriorating and badly need repair and upgrades.

High-speed broadband is also an important part of modern business, and access to it is critical for the survival of small, rural communities as well as local artists and craftspeople. Many firms can locate almost anywhere if they have access to high-speed broadband and other communications. Major investments in broadband would almost certainly increase private investment and influence the location decisions of firms.

Poverty and Inequality Reduction

New Mexico could also adopt policies to reduce poverty and lessen inequality for its citizens. Minimum wage laws could be adopted at the state and local levels. There is little evidence to support the widely held view that increasing the minimum wage reduces employment. State law in New Mexico currently requires a minimum wage that is slightly above the national minimum wage ($7.50 and $7.25, respectively). Santa Fe, referring to a "living wage," raised its minimum wage to $10.66 per hour—the second-highest in the nation, behind San Francisco's $10.71 per hour. Albuquerque and Bernalillo County also have raised their minimum wages to levels above the national average. Las Cruces is debating an increase. No economy ever gets very far in the economic development game with a deliberate policy of paying low wages. To provide further assistance to low-wage workers as well as strengthen incentives to work, New Mexico could also increase the state Earned Income Tax Credit.

New Mexico's tax structure, as discussed earlier, is regressive and could easily be reformed in a way that helps the poor without discouraging private sector economic activity. Investments in infrastructure and education and the adoption of a long-range economic development strategy are also key elements in attacking New Mexico's poverty and inequality. New Mexico has wide-ranging policy options.

New Mexico 2050

What will the New Mexico economy look like in the year 2050? There is nothing automatic about economic growth or economic development. Without a new direction—a new strategy—New Mexico's economy in 2050 could look surprisingly like the New Mexico economy of 2014.

But we are optimistic. We envision that by 2050, the technologies developed by New Mexico businesses will be used to deal with a variety of environmental and other problems and that by then New Mexico will provide an environment that nurtures promising start-ups into thriving businesses that choose to be headquartered within the state.

Our vision is that of a dynamic economy in which businesses in many industries are able to prosper, finding here an educated and trained workforce, supply chains able to produce to demanding specifications, other entrepreneurs from whom to learn and with whom to collaborate, and eager if demanding local investors. In this vision, capital will be attracted to New Mexico because things will be happening here. We see a real possibility that New Mexico residents, businesses, educational institutions, and governmental agencies will work together to accelerate the process of economic growth throughout the state.

New Mexico has the opportunity to adopt a new approach to economic development and a set of policies designed to provide economic opportunity for the people of the state. New Mexico does not lack the resources to invest in its own physical and human capital. If New Mexicans make the right policy choices, there is no reason why per capita incomes in the state could not catch up to the national average by 2050. New Mexico would then be in the middle of the pack—ranking about twenty-fifth among states in per capita income, instead of forty-fifth. But economic development in the state offers much more than improved rankings. Economic development as described here could also result in serious reductions in poverty and inequality and increased opportunities for all New Mexicans to thrive.

Notes

1. All data in this paragraph are from U.S. Department of Commerce, Bureau of Economic Analysis, Regional Accounts, www.bea.gov, accessed August 2013.

2. The data in this section are from U.S. Department of Labor, Bureau of Labor Statistics, Quarterly Census of Employment and Wages.

3. New Mexico State University Agricultural Experiment Station / Cooperative Extension Service, *The U.S. Dairy Industry and International Trade in Dairy Products*, Technical Report 42e, September 2005.

4. Dairy Producers of New Mexico website, http://www.nmdairy.org/.

5. Dale M. Doremus, "Environmental Regulation of New Mexico's Dairy Industry," in *Water Resources of the Lower Pecos Region, New Mexico: Science, Policy, and a Look to the Future*, ed. Peggy S. Johnson, Lewis A. Land, L. Greer Price, and Frank Titus, Decision-Makers Field Guide 3 (Socorro: New Mexico Bureau of Geology and Mineral Resources, 2003), 76–79, http://www.nmenv. state.nm.us/gwb/New_Pages/docs_policy/DoremusDecisionMakers.pdf.

6. U.S. Department of Energy, Energy Information Administration, State Energy Profiles, New Mexico, http://www.eia.gov/state/?sid=NM, accessed February 27, 2014.

7. New Mexico Energy, Minerals, and Natural Resources Department, *Annual Report 2013*, http://www.emnrd.state.nm.us/.

8. New Mexico Tax Research Institute, *Fiscal Impacts of Oil and Natural Gas Production in New Mexico: Preliminary Report*, January 2014, http://www. nmtri.org/; U.S. Department of Labor, Bureau of Labor Statistics, Quarterly Census of Employment and Wages, www.bls.gov/qcew.

9. "Crude Oil Production, by States," in American Petroleum Institute, *Petroleum Facts and Figures: Centennial Edition, 1959*, pp. 40–41, CD-Rom.

10. Oil production data in the next few paragraphs are from U.S. Department of Energy, Energy Information Administration, Field Production of Crude Oil, www.eia.gov.

11. "Gross and Marketed Production of Natural Gas, by States," and "Crude Oil Production, by States," in American Petroleum Institute, *Petroleum Facts and Figures: Centennial Edition, 1959*, pp. 102–7, CD-Rom.

12. U.S. Department of Energy, Energy Information Administration, Natural Gas Gross Withdrawals and Production, http://www.eia.gov/dnav/ng/ng_prod_sum_dcu_snm_a.htm.

13. Data for 1882–1927 are from Frank E. Kottlowski, *The Economic Geology of New Mexico* (Socorro: New Mexico Institute of Mining and Technology, 1954). Data for 1928–1960 are from U.S. Bureau of Mines, *Minerals Yearbook, 1952*, vol. 2, table 8, p. 55; and U.S. Bureau of Mines, *Minerals Yearbook, 1960*, vol. 2, table 11, p. 60. Data for 1960–2012 are from U.S. Department of Energy, Energy Information Administration, Coal Data, www.eia.gov.

14. U.S. Department of Energy, Energy Information Administration 2013, Electric Power Annual 2013, tables 3.6 and 3.7, www.eia.gov.

15. Brian McDonald and Philip Farah, *New Mexico Uranium Industry: Current Assessment and Outlook* (Bureau of Business and Economic Research, University of New Mexico, 1982), mimeo.

16. U.S. Department of Energy, Energy Information Administration, Uranium Reserves, http://www.eia.gov/uranium/reserves/table1.cfm.

17. U.S. Department of Energy, Energy Information Administration, Electricity Data, Net Generation by State Historical Tables, www.eia.gov.

18. U.S. Department of Energy, Energy Information Administration, Today in Energy, "Most States Have Renewable Portfolio Standards," accessed December 17, 2014, http://www.eia.gov/todayinenergy/detail.cfm?id=4850.

19. Center for Climate and Energy Solutions, Renewable and Alternative Energy Portfolio Standards, http://www.c2es.org/what_s_being_done/in_the_states/rps.cfm, accessed February 23, 2012.

20. U.S. Bureau of Economic Analysis, Local Area Income and Employment.

21. New Mexico Tourism Department, *Annual Report*, September 2013, http://nmtourism.org/resources/research.

22. National Park Service, *2012 National Park Visitor Spending Effects: Economic Contributions to Local Communities, States, and the Nation*, Natural Resource Report NPS/NRSS/EQD/NRR—2014/765, February 2014.

23. Tourism Economics, Inc., *The Economic Impact of Tourism in New Mexico: 2011 Analysis*, http://nmtourism.org/resources/research.

24. "The Culture Rush," in *New Mexico Art Tells New Mexico History*, New Mexico Museum of Art, online exhibit, http://online.nmartmuseum.org/nmhistory/art-architecture/history-art-and-architecture.html.

25. Jeff Mitchell and Gillian Joyce, findings from a UNM Bureau of Business and Economic Research study for the New Mexico Department of Cultural Affairs, not yet released.

26. U.S. Bureau of Labor Statistics, Quarterly Census of Employment and Wages, 2012–2013, and U.S. Census Bureau, 2011 Nonemployer Statistics.

27. New Mexico's infant mortality rates were the highest in the country, and maternal mortality was 20 percent higher than the U.S. average. See Brad Whorton, *New Mexico Public Health Achievements During the 20th Century* (Santa Fe: New Mexico Department of Health, Office of Vital Records and Health Statistics, August 2002), 6. New Mexico gained a reputation for having a "healthful climate," so many stricken with tuberculosis elsewhere filled the state's sanatoria. New Mexican residents often went without the treatment afforded those in the sanatoria. Ibid., 4.

28. Consider the situation of an obstetrician, who faces an annual cost of $85,000 for malpractice insurance even if never sued.

29. Three hospitals have recently shut down their labor and delivery rooms, and the 2014 legislature saw a battle over Sole Community Provider program funds for hospitals.

30. Keith Hall and Robert Greene, *Government-Financed Employment and the Real Private Sector in the 50 States* (Mercatus Center, George Mason University, November 2013), http://mercatus.org/publication/government-financed-employment-and-real-private-sector-50-states.

31. U.S. Census Bureau, *Consolidated Federal Funds Report for Fiscal Year 2010: State and Local Areas*, September 2011. It should be noted that the 2010 federal

expenditures include those associated with the American Recovery and Reinvestment Act, designed to stimulate the economy in the throes of the Great Recession.

32. "History: The Great Depression and World War II," in *New Mexico Art Tells New Mexico History*, http://online.nmartmuseum.org/nmhistory/people-places-and-politics/the-great-depression/history-the-great-depression-and-world-war-ii.html.

33. U.S. Census Bureau, Poverty Thresholds, http://www.census.gov/hhes/www/poverty/data/threshold/index.html.

34. U.S. Census Bureau, American Community Survey 2012, 1-Year Estimates, table S1702.

35. Ibid., table S1701.

36. "Total income" is the sum of the amounts reported separately for wage or salary income; net self-employment income; interest, dividends, or net rental or royalty income or income from estates and trusts; Social Security or Railroad Retirement income; Supplemental Security Income; public assistance or welfare payments; retirement, survivor, or disability pensions; and all other income. Receipts from the following sources are not included as income: capital gains; money received from the sale of property (unless the recipient was engaged in the business of selling such property); the value of income "in kind" from food stamps, public housing subsidies, medical care, employer contributions for individuals, etc.; withdrawal of bank deposits; money borrowed; tax refunds; exchange of money between relatives living in the same household; gifts and lump-sum inheritances, insurance payments, and other types of lump-sum receipts.

37. U.S. Department of Commerce, Bureau of Economic Analysis, Regional Accounts, www.bea.gov, accessed August 2013.

38. For example, women's labor force participation in New Mexico is generally lower than in the United States. New Mexico has a relatively large Hispanic population, and Hispanic women have lower rates of labor force participation. On the other hand, New Mexico has a relatively small African American population, a group in which labor force participation rates are typically very high.

39. U.S. Bureau of Labor Statistics, Geographic Profile of Employment and Unemployment (CPS) for New Mexico, 2003–2012, http://www.bls.gov/gps/.

40. As cited in a presentation by Peter Winograd, professor of education and director of the UNM Center for Education Policy Research, February 2014.

41. New Mexico Department of Workforce Solutions, *Labor Market Review* 42, no. 11 (January 31, 2014), http://www.dws.state.nm.us/Portals/0/DM/LMI/lmrdec13.pdf.

42. New Mexico Public Education Department, Graduation Rates, 2012–2013.

43. New Mexico Public Education Department, http://www.nmped.org.; Stacy Dean and Dottie Rosenbaum, *SNAP Benefits Will Be Cut for Nearly All Participants in November 2013* (Washington, D.C.: Center on Budget and Policy Priorities, August 2013), http://www.cbpp.org/cms/index.cfm?fa=view&id=3899.

44. Annie E. Casey Foundation, *2013 KIDS COUNT Data Book*, as summarized by New Mexico Voices for Children, *2013 KIDS COUNT in New Mexico*.

45. Michael Mitchell, Vincent Palacios, and Michael Leachman, *States Are Still Funding Higher Education Below Pre-Recession Levels* (Washington, D.C.: Center for Budget and Policy Priorities, May 1, 2014), http://www.cbpp.org/cms/?fa=view&id=4135.

46. New Mexico State Legislature, Fiscal Impact Report for HB 167, Reduce Income Tax Rates, January 30, 2003; New Mexico Legislative Finance Committee, *2003 Post-Session Fiscal Review*, June 2003, p. 2.

47. Historical West Texas Intermediate oil prices as available from the U.S. Department of Energy, Energy Information Administration, http://tonto.eia.gov/dnav/pet/hist/LeafHandler.ashx?n=PET&s=RWTC&f=D. In the introduction to its *2004 Post-Session Fiscal Review*, the Legislative Finance Committee noted, "The volatility of the energy industry continues to raise concerns about the prudence of the state's dependence on the oil and gas industry to buttress otherwise weak revenue growth. And, based on conservative revenue estimates and current program levels, the state will be forced to raise revenues or cut programs next year to comply with the constitutional mandate to balance the budget."

48. Louise Story, "As Companies Seek Tax Deals, Governments Pay High Price," *New York Times*, December 1, 2012, http://www.nytimes.com/2012/12/02/us/how-local-taxpayers-bankroll-corporations.html.

49. Research & Polling, *Business Climate Survey*, February 2014. The survey was commissioned by the Greater Albuquerque Chamber of Commerce.

50. The New Mexico Economic Development Department issued a five-year strategic plan (*Innovation Creates Diversification: Five-Year Plan for Economic Growth and Diversification*) in early 2014. Although there are many worthy features in this plan, it is not a long-term development strategy. NewMarc (New Mexico Association of Regional Councils) is also working on a statewide comprehensive economic development strategy with the financial assistance of the U.S. Economic Development Administration. The NewMarc strategy should be available late this year. The New Mexico Jobs Council, created by the legislature in 2013, is assessing job needs in New Mexico in 2023. Other groups are also actively pursuing economic development strategies.

Chapter 2

New Mexico Education

VERONICA C. GARCÍA

NEW MEXICO IS IN CRISIS! NEW MEXICO IS IN CRISIS!!
New Mexico is in crisis!!! Shout it from the rooftops, print it in two-inch, bold-face headlines above the fold in the newspapers, sound the alarm on radio and television similar to Amber and weather alerts, plaster it on billboards, make it the focus of sermons and speeches, list it as a standing item on all agendas, and include it as a major plank of all political campaigns. Am I exaggerating? No! New Mexico is in crisis!!!!

Consider again, as explained in chapter 1, that in 2013 New Mexico was ranked dead last—fiftieth—in child well-being by the respected Annie E. Casey Foundation in its *KIDS COUNT Data Book*.[1] This ranking has implications far beyond educational outcomes and does not bode well for 2050. It seems that New Mexico is typically at the top of all the "bad" lists and the bottom of the "good" lists.

But we must guard against becoming accustomed to bad news, especially in education, accepting that this is the way it's always been in New Mexico and always will be.

We can do something about it. We *must* do something about it. But simple solutions won't work.

New Mexico's crisis in education involves more than our education system, our schools, and our teachers. It also involves poverty and income inequality. It involves health, too, and the status of the family and the community. The disparate outcomes for children of color (race and ethnicity)

51

must be addressed. I will go into all these areas here, explaining both what the present situation in New Mexico is and what should be done about it, taking into account the recommendations in the 2013 policy agenda, *NM KIDS are COUNTing on Us*, developed by New Mexico Voices for Children as well as some important ones that I have come to feel strongly about as a result of having been a teacher, a school principal, a school superintendent, the New Mexico state cabinet secretary of public education, and the present executive director of New Mexico Voices for Children.

I can say from my own experience that the nationally recognized education expert and advocate Diane Ravitch was right when she wrote, "We need broader and deeper thinking. We must decide if we truly want to eliminate poverty and establish equal educational opportunity. We must decide if we want to build a society with liberty and justice for all. If that is our true purpose, then we need to move on two fronts, changing society and improving schools at the same time."[2]

"Changing society" in New Mexico means, among other things and quite basically, that we must do something about poverty and inequality of income.

Poverty and Inequality of Income

Nationwide, inequality of income has been worsening, so that by the year 2012, 10 percent of earners took in more than half of the total income earned by all Americans, up from one-third in 1979 and the highest level recorded since the government began collecting this data a hundred years ago. By themselves, the top 1 percent of earners in 2012 took in more than one-fifth of America's earned income, 22.5 percent. Nearly one in four Americans— almost 25 percent—lives in poverty today.[3]

What about New Mexico? As we saw in chapter 1, in 2012 New Mexico offered, sadly, just about a mirror image of the national picture in the percentage of people living in poverty, our state's percentage exceeded only by Mississippi's, and New Mexico's per capita income was only 82 percent of the national per capita income, making us forty-third among the states in that respect.[4] Income inequality in New Mexico is just as depressing as in the nation—the lowest 20 percent of New Mexico households have only

3.1 percent of the income, while the highest 20 percent have 50.1 percent. And our middle class is shrinking, as many people have been dropping out of it and into poverty.

Child Poverty in New Mexico

About 30 percent of New Mexico's children under age eighteen (29.8 percent), a total of 157,000 kids, were found to be living in poverty in 2012, an increase from 26 percent in 2005.[5] The federal poverty rate is based on an annual income of $24,028 for a family of four and $12,119 for a one-person household.[6] A family with annual income twice the poverty level is considered "low income." Combine the two groups, and we find that half of all New Mexico children live in families that struggle to provide the basic necessities.[7]

Forty-two percent of New Mexico children are so poor that their families have to rely on the Supplemental Nutrition Assistance Program (SNAP, aka food stamps), and 66 percent of New Mexico children qualify for free and reduced-price meals in New Mexico schools.[8]

Poverty is especially bad for children, as the single best predictor of children's success in school is their family's economic level. Sociologist Sean Reardon has shown that in the United States, the school achievement gap between children raised in poor families and those raised in wealthy ones has grown, just as inequality of income has grown, so that in 2014 the gap is larger by 40 percent than it was thirty years ago. The achievement gap between poor children and wealthy ones is comparable to the gap between fourth graders and eighth graders, and rich kids outperform middle-class kids by as much as middle-class kids outperform the poor.[9] The Center on Budget and Policy Priorities has documented how and why income inequality produces this terrible education achievement gap:

> Most evidence on why poor children underachieve points to a lack of learning stimulation and support at home, at child care/preschool and at school. There is considerable evidence that poverty constrains families' investments in material (e.g., books) and psychosocial (e.g., parent time) resources that promote positive child learning. The homes of poor

children are, on average, defined by inadequate access to materials such as books, age-appropriate toys, and computers; low levels and quality of parent-child talk and little parental engagement in learning or school-related activities with their children; and housing conditions that are not conducive to learning (e.g., poor lighting, limited space, and high noise levels). Outside the home, children in poverty are less likely than other children to attend learning-enriched child care centers and preschools, and schools with high concentrations of children in poverty are exceptionally likely to have teacher shortages, high teacher turnover rates, teachers assigned to topics they are not qualified to teach, and instructional practices that are not empirically informed (e.g., cooperative learning and instructional conversation strategies). In addition, compared with middle-class and wealthier children and adolescents, poor youth are less likely to engage in organized out-of-school activities such as clubs, music lessons, and sports.[10]

When schools are graded for success, or the lack of it, the "poorest-performing schools" in New Mexico, as elsewhere, are virtually always in high-poverty areas.

Race and Ethnicity and Poverty in New Mexico

New Mexico is a minority-majority state. In 2014 we were 47 percent Hispanic, 10.2 percent Native American, and 2 percent African American (with a major decrease coming in the share of the state's population that is non-Hispanic white, which will soon drop to 26 percent).[11] Already 74 percent of New Mexico's children are of racial or ethnic minorities.[12] Fifty-one percent of New Mexico's racial and ethnic minority populations have lower incomes than non-Hispanic whites. Thirty percent of all of New Mexico's Hispanic children live in poverty, compared to 13 percent of non-Hispanic white children and 14 percent of Asian American children. The state's Native American children and African American children have even higher rates of poverty (42 percent and 33 percent, respectively).[13]

New Mexico, not unlike other states in the country, had, and has, glaring performance gaps in student achievement and graduation rates, particularly along racial and ethnic lines. The public became more aware of the differences in outcomes when disaggregated student outcome data was required to be publicly reported under the Federal Elementary and Secondary Education Act, more readily known as President George W. Bush's No Child Left Behind law.

Table 2.1. New Mexico high school graduation rates, 2012–2013

	%
TOTAL	70
Asian	86
Non-Hispanic white	77
African American	68
Hispanic	67
American Indian	64
Economically disadvantaged	64
Students with disabilities	60
English-language learners	65

Source: New Mexico Public Education Department

It is clear that there are large disparities and inequities in student outcomes, particularly by race and ethnicity but also by disability, language proficiency, and income. It is easy to see, for example, that a poor, Hispanic, English-language learner is at high risk for dropping out. In some areas, gaps between different groups of students are larger than forty percentage points. As a group, non-Hispanic white New Mexicans tend to earn more, have higher levels of educational attainment, have lower rates of unemployment, and they are less likely to be uninsured. New Mexico minorities, on the other hand, are disproportionately likely to be low income, poorly educated, unemployed, and uninsured. They are also more likely to be incarcerated and to be teen and/or single parents.

Racial and ethnic disparities affect children, and what affects children greatly affects educational outcomes. Unless we change things drastically, as poorly educated children age and join the workforce—or *not*, as the case may be—their lack of educational attainment will have devastating effects not only on our economy but on the quality of life for all New Mexicans.

Family Poverty—and Education

Thirty-seven percent of all New Mexico children, 192,000 of them, lived in families that lacked secure employment in 2011, an increase from 30 percent in 2008.[14] This insecure family employment situation negatively affects children in a number of ways: the lack of secure employment adds stress to the family, and parents are less likely to focus on their children's educational needs.

Children living in poverty, with its resultant family stress, are more likely to experience Adverse Childhood Experiences (ACEs). These include abuse (emotional, physical, and sexual), neglect (emotional and physical), and household dysfunction (mother treated violently, household substance abuse, household mental illness, parental separation and divorce, and incarcerated household member).[15]

At a 2012 summit sponsored by the Robert Wood Johnson Foundation, researchers reported that ACEs such as abuse and neglect can create dangerous levels of stress and derail healthy brain development, with long-term impacts on learning.[16] (Other effects of ACEs correlate with an increase in health problems later in life: alcoholism and alcohol abuse, chronic obstructive pulmonary disease, depression, fetal death, health-related declines in quality of life, illicit drug use, ischemic heart disease, liver disease, risk for intimate partner violence, multiple sexual partners, sexually transmitted diseases, smoking, suicide attempts, unintended pregnancies, early initiation of smoking, early initiation of sexual activity, and adolescent pregnancy.)[17]

It is easy to see how the cycle continues, as children are born into families where they experience high levels of toxic stress, the lifelong effects of which then create the same conditions for their children. Research demonstrates indisputably that such stress has an impact on cognitive (brain) and behavioral development.[18] And it may have a bearing on postsecondary educational outcomes as well.

Health and Poverty—and Education

Nandini Pillai Kuehn, in chapter 4, shows that, particularly before the passage and full implementation of the Affordable Care Act, access to health care was hampered by poverty. People could not purchase the health insurance they needed without help. And, she writes, this was especially true for Hispanics, Native Americans, and African Americans.

Access to health care is critical for success in school. Children need regular checkups in order for developmental delays to be identified and remediated early. The earlier they receive these and other kinds of intervention, the less likely it is that such children will need more costly interventions later. Further, children need routine health care. A child with continued untreated ear infections, for example, is more likely to have trouble reading in school.[19]

Nearly 9 percent of New Mexico's newborns were found in 2010 to be low-birth-weight babies—a health statistic very much related to the poverty status of the mother and to a lack of prenatal care. Low-birth-weight babies tend to be born prematurely, and these babies are at high risk for learning disabilities and impediments to their full development.[20]

New Mexico should restore outreach and simplify enrollment for Medicaid for kids. Medicaid is the single largest provider of health coverage for kids in our state. Unfortunately, thousands fewer children were enrolled in Medicaid in 2014 than in 2011.[21] We should integrate the health insurance marketplace with Medicaid so that there is "no wrong door" for enrollment. Parents are more likely to take their child to the doctor when they have insurance themselves.

The death of any child or teen is a terribly traumatic thing for a family and community, and such a loss contributes to toxic stress for surviving children. The death rate for New Mexico children or teens was thirty-six per one hundred thousand, a 2010 study showed. New Mexico's overall youth suicide rate is one and one-half times higher than the national average, and it is three times higher for Native American youth. New Mexico should expand behavioral health program funding for suicide and bullying prevention. And we should enact gun-safety laws, including mandating child-safety locks to limit unauthorized access to guns.[22]

Nine percent of New Mexico teens—fifteen thousand youth—were found to be abusing alcohol or drugs in 2010–2011.[23] Drug and alcohol abuse is closely linked to poor school performance and a high probability of dropping out, teen involvement with the juvenile justice system, and high-risk behavior such as engaging in unprotected sex; it also can lead to physical and mental health problems, is a frequent factor in youth suicide, and often contributes to ACEs in the home. New Mexico should expand access to behavioral health programs, as well as access to school-based health centers that can provide a safe, accessible place for youth to receive treatment services that they might not otherwise seek or have access to. And we should allow for treatment instead of incarceration for drug and alcohol offenses.

TEEN BIRTHS PER THOUSAND

In 2010, for every 1,000 teenagers in New Mexico, 53 gave birth, for a total of 3,872 teen births.[24] Pregnant and parenting teens are at increased risk for dropping out of school. Teens are also at higher risk for having low-birth-weight babies, which increases the likelihood that their children will have difficulties in school. Teen parents are more likely to end up living in poverty, thus perpetuating a cycle of poverty, with its associated poor educational and health outcomes.

What is to be done? New Mexico should increase funding for teen pregnancy prevention, from early childhood programs to those involving dropout prevention. If young women are doing well in school and have short-term as well as long-range goals, they are more likely to delay pregnancy.

We should expand access to school-based health centers and evidence-based and age-appropriate sex education. Teens need access to health care professionals who can help provide medically accurate information and support as well as assist the teens in making informed decisions.

Again, we should increase funding for the early childhood programs mentioned above. Teen mothers need the most support, through home-visitation programs, quality child care, and pre-K programs. Evidence indicates that teens participating in quality home-visiting programs may delay second pregnancies. Parent coaching can effectively help teen parents interact with their children in developmentally appropriate ways, which can decrease the number of ACEs and ensure that the children will be ready for school.

Poverty is highly correlated with hunger. Forty-two percent of New Mexico children rely on SNAP benefits.[25] We have one of the highest rates of food insecurity for children in the nation. Proper nutrition is critical to proper brain development. Hungry children have trouble concentrating, and this, of course, also adversely affects their school achievement.

New Mexicans should take note that worsening income inequality produces worsening educational inequality. Nationally, talking about people in the top and bottom 25 percent of earners who were born in the 1960s, 5 percent of the poor people went to college, and 36 percent of rich people did. One generation later, among people born in the 1980s, the number of rich people who went to college jumped by 20 percent, while the number of poor people who did so grew by only 3 percent.[26] And since local public school financing significantly depends on local property taxes (although, fortunately, state funding helps to equalize this in New Mexico) and school districts vary widely in property values, rich districts nationally have been found to have higher-quality schools and teachers than poorer districts have.

It's a vicious cycle. Since those with more and better education earn more, inequality of education produces inequality of income, and, in turn, inequality of income produces inequality of education.

What Is To Be Done about Poverty and Income Inequality in New Mexico?

To reduce poverty and income inequality in our state, first, more well-paying jobs are needed (and chapter 1 has spelled out how that can be accomplished). But here, let me say that creating new jobs requires more state and federal investment in school buildings, highways, water and sewer systems, alternative energy sources, and other infrastructure.

New Mexico must also begin more real economic development initiatives while requiring stricter accountability measures in return for tax breaks that are intended to create jobs. Millions of dollars have been lost in New Mexico over the last dozen years due to tax breaks given with the hope of creating jobs, yet these tax breaks have not created significant number of jobs at all. Ineffective tax breaks represent lost revenue that could have provided New Mexico children more opportunity to succeed, graduate from high school, and attend career preparation programs. An educated and career-ready workforce is what most attracts business and industry to New Mexico.

One urgent priority is the need to raise the minimum wage, both in the Unites States and in New Mexico, and to peg it to the cost of living index. Our state has a higher minimum wage than the federal minimum (which President Obama is rightly trying to get raised to $10.10 an hour), but the New Mexico minimum has lost 10 percent of its purchasing power since it was last raised, in 2009. To raise it just to $8.50 per hour would materially help nearly 20 percent of New Mexico's children, those who have one parent working at wages below that level.[27]

Parents must have safe, reliable child care in order to work and look for work. High-quality child care costs more than tuition in our state's universities, so parents often settle for low-quality child care, which also affects the child's readiness for school.[28] New Mexico should restore eligibility for child care assistance to its earlier level of twice the poverty level. Due to past budget cuts, eligibility for New Mexico child care assistance is down to 125 percent of the poverty level. As a result, some five thousand New Mexico children are on a waiting list, making it difficult for their parents to find and keep work unless they place their children in substandard child care settings.[29]

The next most important thing that New Mexico—and the United States—should do to lower child poverty is to enact a more progressive and equitable system of taxation. New Mexico's state and local tax systems are highly regressive; poor people are hit the hardest. For example, a New Mexican with annual income of $17,000 pays more than 10 percent of his or her income in local and state taxes, while an individual with an income of $323,000 pays less than 5 percent.[30] We should restore New Mexico's former corporate tax rates, recently reduced in order to attract industry to the state. As James Jiménez, director of policy research and advocacy integration for New Mexico Voices for Children, has said, "The more we cut corporate taxes—which we've been doing a lot of in New Mexico—the more we have to collect from individuals and working families to make up the difference. It's that or shortchange our public schools, health care, and public safety services."[31]

New Mexico's unfair system of taxation exacerbates the difficulties of working-poor families. Just as we should expand the reach of the federal Earned Income Tax Credit for working Americans, here in New Mexico we should also increase the Working Families Tax Credit, which 26 percent of New Mexico tax filers claim at its present level, as well as the Low-Income Comprehensive Tax Rebate.[32]

At the federal level, unemployment insurance benefits should be extended to assist the long-term unemployed and benefits for child dependents should be restored, both to help tide families over until they can find work and to prevent crisis situations such as homelessness, which bring on the sort of stress related to ACEs.

And homelessness and poor living conditions should be addressed directly. In 2013 in New Mexico, more than eighteen thousand children aged eighteen and younger (eight thousand under age six) were homeless temporarily or for a longer term.[33] Thirty-six percent of New Mexico's children in 2013 were living in households with a high housing cost burden (more than 30 percent of family income spent on housing), which results in the family having less money for other necessities, such as transportation, utilities, food, and medicine, and forces families into poor housing situations, which can pose other serious health and safety hazards for children.[34]

In regard to housing, New Mexico should increase funding for Individual Development Accounts for parents and children. These accounts are public-private partnerships that give low-income New Mexicans financial incentives to save money in order to purchase a home or pay for college. At the federal level, we should save and preserve the Home Loan Protection Act, which protects families from predatory lending practices, and we should increase funding for the Housing Trust Fund, which provides low-interest loans to organizations that build housing for low- and moderate-income individuals.

To fight hunger, state funding should be expanded for the free and reduced-price lunch program and breakfast in the schools, beginning with low-income Title I schools. County and city summer nutritional programs are also in need of support, as are community programs like Cooking with Kids, community gardens, and Farm to Table, which help children learn about the importance of good nutrition, develop a taste for different foods, and learn how to grow and cook nutritious food. And, of course, at the federal level, we should protect and restore funding for SNAP/food stamps.[35]

Forty-three percent of New Mexico children, 208,000 of them, lived in single-parent families in 2012.[36] Such children are more likely to live in poverty, especially children living with single mothers, who still earn less than men for doing the same work. This can affect educational outcomes because children in single-parent homes and those who experience divorce are more likely to drop out of school, become teen parents, and experience divorce themselves as adults.[37] As I've said, New Mexico should restore eligibility for child care assistance for families with incomes up to twice the poverty level, to allow access to quality child care so that the parents can work and to reduce the levels of toxic stress that affect children's ability to learn.

There are too many teen mothers in New Mexico, and they are more likely than not to be living in poverty. We should expand funding for mentoring programs. And since teen mothers also tend to be unmarried mothers, programs that help young women (and men) develop clear life goals and encourage them to postpone parenthood will reduce teen pregnancy rates and reduce the chances that program participants will drop out of school.

Finally, in regard to poverty and educational outcomes, I agree with Diane Ravitch that "poverty is not an excuse, it's a harsh reality."[38] And we have to deal with it—in America and in New Mexico. Why? Because the sad plight of so many of our fellow Americans and New Mexicans ought to offend our consciences. Moreover, it is not in the best interest of those of us who are better off to allow the current levels of poverty and inequality of income to continue. How many industries, for example, would want to come to a state where so many people are living in poverty—unless they are looking for a place where they could pay a nonlivable wage (and have taxpayers make up the difference)?

In New Mexico and in our nation, we want instead a society where fairness is the rule, where all people have an equal chance to succeed and to take care of themselves and their families by working, if they can. We should all realize that we're in this together and that everybody does better when everybody does better. We want to live in a society that is stable, safe, and secure, a society that supports self-esteem, that makes us proud every day to be members of it. Most of us agree—I do—with President Franklin Roosevelt, who said, "The test of our progress is not whether we add more to the abundance of those who have much. It's whether we provide enough for those who have too little."[39]

New Mexico Education

"Public schools exist to give all children equal opportunity, no matter what their zip code," Diane Ravitch says, but she adds, "as we've seen, there is a strong correlation between poverty and family income, on the one hand, and educational outcomes of children and young people, on the other. . . . Schools fail when they lack the resources to provide equal educational opportunity."[40]

I want to discuss what those needed resources are and what kind of real school reform is necessary. But first I want to say something about what we should not do.

What Doesn't Work?

I've sat in countless legislative hearings listening to legislators offer accounts of their humble beginnings, how they themselves successfully made it out of poverty, yet these legislators do not seem to understand why today's children require additional government spending for essential support programs. "I made it," these legislators have said, in effect, "Why can't everybody else?" Hence bad policy is often made or good policy rejected because of the "exceptions." We shouldn't make policy on the basis of exceptions.[41] Still, I want to tell you my own exceptional story.

MY STORY

I grew up in abject poverty. I remember days when the only food in the refrigerator at home for my mother and me was salad dressing. Thank goodness, we received food stamps and food commodities, and I can tell you that the flour, peanut butter, rice, and other staples we got made a huge difference for us, the difference between having full stomachs and going hungry. I can also tell you that the supplemental nutrition support we got was just that, supplemental. It wasn't always enough to adequately feed the two of us.

As I got older, I worked after school. The money I earned, however, went to help pay bills; there was very little left for school yearbooks, pictures, and other school needs. My class yearbook doesn't include my senior picture; I couldn't afford the photography fee.

I can specifically remember which teachers made a difference in my success (and in which grades they taught me). In high school, I was destined to be a dropout, had it not been for the relationship I had with my speech coach and English teacher, Mrs. Anne Watters. She gave of her own time to be with me and other students after school, prepping us for our speech-team competitions. But it was more than just the coaching—it was her mentoring, her genuine interest in us, her caring, and the relational aspect of teaching and learning.

The support of my wonderful teachers was not enough. There were few, if any, in-school support services to help mitigate the impacts of poverty. There were, though, several important government-funded programs that made a difference in my ability to graduate from high school and college, the first in my family to do either, giving me a real opportunity for success.

For example, had it not been for a program at the University of New Mexico, the College Enrichment Program, I would not have made it. My family had no idea about how to support me when I attended college. Off I went for a summer program, living in the dorms the summer before fall semester. There I had an opportunity to develop a network of friends in the same program who were African American, American Indian, Hispanic, and white, all of us poor, all of us first-generation college attendees, and in most cases first-generation high school graduates.

This little cohort served as a support group for me as we all ventured into this alien world. That UNM program must have been expensive, as we were housed in the dorms for two summers. There we were taught study skills (which I resented and thought I didn't need but later found out I did), we took a couple of summer school courses so that we could get ready for a college curriculum, and we were escorted to many cultural enrichment activities—events at UNM's Popejoy Hall, for example, and the famous Santa Fe Opera, as well as field trips around the state, as many of us had never been out of our own local communities.

That worthwhile UNM program continues today, though, due to decreased funding, it presently provides scaled-down support.

I was able to afford college because of a program that was a part of President Lyndon Johnson's Great Society and War on Poverty initiatives—the National Defense Student Loan and Grant Program. If you applied to college and you were low-income, you were eligible for a student loan that was matched to a grant. If, after receiving these and graduating, you taught in a low-income area or in special education, a certain portion of the loan would be forgiven for each year you taught. I started off as a speech and communications major but my interests shifted to special education; and the loan forgiveness feature gave added incentive to my decision, as well as making college affordable. Even with this vital support, however, it was still necessary for me to work during all of my college years.

So I say again and from my personal experience that poverty is not an excuse. But I can tell you that programs that help mitigate the impacts of poverty give children an opportunity to be successful that they otherwise wouldn't have. Once such opportunity is provided, success, of course, is dependent on an individual's own hard work, as well as myriad other factors, but we can't expect children to do it on their own.

Making policy by exceptions doesn't work. And there are a number of other approaches to school reform that don't work either.

MORE COMPETITION DOESN'T WORK

I am concerned about the so-called education reform that has grown out of a combination of President George W. Bush's No Child Left Behind law and

President Barack Obama's Race to the Top initiative. These efforts are grounded in high-stakes student testing, teacher accountability based on test results, and more school choice. No Child Left Behind presumes that all students will reach proficiency, and Race to the Top intends that schools will demonstrate achievement growth every year. If these things do not happen, it means that schools and teachers are "failures."

Behind this approach is a fundamental belief that schools improve if they are forced to compete and that teachers will produce higher test scores if they are "incentivized" to do so by merit pay. These particular "education reformers" use student test data to fire principals and teachers and close schools, to argue for private and corporate management of public schools, and to minimize the value of teacher credentials or experience because some economists say that they do not increase test scores.[42] The quality of a teacher and of a school are measured narrowly by student test scores. Results are skewed by social class, and the cycle of low performance continues.[43]

I am not against accountability, but I am against measuring teacher effectiveness in an arbitrary and punitive way. Given my considerable experience with New Mexico teachers, I know that if they are invited to the table, they will collaborate on constructing a meaningful and comprehensive evaluation system that is fair and just. It is puzzling to me that some would call a teacher evaluation system "ineffective" because it weeds out *too few* teachers who have experience and the proper credentials. What percentage of doctors, dentists, lawyers, architects, or other professionals are fired every year based on evaluations? My guess is that the number is pretty low.

NARROWING SCHOOL CURRICULA DOESN'T WORK

There is understandably a public focus on lower-performing schools, which typically are in high-poverty areas. Responding, "reformers" often move to narrow the schools' curricula to focus on the skills being tested. Out the window go field trips, enrichment activities, music, art, drama, and courses that aren't tested, such as social studies, geography, and history. Children who live in impoverished communities end up getting the opposite of what they need to enhance their learning and to bring context to their learning environment. Physical education is also important; the latest research on building cognitive functioning shows the vital importance of exercise. Also, health experts have noted that the current generation of children is the first that may not outlive their parents, due to childhood obesity and the serious and very expensive health consequences it can cause later in life, such as hypertension, type 2 diabetes, and heart disease.

SIMPLE GRADING OF SCHOOLS DOESN'T WORK

I do not believe that a simple grading of schools—A to F—is an educational reform any more than I believe that weighing yourself and giving yourself a grade will improve your health. Changing your diet and your exercise habits would be reform, just like changing what we do in schools and in our communities would be true reform.

Deborah Jewell-Sherman, the first woman professor of practice at the Harvard Graduate School of Education, has found that "as school districts and states struggled" to meet their yearly benchmark targets that were set under No Child Left Behind, "labeling schools that showed growth but did not meet yearly benchmarks as 'failing schools' contributed to a serious reduction in the public's confidence in its public schools and frequently demoralized the very teachers and administrators tasked with ensuring increased student achievement."[44]

A SIMPLE MERIT PAY SYSTEM DOESN'T WORK

The notion held by some education "reformers" that merit pay and competition will improve educational outcomes is misguided. The National Center on Performance Incentives at Vanderbilt University carried out a definitive study on merit pay. Some economists had speculated that the reason merit pay didn't lead to good results was that the offered bonuses were too small. The Vanderbilt group experimented by offering a bonus of $15,000 for teachers whose students got higher math scores. Over three years, the researchers closely studied the performance of Nashville public teachers in the experimental group as well as a control group of teachers who didn't get bonuses, and they found no difference in math-teaching results.[45] Ironically, within days of the announcement of the results of the Vanderbilt study, the U.S. Department of Education released the first $500 million grant for its Teacher Incentive Fund, established to encourage more local school districts to try merit pay.

At the same time that the Vanderbilt experiment was initiated, New York City started its own version of merit pay. The city paid out $56 million in bonuses but at the end of three years abandoned the experiment. A Rand Corporation study documented the program's failure to produce results: the experiment did not raise test scores, did not increase teacher satisfaction, and was found to be a waste of public money.[46] Likewise, a four-year study of a Chicago teacher advancement program concluded that, while offering merit pay resulted in a somewhat higher teacher retention rate, it had no significant effect on test scores.[47] As Diane Ravitch writes, "Merit pay is the idea that never works and never dies. No matter how many times it fails, its advocates never give up."[48]

What We Must Do, What Will Work

Linda Darling-Hammond of Standard University, a national leader in the field of public education, sums up well what should be done to improve education:

> It's not as though we don't know what works. We could implement the policies that have reduced the achievement gap and transformed learning outcomes for students in high-achieving nations where government policies largely prevent childhood poverty by guaranteeing housing, health care, and basic income security. These same strategies were substantially successful in our nation through the programs and policies of the War on Poverty and the Great Society, which dramatically reduced poverty, increased employment, rebuilt depressed communities, invested in preschool and K-12 education in cities and poor rural areas, desegregated schools, funded financial aid for college and invested in teacher training programs that ended teacher shortages. In the 1970s teaching in urban

communities was made desirable by the higher than average teacher salaries, large scholarships and forgivable loans that subsidized teacher preparation, and by the exciting curriculum and program innovations that
federal funding supported in many city school districts.[49]

It is clear that there is no simple, single solution to New Mexico's education problems. We need a comprehensive approach. Education expert Pedro
Noguera reports that in 2008 a coalition of scholars, policy makers, and
educational leaders issued a policy statement that called for three major revi-
sions in education policy: expand access to learning time through quality
after-school and summer school programs; provide universal pre-K programs; and provide universal health care for children. This reform was called
the Broader, Bolder Approach (BBA) to education. The BBA reform agenda
is part of a larger national effort to develop a comprehensive school-reform
strategy and change the focus and direction of educational policy to include
attention to the social and economic factors arising out of distressed social
contexts within impoverished communities that often undermine schools
and children.

Many of the cognitive and behavioral deficits with which children come
to school begin long before they enter their first classroom. As Diane Ravitch
says, "Achievement gaps begin long before children start kindergarten on the
first day of school. If we are serious about narrowing the gap, we need stable,
experienced staff, [a] rich curriculum, social services, after-school programs,
and abundant resources to meet the needs of these students."[50]

MONEY

On the subject of New Mexico education problems, one often hears conservative budget cutters saying something like, "Well, we can't just throw
money at the problem." Why not make evidence-based investments? What
would they prefer to throw, blame? On the contrary, I believe that if we
really want better schools and better education outcomes in New Mexico, it's
not enough just to point the finger of blame, as some people do—at teachers,
principals, schools, universities, parents, children, communities, the media,

state legislatures, state agencies and departments, the federal government, or Congress. We should be positive. And we're going to have to spend more money, too.

The New Mexico Center on Law and Poverty recently filed a lawsuit alleging that the state of New Mexico is failing to comply with a provision in the New Mexico Constitution that requires the state to establish "a *uniform* system of free public schools *sufficient* for the education of, and open to, all the children of school age in the state" (italics added) and asking the courts to mandate that the state effectively carry out that constitutional requirement. Whether this lawsuit proves to be successful or not, I hope it helps more policy makers come to agree with what a center official said when she announced the lawsuit: "Tracking results and accountability are critical. But we can start with what evidence indicates will work: well-trained and well-paid teachers; adequate numbers of quality teachers' aides; properly trained reading specialists and support services; parental engagement; and integrating music and art into the curriculum. . . . Even with this year's increase in the education budget, we are not back to 2008 levels of funding when adjusted for inflation, when experts and policy makers on both sides of the aisle agreed that our schools were already underfunded."[51]

What needs to be done to improve education in New Mexico will cost money. No way around that.

EARLY CHILDHOOD EDUCATION

If we really want to improve New Mexico education and outcomes, we have to start with the basics—and that means early childhood education.

It is universally accepted that 80 percent of a person's brain development occurs within the first five years of life and that full development is dependent on early nurturing and stimulating experiences. Yet, the 2013 report *NM Kids are COUNTing on Us* showed that from 2009 to 2011, 62 percent of New Mexico's children, then thirty-five thousand children, were not attending any pre-K preschool.[52] That's still largely the situation.

New Mexico's total annual early childhood education budget need is estimated at approximately $409.9 million, but the 2014 state budget provides only

$108 million for that purpose.[53] That's a large funding gap. Fortunately, we have a quarter of necessary funds—even without a tax increase.

A high priority in New Mexico? Getting the New Mexico State Legislature to refer, and the people to vote to adopt, a constitutional amendment to provide new and sustaining funds for early childhood education by annually earmarking for that purpose a small percentage of the income generated from New Mexico's Land Grant Permanent Fund.

New Mexico's multibillion dollar, and growing, Land Grant Permanent Fund is the second-largest state fund in the nation, the largest on a per capita basis.[54] The fund maintained a steady average rate of growth of 11 percent through the country's devastating Great Recession, which began in 2007, and it grew an amazing 13.28 percent in 2013, nearly double its targeted return on investment—winding up that year with a total of almost $13 billion in principal.[55]

Professor James J. Heckman, a Nobel Prize–winning economist at the University of Chicago, is one of the most prominent American advocates of early childhood education. Because he approaches the subject from an economist's point of view, he focuses on pursuing the most cost-effective way to heal economic and social dysfunction in our country. Heckman states that the number of children who are born into disadvantaged environments—at risk for teen pregnancy, crime, poor health, and a lifetime of low earnings—is increasing, and he adds, "The absence of supportive family environments harms child outcomes. The good news is if society intervenes early enough, it can improve cognitive and socio-emotional abilities and the health of disadvantaged children. Early intervention not only enhances the life prospects of children but also has a high benefit-cost ratio and rate of return for society's investment. The longer society waits to intervene in the life cycle of a disadvantaged child, the more costly it is to remediate the disadvantage."[56]

Heckman believes that noncognitive skills like motivation, self-discipline, and the ability to work with others are as important for success in life as cognitive skills. But federal education policy under No Child Left Behind deprioritizes noncognitive skills. Heckman further cites studies like the Nurse-Family Partnership Program, the Perry Preschool Project, and the

Abecedarian Project to demonstrate that investment in early childhood education improves noncognitive skills and has significant long-lasting effects that represent the best return on society's investment.[57]

Similarly, in New Mexico numerous studies, including progress reports on pre-K attendees here, show that children who attend pre-K are more likely to outperform their peers who have not attended pre-K and are more likely to be reading at grade level by grade three.

Arguments against using a small portion of the New Mexico Land Grant Permanent Fund for early childhood education, where it will make the most significant difference in improving educational outcomes and child well-being in our state, are misguided at best. Rhetoric such as "we must not 'raid' the fund" and "save the fund for future generations" make as much sense as a family saving money for a rainy day, then not spending something like seventy-five dollars on preventive dental care for their child, only to spend thousands of dollars later for expensive remedial dental treatment.

There are a safeguards in the proposed amendment to protect the fund from being depleted.

New Mexico is in crisis! Our children are in crisis! There are not currently enough general-fund dollars available to meet the need for early childhood education without this constitutional amendment. But with or without the constitutional amendment, we should increase general-fund spending on early childhood programs, including child care assistance, pre-K, and training/technical assistance for early learning providers. This type of support is vital and, coupled with parent-coaching programs such as home visiting, will reduce the incidence of child abuse and subsequent ACEs, which negatively impact educational outcomes.

We should also, of course, as I've said more than once, restore eligibility for child care assistance to twice the poverty level. State-supported child care allows parents to work so they can better provide for their children. It helps them obtain a higher quality level of child care than they otherwise would be able to afford, and high-quality child care can make a positive difference in a child's school readiness.

New Mexico's pre-K program has been studied and found to be successful at improving student achievement.[58] It should be made universally available to all in New Mexico who want to participate and should eventually be provided as a full-day program.

At the federal level, President Obama's Preschool for All proposal should be passed by Congress. The United States is one of the few wealthy nations that lacks a comprehensive plan for early learning. The president's proposal would be a major positive step forward for our children, increasing their chances for long-term success, and would give states the financial support they need to expand their most effective programs.

NEW MEXICO'S PUBLIC SCHOOLS GENERALLY

The 2011 National Assessment for Educational Progress (NAEP) found that 79 percent of fourth-grade children in New Mexico were not proficient in reading.[59] Lack of reading proficiency by the fourth grade is a major problem for children, because prior to that time they are supposed to be taught the mechanics of reading; after third grade, they are supposed to be reading to learn. Children not proficient in reading by the time they reach the fourth grade will have significant difficulty in mastering other subjects and will be at greater risk for dropping out of school.

As also mentioned in chapter 1, a 2011 NAEP assessment found that 76 percent—think of it, three-fourths!—of New Mexico eighth graders were not proficient in math.[60] When middle school students are behind in math, they will not be prepared for the rigors of algebra and additional math requirements needed to graduate from high school, nor will they be properly prepared for college. And we all know that math skills have become more important in today's high-tech work environment.

A study conducted during the 2009–2010 school year found that 33 percent of New Mexico high school students failed to graduate on time.[61] The lifelong costs of dropping out of high school are indisputable, and dropping out continues the cycle of poverty: children of dropouts are more likely to be dropouts themselves.

What's to be done about these really disturbing facts about New Mexico public education?

Again, research clearly shows that children who receive high-quality early childhood care and education programs start school on track and stay on track. If students have quality pre-K, early learning programs like home visitation, and high-quality child care, they have an increased likelihood of reading at grade level by the fourth grade, of being proficient in math by eighth grade, and of graduating from high school on time.

In addition to the recommendations stated earlier regarding increasing funding for early childhood education, New Mexico should restore K-12 per-pupil funding to pre-recession levels. During the recent Great Recession, New Mexico made some of the deepest budget cuts in the nation in K-12 per-pupil spending, adjusted for inflation.[62]

We also need to increase the number of in-school reading coaches, reading specialists who can provide the additional support for children who come to school with delays, and to improve literacy skills for all children. And we should provide needed math coaches and additional teacher professional development in mathematics.

We should also fund in-school efforts that mitigate the effects of poverty and give children in poverty a fair opportunity for success, including smaller class size, breakfast in the schools, extended day care, and tuition-free summer schools.

We should expand funding for the K-3 Plus program, which adds an additional twenty days to the school year for those grades. This program, primarily for low-income communities, gives students the opportunity to have additional time on task to ensure that they are at grade level by the end of third grade. We should expand K-3 Plus to K-8 Plus. Students who have benefited from the additional support of K-3 Plus do not magically need less support after third grade. Many will, instead, continue to require additional instructional time. It should be noted that countries that outperform our national average on standard assessments offer more than the 6.5 hours of school per day and the 180 school days per year that New Mexico offers its public school children.

We should identify students in ninth grade who require additional learning time and provide them with free summer school, after-school tutoring, and online learning opportunities such as the present in-state and publicly funded program IDEAL-NM (Innovative Digital Education and Learning-New Mexico).

We should provide additional school counselors. Teenagers, particularly those in poverty, require more support in dealing with the high levels of toxic stress to which many are exposed. Current staffing levels allow counselors to provide only the minimum level of counseling. Unfortunately, counselors spend most of their day coordinating testing, class schedules, and transcript checks. In some schools, the overload demands on the time of principals and assistant principals result in counselors being tasked with administrative and student disciplinary duties.

We should increase graduation rates by fully implementing the "high school redesign" (a part of the Richardson administration's Making Schools Work Reform) plans for funding more dual-credit, online, and AP courses as well as relevant service-learning opportunities.

More professional development for teachers on the use of technology is also needed, so that teachers can be better prepared to engage students who would benefit from the use of technology to enhance their learning opportunities.

Finally, schools are at the center of their communities; parent and community engagement are critical in supporting children in school. Evidence shows that community schools that provide wraparound services such as onsite, quality tutoring, school-based health clinics, and access for parents to training in English as a second language, as well as enrichment programs such as dance, music, and art classes, can go a long way toward strengthening schools and improving educational outcomes. They also can engage the family and community by providing a more enriching school experience, which will positively affect truancy. Kids need to be in school; we need to focus on the student-teacher relationship and on how we can make school a more accommodating and inviting place rather than looking at punitive measures to improve school attendance.

TEACHER QUALIFICATIONS AND COMPENSATION

Highly skilled teachers (and principals) are the key to successful schools. We must provide a better level of compensation to help us attract and retain the best and the brightest in the profession. There is too much turnover in New Mexico. Each year, too many teachers (and principals) leave the state or the profession, seeking greener pastures.

Prior to my appointment as New Mexico cabinet secretary for public education in 2002, a broad-based group of stakeholders developed and passed through the legislature a three-tiered teacher-licensure system to be instituted in response to the federal requirement for increasing the share of teachers who are highly qualified and for giving teachers an incentive to acquire master's degrees and/or national board certification. Attached to the system were required increases in teacher pay. Before this three-tiered licensure system was put in place, around 78 percent of New Mexico teachers were certified. Afterward, by 2010, almost 99 percent of our teachers were certified.

Everybody wants doctors, nurses, dentists, lawyers, and accountants, for example, to have a certain amount of required education and certification. We all believe that degrees, training, and certification make a difference in these professions. Yet when it comes to teaching, some are quick to dismiss training as unimportant. Part of this attitude, I think, comes from our personal familiarity with the education setting: most of us have spent at least twelve years in school, more if we attended college.

We feel we are knowledgeable about what good teaching requires and what is important. Teaching expert David F. Labaree has described the situation in a way that anyone who has been a teacher recognizes: teaching is hard and complex work, and it is extraordinarily difficult to construct a good and objective measure of effective teaching. Still, so many nonteacher policy makers and members of the general public believe that teaching is an extension of child rearing. Teaching looks easy because everyone has been in school, because public school teachers are conveying knowledge and skills that adults already have, and because teachers give away their expertise.[63]

SCHOOL HOURS

We have a long tradition of expecting teachers to do much that is required on their own time: to prepare for classes, to create stimulating learning environments and engaging activities, to thoughtfully grade papers, to increase their skills and their own learning, to engage in in-service and staffing meetings about select students, and to meet with parents.

I ask you to consider the following three examples. The basic teacher contract typically runs for 182 days a year and seven hours a day. A teacher who starts at $30,000 per year is earning about $23 per hour and $164 per day. If that beginning teacher were working a standard contract that paid her for an eight-hour day and 220 days per year, she would earn $184 per day, or about $40,480 per year. This seems like a reasonable beginning salary for someone coming out of college with a bachelor's degree. If we were to take a more seasoned teacher with a master's degree earning a current salary of $45,000 per year and extend that contract to an eight-hour day and 220-day contract, that teacher would earn $62,166 per year.

We know that students in other high-performing countries attend school for more hours per day and have a longer school year. In New Mexico, data show that programs like K-3 Plus, which adds twenty days to the school year, get good results and are raising the annual salaries of teachers in the program.[64]

Employing teachers at their current rate and extending their contract to an eight-hour day and a full calendar year would make the profession of teaching more appealing, as the pay would be more commensurate with teacher-education requirements. It would attract more individuals who would love to teach but cannot afford to enter the profession at the current, substandard salaries. It would create a greater and more diverse pool of teachers, and it would give children additional learning time that would significantly mitigate the impacts of high poverty and increase their opportunity to succeed.

Extending the school day and school year, coupled with early diagnosis of student learning problems and targeted intervention, would also obviously be a more effective strategy than third-grade-level retention, which some advocate.[65] Regardless, social promotion versus grade retention as an either/or proposition has been debunked by researchers from the University of California, who have shown that a multitiered approach to addressing academic delays, avoiding the negative impacts of retention, is worthwhile, doable, and preferable.[66]

SCHOOL LEADERSHIP

The school principal is critical to creating a supportive and motivating environment for teachers. In fact, teachers themselves cite the quality of their principal as more important than pay in influencing whether they stay in their teaching positions. And good research on the effects of the school principal shows that leadership is second only to classroom instruction among all school-related factors that contribute to what students learn in school. School leaders improve teaching and learning indirectly and most powerfully through their influence on staff motivation and commitment and on working conditions.[67] New Mexico should do everything it can to recruit and train outstanding school principals.

TEACHING TEACHERS

New Mexico should again fund a program that was started but not continued for an asserted lack of money: a partnership between the New Mexico State Public Education Department and the Golden Apple Foundation to provide support to high school students who decide to major in education. This would provide a pipeline of teachers who have the cultural sensitivity to go back and work in their communities. Congress should resurrect the National Defense Student Loan and Grant program for high-need occupations, including teaching, and provide loan forgiveness for program participants who go on to work in the occupation or profession.

ADULT EDUCATION

Twenty-two percent of New Mexico children, 115,000 children, were found in 2011 to be living in a home where the household head lacked a high school diploma.[68] Children's educational attainment levels are closely tied to the educational attainment levels of their parents. Parents who lack a high school diploma often lack the confidence and skills to help their children with their schoolwork, and they often feel less able to advocate for their children and interact with school personnel on behalf of their children. Parents without high school diplomas tend to earn less money, be stuck in low-wage jobs, and have higher rates of unemployment. These conditions often produce toxic stress in the home, which negatively affects the children and their performance in school.

What is to be done? We should expand funding for adult basic education classes and classes in English as a second language.

UNDOCUMENTED IMMIGRANTS

There are something like 11 million undocumented immigrants in the United States, an unknown but sizeable number of them in New Mexico.[69] Many are what are called "Dreamers," young people who were brought here as minor children by their parents *sin papeles*—without papers, or immigration authorization documents. New Mexico has provided by law that any such young people who graduate from a New Mexico high school are entitled to pay state-resident tuition at any New Mexico college or university; that right should, of course, continue to be recognized, and they should continue to be permitted to receive New Mexico Lottery Scholarships. President Obama, by a 2013 executive order, deferred for two years any federal attempt to deport these young people, allowing them work permits; this order should be made permanent by act of Congress.

Further, Congress should at last pass comprehensive immigration reform to grant permanent residence and a reasonable path to citizenship for all undocumented immigrants who have been living and working in the United States for a time while obeying the law and paying their taxes. It is important that these people be brought out of the shadows and allowed to work openly, educate themselves, receive health care, fully participate in our society and politics, and thereby give a real boost to our economy.

RURAL EDUCATION

Two-thirds of New Mexico's eighty-nine school districts are rural, each with a student population of two hundred or fewer. (One-third of all New Mexico public school students attend the Albuquerque Public Schools.) These small rural school districts are the heart and soul of their communities, not only providing jobs as the largest employer in the community but helping build the local economy through school activities and athletics.

Declining population and dwindling economic opportunities are all too common problems in rural communities around the United States, as well as in New Mexico. Consolidating school districts, and thus closing some small schools, as a way to save money has generally meant that the small town or community where the school closed pretty much closes down, too. Consolidations are, of course, much opposed locally—and are to be avoided, if possible. In 2005 the New Mexico State Legislature adopted a Department of Public Education proposal, the New Mexico Rural Revitalization Initiative, under which local community leaders where a school closing was threatened worked with the school on projects and programs to improve the community's economic health and the school's chances for survival. Twenty-eight school districts participated in this program when it began, a number that grew to forty-five.[70] Unfortunately, this program was eliminated and lost its funding from the legislature. It should be revived.

Regardless, New Mexico needs to strengthen its rural schools.[71] Increasing the opportunity and capacity for distance learning is important. We should ensure that all rural schools have access to broadband and to advanced technological equipment, so they can participate in synchronous and asynchronous coursework. Among rural schools, too, there should be more collaboration and pooling of resources and administrative functions through Regional Educational Cooperatives.[72]

TECHNOLOGY

We should support the implementation of President Obama's Connect Ed Initiative and Connect Educators Plan to improve New Mexico education at all levels, rural as well as urban, by providing broadband high-speed Internet access for all schools, students, and teachers. "Technology offers extraordinary opportunities and capacities to teachers," the U.S. Department of Education has said. "The breadth and depth of educational materials and information available on the Internet can break boundaries, making any subject accessible anywhere, and providing students with access to experts from across town or across the globe."[73] These new technologies will give teachers the tools and flexibility to engage students and personalize the learning experience, as well as share resources and best practices with other teachers.

We should extend New Mexico K-12 education by utilizing another distance learning opportunity, MOOCs (massive online open courses), which provide unlimited participation and open access to classes via the Web.[74]

HIGHER EDUCATION

New Mexico is in crisis, too, when it comes to postsecondary and higher education. The 2011 report of the Complete College America initiative states, "For a strong economy, the skills gap must be closed." By 2020, the report shows, 61 percent of jobs will require a career certificate or college degree. Only 29 percent of New Mexico adults had an associate's degree or higher at the date of the report, which results in a 32 percent skills gap. Graduation rates in New Mexico, the report adds, "are very low, especially if you're poor, part time, African American, American Indian, Hispanic or older." The report further reveals that 57 percent of New Mexico students who enter two-year colleges require remediation, and 12.1 percent of students who enter four-year colleges require remediation.[75]

Table 2.2. Two-year college graduation rates, New Mexico, 2010

	ALL STUDENTS (%)	WHITE (%)	HISPANIC (%)	AMERICAN INDIAN (%)
Certificates				
2005 on time (1 year)	1.8	2.1	1.3	2.5
2005 two years	0.8	0.8	0.8	1.0
Associate's degrees				
2 years	3.3	3.7	2.0	3.7
3 years	5.4	5.4	5.5	6.0
4 years	7.1	6.9	7.5	8.2

Source: New Mexico Public Education Department

Table 2.3. Four-year college graduation rates by ethnicity, New Mexico and U.S. averages

	4 YEARS (%)	6 YEARS (%)
Total		
New Mexico	11.9	40.6
United States	31.3	56.0
White		
New Mexico	15.2	46.2
United States	34.2	58.9
Black		
New Mexico	8.6	32.0
United States	16.4	38.3
Hispanic		
New Mexico	9.2	37.1
United States	21.5	47.8
American Indian		
New Mexico	17.2	37.0
United States	—	21.1

Source: *Chronicle of Higher Education*, College Completion microsite, http://collegecompletion.chronicle.com/state/#state=nm&sector=public_four

Low graduation rates for New Mexico community colleges and four-year universities point toward decreased earning power for the students who don't complete their degrees, a weak New Mexico economy, and poor prospects for state job growth, as industry and business seek an educated and career-ready workforce. In central New Mexico there is a corrective initiative, called Mission Graduate, the goal of which is to see sixty thousand students in the region complete post-secondary degrees between 2013 and 2020. The outcome of this effort will have an impact on New Mexico 2050. Our state cannot expect to thrive economically in a knowledge-based economy with low levels of educational attainment.[76]

What is to be done in New Mexico higher education?

First, think of the New Mexico students. Tuition in New Mexico four-year universities has increased by more than 25 percent since 2008.[77] We should support President Obama's efforts to hold down such increases, which represent alarmingly rising barriers to higher education for so many young people from lower- and middle-income families.

Congress should provide more student grants and low-cost loans, as advocated by U.S. senator Elizabeth Warren.[78] It should find some way to forgive, or ameliorate, the enormous overhanging student-loan debt in this country, which is such a terrible burden for the young people involved and such a heavy drag on the nation's economy.

In New Mexico, we should support policy initiatives to lower the costs of education for students, fully fund Lottery Scholarships, restore the College Affordability Fund, lower student-loan rates, and end the predatory practices of some private, for-profit colleges whose graduates often wind up with crushing debt and poor job prospects.

New Mexico's colleges and universities should maintain or establish programs to support first-generation college attendees, program such as ENLACE (ENgaging LAtino Communities for Education), the College Enrichment Program, and Gear Up, and actively recruit minority staff who have firsthand experience in the cultural and linguistic contexts from which so many students come. We should provide more opportunities for poor and minority students to participate in "jump-start" programs to provide orientation and contextual experience during the summer before college students formally begin their fall coursework.

Experienced professors should be assigned to teach more of the beginning, fundamental college and university courses that are often taught by less experienced graduate students, and there should be an expansion in the offers of synchronous and asynchronous online courses and project-based coursework that minimize the need for regular, face-to-face instruction, so as to increase the flexibility of course schedules and better accommodate working students.

Now consider our college and university institutions themselves. More money is needed, of course. But there are other needs, too.

New Mexico funds twenty-five institutions of higher education: seven four-year universities, ten branch campuses, and eight community colleges with several "twigs."[79] Arizona, by comparison, serves four times as many postsecondary students with fewer state-supported schools. There is no political will for cutting out any of these institutions; many of them could be eliminated only by amendments to the New Mexico Constitution. So it is essential that, under the guidance of the New Mexico State Legislative Finance Committee, the various institutions develop a statewide plan for coordination and alignment of programs and the elimination of duplicative competition among specialized programs where practicable.

I agree with the New Mexico Legislative Finance Committee recommendations for higher education funding-formula changes to provide incentives for improving the cost-effectiveness of services as well as boosting completion rates, on-time graduation rates, and degree-production rates. And New Mexico's higher education institutions will need to continue to curb spending on administration and to review the costs of athletics and general subsidies for enterprises like alumni offices and foundations with the use of instruction and general funds.[80]

New Mexico 2050

Bottom line: New Mexico is in crisis. But New Mexico's situation is not hopeless. By putting our differences aside and coming together for the common good of our children and our state we can turn things around. It won't come quickly, it won't be easy, and there will be no simple solutions.

Not every single thing recommended here will be adopted in New Mexico, of course, but a lot of these proposals will be, especially the priority ones, because more and more of us will come to see that they are the right thing to do and are in our own best collective self-interest.

Real education reform won't come cheap, either, but it can be accomplished—if we have the political will and the courage, as I believe we do, to truly put New Mexico's children first and hold to the ideal that all children deserve be given the opportunity to succeed.

I am going to be optimistic and say that I believe that New Mexicans will consciously decide to support the preservation of public education as a key to maintaining and strengthening a democratic society. It is in the public schools that children from different backgrounds, ethnicities, and walks of life come together and build relationships and understanding that only serve to strengthen our society. We will be vigilant against "reform" strategies that seem constructed to ensure public school failure and to justify the privatization of public schools, schools to be run and governed by for-profit companies and boards of directors, not public boards of education. We will decide that we are going to keep, increase investment in, and strengthen our public schools.

We will also decide, I believe, that we are not going to allow the continued narrowing of school curriculum to focus on certain skills, discarding what we know makes for well-rounded and educated citizens. There are life lessons to be learned in exploring literature and understanding history, becoming aware of past mistakes that we hope future generations will not repeat. It is important for our children—for us, too—to learn of the civil rights struggles and fights for freedom of our predecessors and what sacrifices they made in order for us to be able to live in the kind of society we enjoy today. Critical thinking and the ability to analyze and synthesize information will continue to be important skills in this century and beyond.

We will truly recognize that teaching children how to learn and instilling in them a love for lifelong learning is as essential as teaching discreet skills. We must recognize that we are preparing children for a future we cannot yet fully imagine, just as my teachers over fifty years ago were preparing me for a world that they couldn't fully imagine, either.

We will decide that feeding the spirit is as important as feeding the mind and that cognitive skills are in fact strengthened through music, dance, and art. We will recognize that learning a second language enhances cognitive development as well as improves a student's employability and ability to communicate effectively with more people. Business leaders are right when they say that workers also need the so-called soft skills, such as the ability to show up on time, meet deadlines, cooperate with others, collaborate in groups, and deal with conflict and differences of opinion, as well as creativity, initiative, and impulse control. These are all characteristics that teachers play an important role in instilling in their students. Those skills will be equally as important in 2050 as they are today.

We will show by our actions that we believe that New Mexico, a multicultural state, was right in adopting the only Indian Education Act and Hispanic Education Act in the nation and that these acts should be enforced

and implemented. We will agree that the achievements of the children covered by the acts should be monitored and reported on in an annual status-of-
education report and that the maintenance of language and culture is an
important element in strengthening a child's sense of self and pride, which
enhances the child's overall feeling of efficacy.

Importantly, we will not ignore the longitudinal research findings from
one-way and two-way dual-language models of schooling that demonstrate
the substantial power of bilingual education for enhancing student outcomes
and fully closing the achievement gap. Education researchers Virginia Collier
and Wayne B. Thomas from George Mason University said this about their
relevant study, "We used the word *astounding* in the title because we have
been truly amazed at the elevated student outcomes resulting from participation in dual [language] programs after almost two decades of program
evaluation research that we conducted in 22 large and small school districts
from 15 different states, representing all regions of the United States, urban,
suburban, and rural counties. We continue to be astonished at the power of
this school reform model."[81]

We will continue to believe that support services provided through com-
munity-schools initiatives like after-school programs; tutoring; enrichment
programs; school-based health clinics; provision of counselors, nurses, and
social workers; and extended school days and school years are important to
give poor children and children of color an equitable (fair and just) opportunity to succeed in school.

We will look critically at the policies and funding priorities that continue
the cycle of poverty and lack of educational outcomes. Our school budgets
will provide funding that demonstrates our belief that, while schools can and
must do better, there are issues outside of schools that we as a society have an
obligation to address.

History will show that New Mexico made a bold move in one of the
interventions with the highest leverage, fully investing in early childhood
education and expanding the traditional definition of early childhood to
include children up to age eight. Scientific research and economic forecasts
show indisputably that we can break the cycle of poverty through positive
educational outcomes by investing in the early years (home visitation, quality

child care, increased child care assistance, quality pre-K, and investment in the professional development of the early childhood workforce). We as a state will have explored all options for piecing together the necessary funding, particularly that of taking a very small portion of the Land Grant Permanent Fund, as well as introducing new and innovative income-generating taxes or reprioritizing general fund spending. We will have abandoned the misguided rhetoric of "We can't afford to 'raid' the fund" and "We must save the fund for future generations." If we do all this, by 2050 we will not have lost the current generation and we will see savings in government spending (through less crime, fewer incarcerations, lowered health costs, and less remediation) and will increase our tax base, as we will have more contributing, taxpaying members of society. We will not have placed future generations at risk of living lives of poverty and requiring expensive remediation.

Finally, we will stop demonizing and start supporting our teachers and, for that matter, all educators. Why would anyone want to join this honorable and meaningful profession with the disrespect and lack of autonomy it has endured?

In 2050, New Mexico can be a flagship state. There is no silver bullet, but, working together, we can move from a state at the bottom of the barrel to a high-performing state.

¡Sí, se puede!

Notes

1. State Profiles, *2013 KIDS COUNT Data Book* (Baltimore, MD: Annie E. Casey Foundation, June 2013), http://datacenter.kidscount.org/publications/databook/2013.

2. Diane Ravitch, *Reign of Error: The Hoax of the Privatization Movement and the Danger to America's Public Schools* (New York: Alfred A. Knopf, 2013), 225.

3. Barack Obama, "Remarks by the President on Economic Mobility," White House, December 4, 2013. On inequality of income, see also Annie Lowrey, "The Rich Get Richer Through the Recovery," *Economix* (blog), *New York Times*, September 10, 2013, http://economix.blogs.nytimes.com/2013/09/10/the-rich-get-richer-through-the-recovery/; Joseph E. Stiglitz, *The Price of Inequality*

(New York: W. W. Norton, 2013); Timothy Noah, *The Great Divergence* (New York: Bloomsbury, 2012); and Robert Reich, *Beyond Outrage* (New York: Vintage Books), 2–12.

4. See U.S. Department of Commerce, Bureau of Economic Analysis, Regional Accounts, www.bea.gov, accessed August 2013.

5. U.S. Census Bureau, American Community Survey, 2012 One-Year Estimates, table S1702.

6. U.S. Census Bureau, Poverty Thresholds, http://www.census.gov/hhes/www/poverty/data/threshld/index.html.

7. Sharon Kayne, ed., *NM KIDS are COUNTing on Us: A Policy Agenda for a Better New Mexico* (Albuquerque: New Mexico Voices for Children, September 2013).

8. Stacy Dean and Dottie Rosenbaum, *SNAP Benefits Will Be Cut for Nearly All Participants in November 2013* (Washington, D.C.: Center on Budget and Policy Priorities, August 2013), http://www.cbpp.org/cms/index.cfm?fa=view&id=3899; New Mexico Public Education Department, http://www.nmped.org.

9. Sean Reardon, "The Widening Academic Achievement Gap Between the Rich and the Poor: New Evidence and Possible Explanations," in *Whither Opportunity? Rising Inequality, Schools, and Children's Life Chances*, ed. Greg J. Duncan and Richard J. Murnane (New York: Russell Sage Foundation, 2012).

10. Arloc Sherman, Robert Greenstein, and Sharon Parrott, "Policies to Reduce Poverty," in *Improving the Odds for America's Children: Future Directions in Policy and Practice*, ed. Kathleen McCartney, Hirokazu Yoshikawa, and Laurie B. Forcier (Cambridge, MA: Harvard Education Press, 2014), 206, 207.

11. U.S. Census Bureau, Current Population Survey: Voting Supplement, November 2012; U.S. Census Bureau, Current Population Survey, Population Files by Age, Sex, Race, Hispanic Origin and Non-Hispanic Origin, July 2012. Both obtained from University of New Mexico, Bureau of Business and Economic Research.

12. Veronica C. García, "It's Not an Excuse, It's a Fact: Poverty Hurts Kids," *Albuquerque Journal*, March 21, 2014, A7.

13. Lisa Cacari Stone and Deborah Boldt, *Closing the Health Disparity Gap in New Mexico: A Roadmap for Grantmaking* (Con Alma Health Foundation, May 2006), http://www.borderhealth.org/files/res_798.pdf.

14. Feeding America, "Map the Meal Gap," www.feedingamerica.org/hunger-in-america/our-research/map-the-meal-gap.

15. Centers for Disease Control and Prevention, Injury Prevention and Control, Division of Violence Prevention, Adverse Childhood Experiences Study, www.cdc.gov/violenceprevention/acestudy/.

16. Susan Promislo, "Trumping Aces: Building Resilience and Better Health in Kids and Family Experiencing Trauma," *Culture of Health* (blog), Robert Wood Johnson Foundation, June 19, 2013, www.rwjf.org/en/blogs/culture-of-health/2013/06/toxic_stress_helpin.html.

17. Ibid.

18. Ibid.

19. Teresa Sadowski, The School Speech Therapist, www.theschoolspeechtherapist.com.

20. "Estimated Rates of Preterm Birth per 100 Live Births, 2010," in *Born Too Soon: The Global Action Report on Preterm Birth* (March of Dimes, 2012), http://www.marchofdimes.org/mission/globalpreterm.html.

21. New Mexico Human Services Department, Monthly All Children Eligibility Reports, 2010–2013.

22. New Mexico Suicide Prevention Coalition, http://www.nmsuicideprevention.org.

23. Kayne, *NM KIDS are COUNTing on Us.*

24. Ibid.

25. Ibid.

26. Study by the Russell Sage Foundation quoted in Steve Hargreaves, "How Income Inequality Hurts America," CNNMoney, September 23, 2013, http://money.cnn.com/2013/09/25/news/economy/income-inequality/.

27. Gerry Bradley, *New Mexico's Wage Race to the Bottom: Raising and Indexing the State Minimum Wage to Break the Free Fall* (New Mexico Voices for Children, January 2013).

28. Kayne, *NM Kids are COUNTing on Us.*

29. New Mexico Human Services Department, Monthly All Children Eligibility Reports, 2011–2013.

30. *Who Pays? A Distributional Analysis of the Tax Systems in All 50 States*, 4th ed. (Institute on Taxation and Economic Policy, January 2013).

31. New Mexico Voices for Children, "Report: State Corporate Income Tax Revenue Eroding," press release, April 14, 2014.

32. Figures for the share of filers claiming the Working Families Tax Credit are taken from 2010 federal income tax returns.

33. Kayne, *NM Kids are COUNTing on Us*; National Alliance to End Homelessness, http://www.nmeoc.org/advocacy-policy/campaigntoendhomelessness.

34. Ibid.

35. Dean and Rosenbaum, *SNAP Benefits Will Be Cut for Nearly All Participants*.

36. Kayne, *NM Kids are COUNTing on Us*.

37. "Teen Pregnancy and Divorce," Pregnant Teen Help: Teen Pregnancy, Statistics, Prevention and Facts, January 3, 2012, http://www.pregnantteenhelp.org/teenage-pregnancy-divorce.

38. Ravitch, *Reign of Error*, 224.

39. Quoted in Marian Wright Edelman, afterword to McCartney, Yoshikawa, and Forcier, *Improving the Odds for America's Children*, 217.

40. Ravitch, *Reign of Error*, 224.

41. Ibid., 225.

42. Ibid., 18.

43. David F. Labaree, "Targeting Teachers," in *Public Education Under Siege*, ed. Michael B. Katz and Mike Rose (Philadelphia: University of Pennsylvania Press, 2013), 36–39.

44. Deborah Jewell-Sherman, "The Past as Prologue to the Future," in McCartney, Yoshikawa, and Forcier, *Improving the Odds for America's Children*, 75.

45. M. G. Springer, D. Ballou, L. Hamilton, V. Le, J. R. Lockwood, D. McCaffrey, M. Pepper, and B. Stecher, *Teacher Pay for Performance: Experimental Evidence from the Project on Incentives in Teaching* (Nashville, TN: National Center on Performance Incentives, Vanderbilt University, 2010).

46. Sarah D. Sparks, "Study Leads to End of New York City Merit-Pay Program," *Education Week*, July 20, 2011.

47. Steven Glazerman and Allison Seifullah, *An Evaluation of the Chicago Teacher Advancement Program (Chicago TAP) After Four Years* (Washington, D.C.: Mathematica Policy Research, March 7, 2013); Nora Fleming, "Some Efforts on Merit Pay Scaled Back," *Education Week*, September 21, 2011.

48. Ravitch, *Reign of Error*, 122–23.

49. Linda Darling-Hammond, "Why Is Congress Redlining Our Schools?," *Nation*, January 30, 2012.

50. Ravitch, *Reign of Error*, 59.

51. See Gail Evans, "Schooling Poor Kids Requires More Funding," *Albuquerque Journal*, April 6, 2014, B3.

52. Kayne, *NM Kids are COUNTing on Us*.

53. *Reclaiming the Promise: Solutions to New Mexico's Early Learning Crisis* (Albuquerque: OLE Working Parents Association and New Mexico Early Educators United, 2014).

54. Invest In Kids Now, "New Mexico Has the Second Largest Fund and the Lowest Fourth Grade Reading Scores," fact sheet, n.d., accessed November 19, 2013, http://www.investinkidsnow.org/.

55. Milan Simonich, "State Endowment Hits $17 Billion: Investments for Year Almost Double Targeted Goal," *NM Capitol Report: A View from the New Mexico State Capitol*, August 13, 2013.

56. James J. Heckman, "Schools, Skills & Synapses," (working paper 14064, National Bureau of Economic Research, Cambridge, MA, June 2008), http://www.nber.org/papers/w14064.pdf?newwindow=I.

57. Ibid.

58. Jason T. Hustedt, W. Steven Barnett, Kwanghee Jung, and Linda D. Goetze, *The New Mexico PreK Evaluation: Results from the Initial Four Years of a New State Preschool Initiative, Final Report* (National Institute for Early Education Research, Rutgers University), http://nieer.org/pdf/new-mexico-initial-4-years.pdf.

59. Kayne, *NM Kids are COUNTing on Us*.

60. Ibid.

61. Ibid.

62. Michael Leachman and Chris Mai, *Most States Funding Schools Less Than Before the Recession* (Washington, D.C.: Center on Budget and Policy Priorities, September 2013), http://www.cbpp.org/cms/index.cfm?fa=view&id=4011.

63. Labaree, "Targeting Teachers," 36–39.

64. New Mexico Legislature, Finance Committee, *Developing Early Literacy in New Mexico*, report 12–05 (Santa Fe, December 7, 2012), http://www.nmlegis.gov/lcs/lfc/lfcdocs/perfaudit/Developing%20Early%20Literacy%20in%20New%20Mexico.pdf.

65. Jane L. David, "What Research Says About Grade Level Retention," *Education Leadership* 65, no. 6 (March 2008): 83–84.

66. Shane R. Jimerson, Sarah M. Woehr, and Amber M. Kaufman, "School and Home: Grade Retention and Promotion; Information for Parents," National Association of School Psychologists, 2007.

67. *Leadership Matters: What the Research Says About the Importance of Principal Leadership* (Reston, VA: National Association of Secondary School Principals; Alexandria, VA: National Association of Elementary School Principals, 2013), http://www.naesp.org.

68. Kayne, *NM Kids are COUNTing on Us*.

69. See Fred Harris and Demetria Martinez, *These People Want to Work: Immigration Reform* (Kindle e-book, 2013).

70. Diette Courrégé Casey, "New Mexico Rural Initiative Shows Promise, Disappears," *Rural Education* (blog), *Education Week*, October 24, 2011, http://blogs.edweek.org/edweek/rural_education/2011/10/new_mexico_rural_initiative_shows_promise_disappears.html.

71. Ibid.

72. Steve Nelson, "Leveraging the Unique Features of Small, Rural Schools for Improvement," *Lessons Learned* 1, no. 5 (December 2010), http://educationnorthwest.org/resource/1349.

73. "Supporting Educators to Innovate Through Technology," *Homeroom* (blog), U.S. Department of Education, www.ed.gov/blog/2014/04/supporting-educators-to-innovate-through-technology/.

74. "Massive Open Online Course," *Wikipedia*, last modified October 28, 2014, http://en.wikipedia.org/wiki/massive_open_online_course.

75. New Mexico state data, 2011, Complete College America, completecollege.org/college-completion-data/.

76. Ibid.

77. Michael Mitchell, Vincent Palacios, and Michael Leachman, *States Are Still Funding Higher Education Below Pre-Recession Levels* (Washington, D.C.:

Center on Budget and Policy Priorities, May 1, 2014), http://www.cbpp.org/cms/index.cfm?fa=view&id=4135.

78. See Katrina vanden Heuvel, "Sen. Warren Leads Fight to Reform Student Debt," *Washington Post*, April 27, 2014.

79. "New Mexico Public Colleges (4-Year): Graduation Rates," *Chronicle of Higher Education*, College Completion microsite, http://collegecompletion.chronicle.com/state/#state=nm&sector=public_four.

80. *Higher Education: New Mexico State University and University of New Mexico*, report to New Mexico Legislature Finance Committee, August 11, 2010.

81. Virginia P. Collier and Wayne P. Thomas, "The Astounding Effects of Dual Language Education for All," *NABE Journal of Research and Practice*, no. 2 (Winter 2004): 1–2.

Chapter 3

New Mexico Health and Health Care

NANDINI PILLAI KUEHN

THE HEALTH CARE SECTOR IN THE UNITED STATES AND IN
New Mexico is on the verge of monumental change. The federal Patient Protection and Affordable Care Act (ACA) was signed into law in 2010, and the
New Mexico Health Insurance Exchange, the vehicle that enables New Mexicans to purchase subsidized, affordable health insurance, moved into place
in 2013.

In order to understand the full impact of the reforms and the future, it is
necessary to step back a few years and describe how this system came to be.
That will also provide a baseline with which to measure the changes the law
prescribes and to measure the possibilities for the future.

2014 State of Affairs in New Mexico

New Mexico had for many years the second-highest uninsured rates in the
nation. Most of the state is designated as medically underserved, and large
parts of the state are declared rural and frontier. Access to health care is
hampered by poverty, which means people cannot purchase the health insurance they need without help. Even for those with coverage, transportation to
health centers is a problem exacerbated by long distances, access to specialists
is poor, and there is almost no follow-up care. Table 3.1 summarizes population characteristics that affect health outcomes in New Mexico and the
United States.

Table 3.1. Health insurance coverage, poverty, and median income, New Mexico and United States

	NEW MEXICO	UNITED STATES
Total population, 2013	2,085,287	316,128,839
No. (%) uninsured, 2010–2012	429,000 (21)	46,339,500 (15.4)
No. (%) children, 0–18, uninsured, 2010–2012	74,000 (13)	7.2 million (9)
No. (%) served by Medicaid, 2010	574,914 (28)	— (21)
Median household income, 2008–2012	$44,886	$53,046
Persons below poverty level, 2008–2012*	19.5%	14.9%

* Federal Poverty Levels for 2014 were $11,670 for a single individual; $23,850 for a family of four. U.S. Department of Health and Human Services, ASPE, 2014 Poverty

Source: U.S. Census Bureau, QuickFacts for New Mexico; New Mexico Human Services Department/Insure New Mexico, New Mexico Facts-at-a-Glance, January 2014.

Race and Ethnicity

Epidemiologists and other analysts have consistently documented that health status and health outcomes are related to population demographics such as race and ethnicity. Access to insurance is a vital ingredient in getting access to health care, but minority populations are disproportionately uninsured due to poverty. New Mexico's minority-majority population is an important factor related to health disparities and health equity deficits in the state. As long as health outcomes of minority populations are poorer than those of the white population and as long as minority populations continue to grow at higher rates than the white population, health disparities in New Mexico will increase, and so will the strain on health care and social services. This needs to change. The ACA set in motion wheels that will lead to greater scrutiny of these trends and move the system toward greater equity as reforms in the health system take hold.

As a minority-majority state, New Mexico has always faced daunting health challenges. Forty-seven percent of this state's population is Hispanic, and Native Americans amount to 10.2 percent. African Americans and Asians form a very small minority of New Mexico's population.

Medicaid covers the costs for about 70 percent of the births in New Mexico. A state report identified this Medicaid population as "disproportionately Hispanic, Black and American Indian."[1] Most mothers were single and were in their teens. Pregnant women covered under fee-for-service Medicaid are less likely to receive prenatal care and have the highest percentage of low-birth-weight infants (weighing less than 5.5 pounds). The largest component of the fee-for-service population under Medicaid continues to be Native American.

In his foreword to the U.S. Center for Disease Control and Prevention's *Health Disparities and Inequalities Report 2013* Thomas R. Frieden says that variations in death and illness vary by gender and by race and ethnicity. Cardiovascular disease is the leading cause of death in the United States. He adds, "Non-Hispanic black adults are at least 50% more likely to die of heart disease or stroke prematurely (i.e., before age 75 years) than their non-Hispanic white counterparts."[2]

The New Mexico Health Department's analysis of key health indicators reinforces this finding for minority populations in New Mexico.[3] It notes that Native Americans had the highest or worst rates for late or no prenatal care, deaths from diabetes, obesity, youth suicide, and alcohol-related deaths, as well as the highest death rates from treatable and preventable conditions such as diabetes, influenza, and pneumonia. African Americans in New Mexico had the worst rates for infant mortality, HIV infections, homicide, and adult smoking. Hispanics had the worst rates for teen births, pertussis, and adults with diabetes not receiving treatment. White populations are not immune to health risks, and whites had the highest rates for fall-related deaths, suicide, and drug overdose in New Mexico.

Even a cursory review of this situation indicates that many of these outcomes should be preventable if health care of equal quality were available to all and if accountability were defined and measured.

Socioeconomic Indicators

There is also an increasing understanding of the impact of socioeconomic factors like income, education, employment, and housing on health status. Minority populations in New Mexico have higher levels of poverty than whites. In New Mexico, 25 percent of Native American families, 20 percent of Hispanic families, and 19 percent of African American families have incomes below the poverty level, compared to 7 percent of New Mexico non-Hispanic white families.[4] Since access to health care is dependent on having health insurance and since the cost of health insurance is beyond the means of those with marginal incomes or in poverty, the predictors for health disparities line up with almost impossible odds for minority populations.

Because socioeconomic factors often overwhelm our ability to reach good health status for minority populations the system needs to encompass a wider scope of corrective action—with education, employment, and good housing as equal partners in our endeavor to achieve good health status.

Early Childhood

Sobering statistics show that triggers for chronic behavioral and physical health problems and interventions begin much earlier than when some individuals access the health care system (and their problems are not diagnosed) or confront correctional systems (because of their behavioral health or substance abuse problems).

As noted in chapter 2, researchers have found through surveys and analyses of health data that adverse childhood events leave a marked impact that lasts into adulthood. These events include physical, psychological, and sexual abuse, violence in the home, substance abuse in the home, and neglect. New Mexico data illustrate that the higher the number of such events experienced by individuals, the higher the risk of illicit drug use, alcoholism, and suicide.[5] Studies have also indicated that positive early childhood interventions are the best indicators for high school graduation and that, in turn, a high school education "is the leading health indicator for adults, even when controlling for race and income."[6]

Ensuring good health in adults therefore begins with programs that assist parents to develop good parenting skills, such as home visits by trained health workers to newborn babies. These visits also detect any potential risks to the child and help with early mitigation of abuse or exposure to risk. Following home visits, early childhood education maximizes children's developmental capacity and detects problems (often correctable) early to make sure that there are few if any lifelong deficits for children. These services are invaluable for fostering school readiness and preparing children to cope with social and educational challenges as they develop into adults.

In addition to poor health status, the repercussions of adverse childhood events have wide-reaching societal costs. They include repeated encounters with the juvenile justice system, need for special educational services, and repeated incarceration, not to mention repeated use of emergency health services. In all these situations, prevention in the form of home visiting and early childhood education are cost-effective investments and are society's best hope for mitigating self-destructive behavioral health problems among adults.

These critical social and demographic complexities challenge notions that expanding health care access by itself will automatically yield better health. These complexities also may overwhelm efforts to implement a one-dimensional solution. We cannot wait, however, to improve access to health care until all of the socioeconomic issues have been resolved. Health needs are pressing and, for many people, being physically functional and healthy is instrumental for coping with the systemic barriers they face.

In addition to expanding health insurance coverage, the ACA provides a subset of additional funding for supportive services and expands mental and behavioral health programs. It also has provided additional state funding for home visiting in New Mexico.

Impact of the Uninsured

Estimates of the number of uninsured individuals in New Mexico vary from study to study, but there is consensus that more than 400,000 people in New Mexico had no health insurance coverage prior to enactment of the ACA. In addition, the state has estimated that about 108,000 individuals were eligible for State Coverage Insurance. This program had just 35,130 enrollees as of December 2013 because New Mexico was unable to subsidize additional enrollees.[7]

Both the New Mexico Coverage Initiative, which offers state-subsidized coverage to low-wage employees, and the New Mexico High Risk Pool, which offers coverage to those with health risks that were considered "uninsurable," hardly made a dent in the uninsured numbers. It would have been impossible for a small, impoverished state to raise the revenues necessary to address the health care needs of those who had no means to purchase coverage.

There are human as well as economic costs of having large numbers of uninsured in a state. The Institute of Medicine in 2002 estimated that 18,000 deaths in the United States each year could be prevented through insurance coverage; in 2006 the Urban Institute used the same methodology and estimated that the number had risen to 25,000 preventable deaths per year. Families USA in 2006 reported that there were 260 deaths in New Mexico each year for the same reason.[8]

Researchers have also documented that 62.1 percent of bankruptcies in the United States have a medical cause, that 75 percent of these individuals who filed for bankruptcy had health insurance, and that the share of bankruptcies attributable to medical problems rose by 50 percent from 2001 to 2007.[9]

From a business perspective, high numbers of uninsured result in huge levels of bad debt for health care providers. For many uninsured people with serious illnesses, the only source of care has been hospital emergency departments, which are also the most expensive setting for service. If an uninsured person is unfortunate enough to require admission to the hospital, costs for that admission could run into tens of thousands of dollars, which the patient could never hope to pay and the service provider could not hope to recover. These uncompensated costs become incorporated into premiums. It is estimated that individual premiums cost an average of $410 more per year, while family premiums cost $1,200 more, as a consequence of bad debt covered by hospitals and other providers. According to a Kaiser Family Foundation report, in 2013 the cost of "uncompensated care" across all health care settings for uninsured people nationally totaled $84.9 billion dollars, with 60 percent of that care provided in hospitals.[10] Losses of this magnitude are unsustainable.

WHO WERE OUR UNINSURED?

The most current information about New Mexico's uninsured was provided by a survey conducted in May 2011 by experts at Research and Polling.[11] A majority (55 percent) of survey respondents who were uninsured were currently employed, while 45 percent were not; of those employed, 25 percent had full-time, year-round employment and 10 percent were self-employed. A large number were either seasonal or part-time workers. The higher the level of education and the higher the income level, the more likely that the individual had health insurance. Within the uninsured, 27 percent had lost coverage or dropped it in the previous nine months; 40 percent had lost coverage in the last year.

Thirty-eight percent of those surveyed had never had health insurance as adults. Significantly, the majority of these were under age twenty-five or had limited education. Forty-four percent of Hispanics and 51 percent of Native Americans were likely to have never had health insurance. (It is important to understand that the Indian Health Service [IHS] is not health insurance. IHS is a health care delivery system, with clinics and hospitals that provide health care to Native Americans, but it is poorly funded and unable to meet the serious health needs of this population.)

The highlight of the findings from this survey is that a majority of New Mexico's uninsured were actually employed, although only 25 percent had full-time, year-round employment. Large numbers of part-time and seasonal workers in low-wage positions are not offered health coverage by their employers. Depending on employers to step up and cover all their employees may not work in the real world.

Building on Employer-Based Insurance

The ACA is based on the employer-coverage system that has historically been the source of health care coverage for working individuals and families in the United States. However, that system has been steadily eroding over time, and employers are often unable to continue to provide this coverage. In a report for a New Mexico health coverage initiative in 2006, Mathematica Policy

Research noted that 79 percent of private sector workers were in firms that offered coverage, but only half of those workers were actually enrolled in employer-sponsored coverage.[12] In addition, 40 percent of workers in small businesses (fewer than twenty-five employees) were offered coverage; of these, only one-third were eligible for coverage, and just 26 percent enrolled.

The most recent (2013) Employer Health Benefits Survey from Kaiser notes that average individual premiums stood at $5,884 annually and family health coverage cost $16,351. Worker contributions to these premiums have increased 89 percent since 2003, while during this period wages increased 1.8 percent. In addition, workers faced an average annual deductible of $1,135 for single coverage, and a sizeable majority (74 percent) paid co-payments for office visits.[13]

Hence, employer-based coverage has not been universal, nor has it always been affordable. Employers were never required to offer coverage, and small businesses often did not provide family coverage (although large employers did). When confronted with major increases in their costs for covering employees, employers often chose plans with higher coinsurance payments and shared costs with employees. Employees turned down coverage primarily because they found their share of the costs to be too much or because they could get better coverage under a spouse's plan at another employer. This often resulted in employees with the most pressing health problems taking up coverage, while many others opted out of coverage altogether. Adverse selection (where only those with health needs purchase health insurance) only added to the upward spiral of premium costs.

Finally, it is important to summarize the world in which health insurance plans operated prior to the ACA and over which states had little or no control. Plan administrators were free to deny coverage to new enrollees with high-risk conditions, to deny coverage retroactively if they discovered any cause that they objected to (rescission), to set limits on the maximum payout annually or over a lifetime, and to deny payment for services at will. This meant that people who had chronic illnesses that implied longtime and steady use of the health system often found it impossible to change jobs or, if they did change jobs, to get insurance coverage that covered preexisting conditions. Individuals who had a sudden, catastrophic health crisis could reach their maximum dollar limits in a very short time and then be deemed "uninsurable," regardless of how long they had paid their premiums.

Health Care Workforce Challenges

A final challenge in New Mexico's health care scene comes from shortages at every level of the health care workforce. A recent report indicated that thirty-two of thirty-three New Mexico counties are designated as Health Professional Shortage Areas, medically underserved areas, or areas with medically underserved populations. We have significant shortages of primary-care physicians, dentists, and nurses.[14]

Until the ACA emerged, with its opportunities, the health coverage situation that New Mexicans confronted was dire indeed. The state had high levels of uninsurance among adults, many of whom were working but could not get affordable coverage through their employers. Employers, who had always been considered the primary source for health insurance coverage, often did not provide coverage, did not have to cover families, and faced unsustainable growth in the cost of offering health care coverage. Insurance plans could refuse to cover individuals, alter coverage options without many restrictions, and raise premiums mostly at will. With a population that was poor and had a significant record of health disparities, New Mexico did not have the resources to invest in the strategies that were required to turn this situation around. Added to this was significant health care workforce shortages in New Mexico, which the state could not afford to correct on its own.

With the advent of the ACA, New Mexico finally has the resources to make investments in its infrastructure and can hope to set the course toward a future in which its citizens can access health care without fear of bankruptcy.

How Is Health Care Changing in New Mexico?

When the ACA was signed into law in 2010, it sought to make more changes to our health system than any other reform effort had in the past. While the central core of the law aimed to change the health insurance system and make insurance affordable for everyone who was uninsured, the ACA also included strategies to change the delivery system through public-program reform, to provide incentives for the development of innovative alternative service delivery models, to focus on health outcomes, and to expand the health care workforce.

Primarily, the law gives each state flexibility in creating a state-based health insurance exchange. Residents of states that opt out can use the federal exchange to purchase affordable insurance. Another reform offered states the option to participate in Medicaid expansion.[15] New Mexico accepted participation in Medicaid expansion, entitling 170,000 single adults to coverage they had never had in the past.

ACA-PRESCRIBED INSURANCE REFORMS

Passage of the ACA initiated a set of systemic changes in the fall of 2010, while others were queued up to be phased in over three years. The most important of these changes related to the way in which insurance plans structured coverage. Accompanying these insurance mandates, the law also expanded the benefits provided by insurance plans. New Mexicans benefited from all of these changes.

- Insurance plans were required to allow children to stay on their parents' or guardians' coverage until age twenty-six. An estimated thirteen thousand New Mexico children qualified in September 2010 to do this.
- Plans could not charge co-pays or deny coverage for preexisting conditions for children. These changes helped 122,000 New Mexico children that first year.
- Seniors on Medicare received rebates that helped cover the "donut hole" in their prescription coverage and discounts for generics. These provisions helped more than twenty-two thousand New Mexico seniors. Changes were also set in motion to close the "donut hole" in 2020.
- Medicare decreed that seniors could get preventive services with no

co-pays as well as one annual wellness visit each year. More than 265,000 New Mexico Medicare enrollees benefited from these provisions.

- Insurance plans were required to spend at least 80 percent of their premiums on medical care or to rebate the balance to their enrollees. These rebates began in 2012.

The New Mexico Department of Insurance was authorized to determine what plans qualified for sale on the New Mexico state exchange and, in conducting insurance-rate reviews, to challenge inappropriate or unjustified rate increases. And New Mexico received $37.5 million to expand the existing high-risk pool to include additional individuals who had earlier been deemed "uninsurable." This was a bridge until the exchange could enroll them in commercial plans in 2013.

Effective as of 2013, when enrollment in the exchanges began, all eligible residents were required to enroll in health insurance coverage—commonly known as the individual mandate.[16] This requirement was intended to prevent people from purchasing insurance only when they were sick, and it helped the exchange enroll a larger group of healthy purchasers to spread risk and cost.

All insurance plans also had to comply with the following:[17]

- No denial of coverage or exclusions for preexisting conditions
- No retroactive denial of coverage
- No additional premium charges for women
- No maximum annual or lifetime benefits
- Establish a threshold to limit the maximum annual out-of-pocket costs for enrollees
- Provide a set of minimum essential benefits that include physical as well as mental health coverage

Individuals eligible to purchase coverage on the health insurance exchange were entitled to federal subsidies if their income was under 400 percent of the federal poverty level. This provided an entirely new opportunity for low-income Americans to purchase health insurance.

One strategic change that the ACA introduced was to require all providers and health insurance plans to begin tracking and reporting information about race, ethnicity, and gender for those enrolled in public programs (Medicaid and Medicare). This signaled an intent to build a population database to review the law's impact on racial and ethnic disparities as well as to determine whether changes to benefits (which made prevention and wellness part of the core business of plans and providers) were yielding the desired results.

A second strategic change made by the ACA was to introduce special provisions for Native Americans through the Indian Health Care Improvement Act. It is now possible for Native Americans to purchase insurance at subsidized rates through the exchange and use it either at the IHS (thereby allowing the IHS to bill for its services) or directly with any provider of their choice.

Insurance Reform and the New Mexico Health Insurance Exchange

In New Mexico, legislation was passed in April 2013 to set up the New Mexico Health Insurance Exchange (NMHIX), with a mandate that it be ready for business when open enrollment began on October 1 of the same year. The federal government provided a special dispensation to a few states, including New Mexico, allowing them to operate a state exchange but giving them permission to use the federal exchange until New Mexico's own system would be ready in 2015 (a two-year extension). The "state exchange" designation allowed New Mexico to apply for and receive federal funds to do its own marketing and to hire community assisters and navigators to help with enrollment. In 2012, prior to the formal designation of this exchange, New Mexico received around $35.2 million from the federal government; when open enrollment was initiated in 2013, New Mexico had about $95 million dollars to fund exchange operations.

Expanded Medicaid

The expansion of Medicaid is probably one of the most profound reforms fostered by the ACA. The New Mexico Health Insurance Exchange reported in April 2014 that New Mexico had enrolled over 112,000 persons in the expanded Medicaid program.

New Mexico agreed to participate in the Medicaid expansion, which extended Medicaid eligibility to single, childless adults with incomes up to 133 percent of the federal poverty level if they were not currently eligible for Medicaid and could not afford health insurance at any cost. The federal government covers 100 percent of the expenses related to this expansion for the first three years. After that, the state must pick up 10 percent of the costs, with the federal government picking up 90 percent. It is estimated that 170,000 New Mexicans could be enrolled in this expanded Medicaid program. This piece of the reform effort has been very successful to date. Recent figures available from the Centers for Medicare and Medicaid Services (CMS) indicate that the second open enrollment period that started in November 2014 has been very successful, and New Mexico stands to meet or exceed its target for Medicaid expansion (and to do well for non-Medicaid enrollments on the exchange).[18]

It is anticipated that New Mexico's Medicaid expansion would provide a major economic boost for the state. Analysts have pointed out that, since Medicaid is delivered through private insurance plans, the state could actually see increased revenue from the premium taxes paid by all managed care organizations (MCOs) that contract to provide services under Medicaid and that there would be additional gross receipts revenue from providers who would serve these enrollees. These two taxes, it was estimated, would add an estimated $451.2 million to $622.4 million to state coffers.[19] In addition, all enrollees in the New Mexico Coverage Initiative, to which the state contributes funding, were covered under the new Medicaid expansion, which meant the state saved its share of the funding for use in other priority programs in New Mexico.

What New Mexico Needs to Do

The ACA has mandated specific changes in the policy and structure of insurance plans, addressing the scope of coverage, benefits required, and reporting requirements. In order to ensure that New Mexico is implementing these requirements consistently and effectively, there needs to be an organized effort to monitor insurance providers and hold them accountable for the outcomes.

Monitor the New Mexico Health Insurance Exchange

The status and effects of NMHIX should be closely monitored. Because NMHIX got a late start and because of problems with the federal exchange, on which New Mexico depended, enrollment numbers for the first open enrollment period were really low. Initial projections estimated that New Mexico would enroll up to eighty thousand individuals and small-business employees on the exchange. As of May 2014, the state may not have reached more than 25 percent of these projections, with a total of around thirty-five thousand individual and small-business enrollees.

The board of the Exchange has the primary authority for oversight. The board is composed of members appointed by the governor and the legislature. The legislature is deeply vested in the success of this enterprise, since the notion of extending health insurance coverage to all New Mexicans has been its focus for decades. At the very least, appropriate committees of the legislature should ask for a standing report from the board chair and the CEO of NMHIX on enrollment figures, the number enrolled through community outreach and brokers, and the status of the "no wrong door" policy.

ENROLLMENT

NMHIX should provide a closer accounting of enrollees on both the individual exchange and the small business portal. Current numbers on individuals come from the federal government, but when NMHIX develops its own enrollment capacity these numbers should be generated in-house. The exchange should track premium payment patterns and "churn" in coverage that disrupts access, continuity of insurance coverage, and provider payment. The NMHIX should also have a strategy for reaching out to communities and families that could benefit from health care coverage.

NUMBER ENROLLED THROUGH COMMUNITY OUTREACH AND BROKERS

The exchange has invested significant resources in training community members to enroll people looking for coverage, and the success of this endeavor needs to be monitored. If necessary, the exchange should plan for additional training and coordination for outreach workers in order to ensure that those in the community who are entitled to coverage with subsidies through the exchange feel encouraged to apply for insurance. Agencies that have been contracted to provide this service need to be supported to meet their targeted goals and activities.

"NO WRONG DOOR" POLICY

The ACA prescribes a "no wrong door" policy, which requires the exchange and Medicaid to coordinate closely. Coordination ensures that people who apply for Medicaid and are not qualified will be transitioned to commercial plans on the exchange in a seamless way. Similarly, if someone with commercial insurance has a loss of income and becomes eligible for Medicaid, he or she should be able to transition (also seamlessly) into that program. At present there are no systems to monitor the effectiveness of this coordination.

Report from the Department of Insurance

Given the expanded scope of the Department of Insurance to monitor plans under the ACA, the legislature needs to schedule reports to review the department's work. Specifically, the department should be asked to provide a report on rate increases that have been requested and approved. It should also report on other insurance-related action regarding certifying qualified health plans on the NMHIX or other regulations that might affect the coverage system adversely.

Based on these reports, the Legislative Health and Human Services Committee should consider whether new legislation is required for additions to the scope and authority of the exchange and consider the need for additional oversight for this entity or for external review and assessment.

Support ACA-Initiated Transformative Forces

As noted in the introductory section, New Mexico has never been able to implement health reform in a multidimensional manner because it could not afford to do so and it could not change insurance plans the way the federal law was able to do. The ACA actually goes much further in reforming the system to address issues that have been barriers for New Mexico for decades. The state legislature can take the lead in overseeing policies that are needed to support full implementation of the ACA in New Mexico.

Although the legislature can provide some monitoring of the health care system, a better option might be to examine whether to commission external experts to assist the legislature in providing reports or to ask existing agencies to provide special reports.

CENTENNIAL CARE

The New Mexico Human Services Department has implemented structural changes to Medicaid through the creation of the Centennial Care program and has introduced new requirements for MCOs to manage risk among their patients. At the heart of Centennial Care's new approach is the requirement for MCOs to demonstrate "care coordination" principles. All enrollees are to receive a three-level health risk assessment. Based on risk, Centennial Care requires MCOs to focus on secondary and tertiary prevention. Centennial Care has also asked its MCOs to examine payment reform in order to pay providers in its network for outcomes rather than processes. These changes will not be evident for a while, but the legislature should target reports at least biennially to ensure that these objectives are on track, with a full report to be made in a year.

The legislature needs to track the success of Centennial Care and expanded Medicaid in improving services for enrollees by requesting specific reports:

1. General enrollment statistics, broken down by geography, race, ethnicity, age, and gender of the people in Centennial Care and with the numbers triaged at levels 1, 2, and 3;
2. The key problems for people at level 3 and the strategies being used to address these problems; and
3. The number of patients who have been assessed co-pays once and more than once.

MONITOR HEALTH DISPARITIES

Each year the Department of Health provides several reports on the health of New Mexicans, on racial and ethnic disparities, and on behavioral health risks that adults and youth in our system face. As more and more individuals get health insurance coverage, these existing reports and disparity measures should be used to monitor the system and to make targeted changes.[20] Examples of questions that should be raised include: Have Native Americans with Medicaid shown better outcomes for prenatal care or for deaths from diabetes? Does the data show whether an increased number of Hispanics are able to access diabetes services?

HEALTH CARE WORKFORCE DEVELOPMENT

Multiple educational and training institutions in New Mexico have received funding to expand the state's health care workforce. The legislature should require a report about how that funding was used and the benefits that have accrued to the state. It may be necessary to contract with a consultant to provide such a report. It is possible that this report could be coordinated through CMS, which made the decisions about funding for expansion and training programs.

Alternative Service Delivery Systems

TELEMEDICINE

Payment for telemedicine is an explicit provision in the ACA. Is telehealth being reimbursed in New Mexico, and if so, how? Several pilot programs are in place, and a briefing session would enlighten legislators and highlight any enabling legislation required. If successful models emerge, they should be examined and highlighted for duplication and replication.

PATIENT-CENTERED CARE

An emphasis on patient-centered, team-based care, as in the patient-centered medical home model, is gaining a foothold in New Mexico primary-care sites. This challenge to the existing fee-for-service model could be a game changer if successful. Links to outcomes and pay for performance or value-based purchasing are among the strategies being tested to connect evidence-based standards of care and outcomes with compensation.

ALTERNATIVE PROVIDER COMPENSATION

Centennial Care has also signaled that MCOs should look at different ways of compensating providers within its networks for outcomes-related care or based on pay-for-performance metrics. New Mexico's shortage of health care workers has been well documented. A report to the Legislative Finance Committee in 2013 pointed out that the state needs to examine "smarter" service-delivery models that "target level of care to level of need."[21] Both the Legislative Finance Committee and the Health and Human Services Committee need to examine solutions and pass legislation required to support new service systems and new ways of expanding the health care workforce and retaining health professionals in New Mexico.

PAYMENT REFORM

The ACA has issued a clear challenge to the dominance of the fee-for-service system in publicly funded programs such as Medicaid and Medicare. The act established the Center for Medicare and Medicaid Innovation to test a series of innovative approaches to system and payment reform. The Commonwealth Fund has identified twenty payment- and delivery-reform models to be tested by the center.[22] The greatest emphasis in all of the innovation models is on moving away from fee-for-service models to global fees and outcomes-based arrangements. These reforms will be particularly important as team-based care models using patient-centered medical homes are implemented to improve patient outcomes and to use scarce physician resources more effectively. The legislature should regularly look for local and other success indicators for team-based care.

New Mexico Health Care in 2050

Forecasting forty years into the future is difficult at best. It appears more difficult if one looks back and realizes that the U.S. health system has gone through regular and unpredictable upheavals during the past four decades, with major gains in the 1970s and 1980s as well as significant breakdowns, frustrating reform enthusiasts. No doubt some of the problems we are working on now will be addressed in the next three or four decades, but new problems driven by cost and technology (not to mention politics) are bound to arise. This is the never-ending cycle of reform, and it shows why the ACA targeted its reform agenda at all levels of the health system instead of tinkering around the edges.

The reform process that the United States is engaged in was initiated because we had a broken system with exorbitant, spiraling costs. There is no serious disagreement about that. Costs of every component of the health care system were rising faster than the system could support, and something clearly needed to happen to change this trajectory.

The United States spends more per capita on its health care system than any other industrialized nation. In its most recent report, the Organization for Economic Cooperation and Development indicated that the United States spent $8,508 per capita on health care in 2011, compared to an average of $3,322 per capita among nations in the organization. Such high expenditures could be justified if our system was measurably better—in terms of health outcomes and longer life expectancy, to mention two measures—than those in countries that spend less. However, health care experts bemoan that this is not the case. Says one, "It is hard to ignore that in 2006, the United States was number one in terms of healthcare spending per capita but ranked 39th for infant mortality, 43rd for adult female mortality, 42nd for adult male mortality, and 36th for life expectancy."[23] A Commonwealth Fund study ranked the United States last among seven developed nations for quality of care, measured in terms of access, patient safety, coordination, efficiency, and equity.[24] Such facts have fueled a question now being discussed in academic and government circles, as well as among the public: why do we spend so much to get so little?[25]

The ACA aims to save up to a trillion dollars by offering incentives for evidence-based prevention and evidence-based care and by monitoring and paying for outcomes rather than inputs. Through such interventions, the law hopes to change the trajectory of health spending by shifting the system away from volume-based care in order to improve value and health outcomes.

Before I examine New Mexico scenarios for 2050, it is important to address the elephant in the room: will the ACA be repealed in the near future?

Will the ACA Be Repealed?

A dramatic and full-scale repeal of the ACA is very unlikely to happen now or in the near future, even though repeal has been and continues to be a battle cry for opponents of the law. Part of the reason that repeal is unlikely relates to the risk of returning to the broken, very expensive system that the ACA attempts to reform.

First, it is safe to say that any proposal to repeal the ACA in the short term will be vetoed by President Obama, who sees the act as his signature accomplishment. Contrary to the forecasts of most critics, and despite the very rocky start to open enrollment, the federal exchange was incredibly successful, signing up almost 7 million people nationally by May 2014). In addition, nationally over 3 million new Medicaid and Children's Health Insurance Program recipients were also on the rolls by that same time, thanks to expanded Medicaid. These numbers are only going to increase with each enrollment period. In addition, 5 million Americans have enrolled in plans that meet ACA standards outside the exchanges, according to a Congressional Budget Office estimate.[26]

But what about the next U.S. president, who might ride into office on the promise of repeal? Part of the motivation behind the frantic push for repeal is to make sure the ACA never takes hold, because that would complicate the task of tearing it down wholesale if a repeal-directed president were to be elected in 2016. The repeal zeal will fade as enrollment numbers inevitably continue to increase.

Eliminating the reforms made to insurance rules of coverage would also be challenging. The federal government could not easily justify reinstating the option for insurance plans to deny coverage for preexisting conditions or returning to the time when people could face bankruptcy because the cost of an unexpected catastrophic illness exceeded their maximum allowable benefits. As baby boomers join the Medicare rolls, they are unlikely to be willing to go back to the "donut-hole" design for pharmacy coverage or to be amenable to paying additional fees for screening and wellness visits.

More importantly, the economic effects of the ACA will pose their own challenge to repeal. Any proposal that would disenroll hundreds of millions of recipients of Medicare and private insurance would have to consider the serious economic impact on providers and insurance plans. By signing up enrollees in Medicaid or commercial insurance, providers have experienced a positive change in their financial risk, compared to the time when communities had vast numbers of uninsured. With repeal, jobs created to serve the Medicaid expansion and the newly insured would be lost. States would lose tax revenues if the health sector lost jobs or if coverage expansions were cancelled. The financial impact on hospitals and insurance revenues would be massive, and local and state governments as well as the federal government would face the challenge of bailing out the system and not having any way to achieve their reform goals.

Even if all this were somehow accomplished, the system would then revert to its disastrous and expensive excesses. It is important to remember what that means. Prior to the implementation of the ACA, all forecasts indicated that health costs were spiraling upward, out of control. Repeal would take us back to those times. Prior to implementation of the ACA, the CMS estimated that U.S. health spending would increase from $2.4 trillion in 2008 to $4.4 trillion in 2018.[27] In addition, health care costs were predicted to grow to 20.3 percent of GDP by 2019. The Urban Institute also estimated that with no reform, the number of uninsured could grow from around 45 million in 2009 to 57.5 million in 2014 and around 66 million by 2019.[28] Without reform, family premiums were estimated to grow from $13,100 in 2009 to $22,440 by 2019.[29]

Any attempts at wholesale repeal of the ACA would inevitably bring back this dire financial reality. State and federal governments would be plunged into confronting crisis after crisis in caring for ever-increasing numbers of uninsured, spiraling premium increases, and a massive loss of jobs in the health sector that would financially hurt both providers and insurance plans.

More likely, opponents of the ACA would choose not to repeal it but to tinker with some sections to make it look like they had dismantled portions of the law without compromising the more user-friendly components. Those options are examined below.

Two Health System Scenarios for 2050

It should be apparent that all sorts of external forces (economic depressions or recessions or major world crises that materially engage the United States, for example) could derail reform, regardless of the politics. However, I will discuss two potential scenarios that consider how the United States and New Mexico's health care system could change between now and 2050.

SCENARIO I: THE AFFORDABLE CARE ACT MORPHS INTO GENERIC UNIVERSAL COVERAGE

Under this first scenario, most of the insurance reforms and all of the health system reforms in the ACA would be implemented successfully, thus changing the landscape and introducing a different set of incentives that eliminate the last vestiges of barriers to coverage. While disgruntled opponents and attempts to fight the ACA would not be eliminated under this scenario, it assumes that the benefits of providing coverage to most people will be seen as supporting social justice goals as well as being consistent with sensible business practices.

This is the ideal scenario.

It assumes that administrators at the state and federal levels who are friendly to health reform will smooth out structural barriers that contribute to increases in health care costs, thereby consolidating the gains on which a sustainable system could be built by 2050. These could include the following:

- Health insurance exchange marketplaces will be strengthened to better manage coverage plans and to negotiate directly with insurance companies on behalf of exchange participants in order to get the best coverage affordable. In addition, exchanges will report on plan costs, out-of-pocket costs, and differences between plan requirements in ways that make sense to consumers as well as on health outcome results or the quality of various incentives within plans sold on the exchange.
- As a consequence of having opportunities to purchase affordable individual coverage, ownership of insurance plans will shift from employers to individuals and insurance coverage will become portable. Portability is a key benefit that has been missing from the system. Tax benefits for employers for providing this coverage will shift to individual tax benefits. This shift will not occur in one easy step and, interestingly, will necessitate changes to the law's requirement that employers provide health care. But in time, with new contractual relationships and increased individual-coverage purchasing capacity facilitated by the exchange, more people will purchase their own insurance, which they can carry with them when they change jobs. This will take small employers with low-wage employees out of the insurance-provision business altogether. Large employers may phase out their involvement in time.
- By 2050, with the changes set in motion by the ACA, the health care

sector will be massively transformed, optimizing digital capacity for care management and cost tracking and establishing real-time quality parameters for providers.

» Electronic health records will be the norm. The ACA offers incentives for the transition to electronic health records, and providers who comply with "meaningful use" criteria are being financially rewarded. Electronic recording (including voice detection) and real-time reporting of health information will become the norm over the next decade in New Mexico, and by 2050 there will be secure information sharing between providers who care for the same patient, which will eliminate duplication of services and thus reduce costs. With this change, penalties could be imposed on providers if diagnostic testing is duplicated outside of evidence-based protocols.

» New technical devices will help patients understand and manage chronic conditions through alerts, prompts, and reminders. Patients will be able to communicate directly with their health care team though these devices.

» Telemedicine will be inexpensive and widespread and a primary source for specialist coverage in rural New Mexico. This technology has struggled to survive outside of research institutions or universities because insurance plans have not known how to compensate providers for its use. The ACA recognizes telemedicine as a legitimate care mechanism and has created opportunities for compensation for telehealth in its public programs. This will transform care in rural New Mexico. New hubs will emerge in both clinics and hospitals that will save patients hundreds of hours in travel to regional and urban centers. These hubs will be centers for regular conferences or for actual care, delivered through primary-care systems and directed by specialists if necessary.

» Primary-care physicians will take their rightful places as leaders and coordinators for all prevention and secondary prevention of chronic care, in both physical and mental health. They will, however, work as part of teams that ensure the kind of follow-up and management that turns the corner on costs by reducing preventable hospitalizations for diabetes, hypertension, obesity, and substance abuse.

» Alternative compensation for providers will be the norm by 2050. Fee-for-service will cease to be the dominant strategy for provider compensation in primary care. As was recommended by the American College of Physicians, the system will replace volume-based care with "care coordination payments for physicians working with health teams."[30] More clinical providers will be compensated through pay-for-performance schemes based on how well they manage chronic diseases, with shared savings, outcomes-based compensation, and bonuses for performance markers that are better than those of their peers. Each one of these systems needs further developmental work, but the pilot programs in place right now should yield the information to begin the process of development in the next decade, with further refinement, more variations, and more focus by 2050.

» Specialists may continue to work within fee-for-service models, but more surgeons or clinical interventionists will be compensated through "bundled payments" arrangements that include accountability for recovery from procedures.

» Quality metrics for emergency rooms and hospitalizations will be refined and will allow these places to deflect admissions by alerting primary-care teams to manage acute episodes more effectively. They will also be able to track whether repeat admissions were preventable and flag those that are a consequence of inadequate or poor discharge planning.

» Health equity will be achieved as more minorities become providers and key players in the health care delivery system and as care is systematically delivered in a culturally sensitive and effective manner and the system is held accountable for disparities.

» By 2050 the health care workforce will be large enough to meet the need. With all the incentives currently in the system to improve compensation for primary caregivers, the number of primary-care physicians will substantially increase, and the system will

concurrently add a significantly higher number of midlevel providers, such as nurse practitioners and physician assistants. Additional
support staff, critical to the team, will emerge, including community health workers or long-distance team members within rural
communities. Pharmacists and others who currently occupy almost
invisible retail roles will emerge as special leaders for clinical management that depends on medication management. Other clinical
roles that will expand in scope are those of therapists, counselors,
behavioral health specialists, and alternative medicine providers.
New supporting roles will emerge to handle the transition to high-
tech care. New clinical roles still being shaped will be established
(such as dental therapists to provide rural communities with
high-quality care to prevent dental problems). Additional midlevel
clinical positions could also develop for other chronic management
and prevention concepts.

»   Well before 2050, best-practices standards will have emerged to
    demonstrate beyond any shadow of a doubt the value the ACA's
    investments in home visits and early childhood education programs.
    By 2050, these services will be available in all communities. New
    service-delivery systems will emerge that build on telehealth care,
    home-based care, or mobile services to reach those who need rou-
    tine follow-up, those who are housebound, and rural populations.

»   The ACA's reporting requirements will make available information
    about the costs of the entire health system, allowing better decision
    making. By 2050, these data will routinely inform health policy,
    planning, and evaluation. Hospital and emergency costs will be
    heavily scrutinized, and it is likely that there will be ways of com-
    pensating hospitals other than per discharge or by the number of
    bed days. Small rural hospitals in particular will be compensated
    for serving needs in local communities and working with major
    regional centers to manage cases using telemedicine.

»   Finally, by 2050 a uniquely U.S.-flavored coordinated-payer system
    will emerge through state initiatives to knit together the various
    components of our health system. In the next decade, state-based.

integrated health systems will emerge in some states that will set in motion health coverage alternatives that will take hold in the second half of this century. Under specific provisions of the ACA, states can apply for a waiver to amend key provisions of the exchange so long as they continue to support the same or higher levels of enrollment, do not reduce benefits, and do not contribute to the deficit.

These crucibles of experimentation with near-universal health coverage will be the ACA's most valuable contribution to reducing fragmentation in our health care system; such changes will reduce administrative costs, because each different coverage system has made different administrative demands on providers. These experimental crucibles will be formally recognized and will be either copied or adapted from different parts of the country to meet local needs.

If the changes set in motion through the ACA are enhanced and supported during the next decade, by 2050 the country can expect to have a system that will have dramatically turned the cost curve by introducing low-cost, effective care that is evidence based and outcomes driven for all populations.

Also, if we leave the ACA to do its work, a system may develop that is more in line with "the American way"—that is, a blend of local structures and solutions with the common theme of care integrated across systems. There will be a "free-market" component; the act will make public programs more efficient and accountable and therefore ensure their survival. And it will provide a role for commercial plans that leave them independent yet regulated enough to deliver good health care outcomes as their core business. We could have an equilibrium of sorts that is uniquely American.

SCENARIO 2: PARTS OF THE ACA ARE RETAINED BUT
DIFFERENT CHANGE AGENTS ARE INTRODUCED,
LEADING TO A DIFFERENT MODEL OF UNIVERSAL COVERAGE

Under this scenario, sometime between now and 2050 there will be additional tinkering with ACA-introduced structures that will insert different political priorities for funding and maintaining our health system. Certain components of the ACA will be implemented fully, but there is the risk of losing others to politics or capacity issues. It is also possible that under this scenario, with fewer regulatory aspects of the ACA in place, more components of the health system will be likely to collide or collapse, leading to a crisis that eventually will require dramatic changes in our health system. The shape of the resulting health system could depend on how much of the ACA gets derailed. This will be a more turbulent scenario, but in the end, it is likely to provide universal coverage as well because high numbers of uninsured are a drag on the economy.

Whatever the changes contemplated in this scenario, new policies will stop short of reintroducing the more egregious flaws of the earlier health insurance system. However, proponents will look at introducing more "market forces" that may be seen as generating cost savings.

There are some changes that could occur in the short term and continue for the near future under this scenario:

- Make health insurance exchanges much more like website sales enterprises. Exchanges will be limited to hosting plans and providing a vehicle for enrolling individuals; they will not act as value-based purchasers of affordable, high-value plans. The exchanges will not have a role in shaping coverage benefits or reporting on quality and costs, so the battle over how to control costs could last longer.
- Exceptions will likely be made to the availability of catastrophic plans, which under current ACA provisions are not allowed to be sold on the exchanges except to a very small group of youth. The number enrolled in such plans would stay small, however, because alternative plans would be more appealing to older adults.
- Many of the systemic changes initiated by the ACA will continue through 2050 under either scenario. Telehealth will be a major player in rural health care delivery, electronic health records will be a normal part of the health system, and there will be secure sharing of essential health information to ensure that duplication and costs are controlled. New service systems will emerge and there will be more evidence-based management, since that will be the most effective cost-control

mechanism available (and cost savings are decidedly a nonpolitical issue). All of the new practitioners identified in the earlier scenario will emerge under this one. None of these alternatives are inherently likely to be targeted for reduction or elimination by repeal-minded politicians.

- While public policies may not target health equity, the expansion of Medicaid and the availability of data will continue to inform the system and challenge health policy through 2050. In New Mexico, the changes initiated by Centennial Care should turn the corner on costs and should demonstrate the extent to which care management will control costs and improve health. Given that minority populations will continue to dominate enrollment in Centennial Care and the Medicaid expansion, data will show whether these interventions change the health status and the disparity pictures in the next decade.

POTENTIAL TURBULENCE

In scenario 2, the biggest issue that could catapult our health system into turbulence will be the question of how or whether to fund Medicaid and whether Medicare can survive under a voucher system. Under full implementation of the ACA, there are structures in place to assess and advise officials in the U.S. Department of Health and Human Services on how to keep both Medicaid and Medicare whole. If those elements of the ACA are sacrificed, as they are bound to be in this scenario, then it is likely that proposals from the past will emerge to haunt the future.

In the political climate of the next decade, using block grants to fund Medicaid may emerge as an option, and it is possible that before 2050 some form of block-grant funding may even be implemented. The concern here, of course, is that block-grant levels will never be increased, even if fortunes within states fall and Medicaid-eligible numbers increase. For New Mexico, the good news could be that, with the state's acceptance of Medicaid expansion, the full budget for Medicaid could look richer, and this could benefit the state for a short period of time. However, this is not a long-term solution to addressing the needs of low-income adults, children, and families and this "solution" will be challenged regularly as more problems emerge within smaller, less populated, and impoverished states like New Mexico.

Medicare, with its rising costs, is another lightning rod for politically driven reform. The ACA, if allowed to work, could develop solutions that maintain the integrity and structure of the program. The law specifically forbids any reduction of benefits, so, changes to Medicare that are built into the law are balanced with a series of changes to ways in which plans are paid for; there are also provisions for savings through changes in the health care delivery system and aggressive monitoring of waste, fraud, and abuse. The Center for Medicare and Medicaid Innovation has funded pilot programs and innovation grants to look at alternative service-delivery and payment systems that could work for the Medicare population. The net impact of these changes was intended to keep the Medicare system solvent for at least another decade, with specific entities within the law charged with coming up with long-term solutions for sustaining this program. However, about a decade from now, the solvency of Medicare will demand attention, and the ACA-based proposals may be rejected in favor of considering a voucher system.

Such changes to Medicare will face stiff opposition as more baby boomers welcome their freedom from commercial insurance under Medicare. Under some voucher plans, the existing complexities of insurance (described as "consumer choice") could follow the elderly until the end, and without standardized benefits, the unpredictability of costs will be a major side effect. Such systems do not take into consideration the problem of the elderly making coverage decisions at a time when they are more frail and battling dementia and other cognitive problems. There is no question that under most voucher programs, two sets of beneficiaries will evolve. One group of beneficiaries will pay more for a similar basket of services, while a second group of Medicare beneficiaries will emerge that is less wealthy and will require subsidies or have to accept lower benefits.

The question of converting to a voucher system could cause a major battle, and that likely would be a major turning point for additional system reform. With such anticipated battles, it is possible that even before 2050 the nation will look for a different solution to address our health care needs.

It is in this context that the system could begin to seriously consider a consolidation of plans, not quite producing one universal plan but instead creating a three-part alliance between programs to cover the most vulnerable populations (the very young, the very poor, the disabled, and the very old) and insurance plans that cover everyone else. Given the current trend of consolidation of insurance plans across the country, there may be only a few national insurance plans remaining by 2050, and this could make negotiation easier and coordination among and between states more feasible.

New Mexico 2050

The Health Care System

The future, given what we know now, is likely to offer some challenges. With full-scale repeal of the ACA being off the table, the best-case scenario (scenario 1) and the moderate-case scenario (scenario 2) will likely combine to produce the following:

- The wheels set in motion by the ACA will continue to protect public programs, which will demonstrate through new accountability standards that they can deliver high-quality health outcomes for the populations they serve. New Mexico will depend on public programs to keep its uninsured numbers at bay.
- Insurance plans will be more regulated and held more accountable for managing health risks than they have been in the past.
- The United States (and thus New Mexico) will in 2050 have a version of universal health coverage that will blend government and private plans.

The Level of Health in New Mexico

Because of the changes initiated now and likely to prevail for the next five to ten years, the health of New Mexico's people will steadily and markedly improve—across all segments of our state's population. These changes can be tracked and measured and will justify the programmatic changes initiated in

Medicaid and Medicare. And with this evidence, it is likely that evidence-based practice will also be supported through commercial plans.

These changes will come about because of the data infrastructure that is being built now. But they will also happen because we will significantly increase our health care workforce, reduce the harmful effects of poor socio-economic factors and adverse childhood events, meaningfully increase our investment in early childhood education, and improve education outcomes generally (as discussed in chapter 2), and we will make substantial headway on cutting our presently very high levels of income inequality and poverty (as discussed in chapter 1).

Quite simply, the health of New Mexico's people will steadily and markedly improve because of the growing implementation, one way or another, of universal health coverage for all and because the quality of that health care will be better.

Notes

1. Office of New Mexico Vital Records and Health Statistics, "Medicaid Paid Births," 2003. See also Legislative Finance Committee, *Prenatal to 3: Lifelong Health and Brain Development Impacts*, June 2012.

2. Centers for Disease Control and Prevention, *Health Disparities and Inequalities Report: United States, 2013.*

3. New Mexico Department of Health, *Health Equity in New Mexico: A Report on Racial and Ethnic Health Disparities*, 8th ed., October 2013.

4. KIDS COUNT Data Center website, www.datacenter.kidscount.org; data from New Mexico Voices for Children.

5. Ronald E. Voorhees, "Our Children Our Future: Developmental Screening" (workshop, May 26, 2006).

6. David R. Williams, *Opportunities to Improve Health by Investing in People and Places* (Robert Wood Johnson Foundation, Commission to Build a Healthier America, 2013).

7. "New Mexico Facts at a Glance," Insure New Mexico, New Mexico Human Services Department, January 14, 2014.

8. Institute of Medicine, *Care Without Coverage: Too Little Too Late*, 2002; Urban Institute, *Uninsured and Dying*, 2006; and Families USA, *Dying for Coverage in New Mexico*, March 2008.

9. David U. Himmelstein, Deborah Thorne, Elizabeth Warren, and Steffie Woolhandler, "Medical Bankruptcy in the United States, 2007: Results of a National Study," *American Journal of Medicine* 122.8 (2009): 741–46.

10. Teresa A. Coughlin, John Holahan, Kyle Caswell, and Megan McGrath, *Uncompensated Care for the Uninsured in 2013: A Detailed Examination* (Kaiser Family Foundation, May 30, 2014).

11. Research and Polling, *Uninsured Household Adult Survey* (New Mexico Office of Health Care Reform, New Mexico Human Services Division, May 2011).

12. Deborah Chollet, et al., *Quantitative and Comparative Analysis of Reform Options for Extending Health Care Coverage in New Mexico* (Mathematica Policy Research, June 2007).

13. Kaiser Family Foundation and Health Research Educational Trust, "Summary of Findings," *Employer Health Benefits Survey*, 2013.

14. New Mexico Health Policy Commission, "Recommendations to Address New Mexico Health Care Workforce Shortages," January 2011.

15. The Medicaid expansion provision was originally mandated in the law, but the Supreme Court ruled that states could not be mandated to comply with it. However, in the same ruling in June 2013, the Supreme Court let stand the "individual mandate," which required all individuals to purchase insurance or pay a penalty. This provision was key to universal coverage and could have significantly weakened the ACA's impact if it had been struck down.

16. The individual mandate was upheld by the Supreme Court on June 28, 2013. However, the law does have a significant number of exemptions for individuals, including hardship.

17. "Grandfathered Health Plan," Healthcare.gov glossary, https://www.healthcare.gov/glossary/grandfathered-health-plan/. Group health plans established before March 23, 2010, did not have to comply with the ACA unless they changed plan benefits significantly.

18. As reported at ACASignups.net, http://acasignups.net/.

19. New Mexico Voices for Children, *The Economic Benefits of Health Care Reform in New Mexico*, June 2011, updated August 2011.

20. New Mexico Department of Health, *Health Equity in New Mexico*.

21. New Mexico Department of Health and Allied Agencies, *Adequacy of New Mexico's Healthcare Systems Workforce*, report to the Legislative Finance Committee, 2013, p. 8.

22. Stuart Guterman et al., "Innovation in Medicare and Medicaid Will Be Central to Health Reform's Success," *Health Affairs* 29.6 (2010): 1188–93.

23. J. Doe, *WHO Statistical Information System (WHOSIS)* (Geneva: World Health Organization, September 2009).

24. Karen Davis, C. Shoen, and K. Stemikis, *Mirror, Mirror on the Wall: How the Performance of the U.S. Health System Compares Internationally* (Commonwealth Fund, 2010). The countries studied were Australia, Canada, Germany, the Netherlands, New Zealand, the United Kingdom, and the United States.

25. Christopher J. L. Murray and Julio Frenk, "Ranking 37th: Measuring the Performance of the U.S. Health Care System," *New England Journal of Medicine* 362 (2010): 98–99.

26. Department of Health and Human Services, "Health Insurance Marketplace Summary Enrollment Report for the Initial Annual Open Enrollment Period," ASPE Issue Brief, May 1, 2014, http://aspe.hhs.gov/.

27. Centers for Medicare and Medicaid Services, National Health Expenditure Projections, 2008–2018, www.cms.hhs.gov. See also A. Sisko et al, "Health Spending Projections Through 2018: Recession Effects Add Uncertainty to the Outlook," *Health Affairs*, March/April 2009. The authors use CMS data for their analysis and also emphasize that public spending will outpace private.

28. Urban Institute, *Health Reform: The Cost of Failure*, May 2009.

29. Centers for Medicare and Medicaid Services, National Health Expenditure (NHE) Fact Sheet, 2007, www.cms.hhs.gov.

30. American College of Physicians, *Achieving a High-Performance Health Care System with Universal Access: What the United States Can Learn from Other Countries*, December 2007. The American College of Physicians represents over 124,000 physicians.

Chapter 4

New Mexico Demographics and Politics

GABRIEL R. SÁNCHEZ AND
SHANNON SÁNCHEZ-YOUNGMAN

PRESIDENTIAL POLITICS HAS A LOT TO DO, OF COURSE, WITH numbers. The U.S. Electoral College system pushes candidates and their strategists to follow paths that will most likely gain them the necessary and decisive 270 electoral votes. So, given the relatively small number of electoral votes that New Mexico can provide a presidential candidate (only five, compared to thirty-eight in neighboring Texas, for example, or eleven in Arizona, nine in Colorado), one might assume that New Mexico would be irrelevant in the presidential campaigns and elections every four years. But that's not what our recent history shows.

New Mexico Is a Minority-Majority State

The relative national interest in New Mexico's voting and politics has been driven largely by the state's unique demography, political history, and political competitiveness. As national party strategists increasingly recognized the growing political importance that Hispanics would have in presidential elections, they began to give more attention to New Mexico's heavily Hispanic electorate.[1] Hispanics or Latinos—we will use the terms interchangeably— currently make up 47 percent of New Mexico's population, the largest Hispanic percentage in any state in the nation.[2] Combining New Mexico's Hispanic population with its Native American community (which constitutes 10.2 percent of the state's population) makes New Mexico one of the

129

few minority-majority states in the country. And the youthfulness of the present New Mexico Hispanic and other minority populations ensures that the state will become increasingly minority-majority over time.

Hispanic Political and Governmental Representation

Their strong electoral participation and historical political importance and influence have led to high levels of descriptive representation in New Mexico for both Hispanics and Native Americans. For example, the proportion of Hispanics in the New Mexico State Legislature is about the same as the proportion of Hispanics in New Mexico's general population, and New Mexico is the only state to have such relative parity in population and legislative representation. Further, Hispanics hold several key positions in statewide offices, on county commissions, city councils, school boards, and in other local government offices. In 2010 Susana Martinez became the first Latina governor in U.S. history, but she is the sixth Latino governor of New Mexico.

Governor Martinez has emerged as a national political figure who is on a select list of Republicans frequently mentioned as potential vice presidential candidates for 2016. She had a prime-time speaking role at the Republican National Convention in 2012. And in 2013 she was featured as one of *Time* magazine's one hundred most influential people in America.[3] The national political prominence of Governor Martinez is a continuation of the high-profile status of New Mexico governors, begun with her predecessor in the governor's office, Bill Richardson. Also a Latino, Richardson was a Democratic presidential candidate in 2008 and was therefore very much in the national news during that campaign season, and thereafter.

At the federal level, two of the three New Mexico members of the U.S. House of Representatives are Hispanic, rounding out a Latino or Hispanic descriptive representation in New Mexico that is deeply rooted in the state, across time and multiple levels of office.

Native American Political and Governmental Representation

Although not as well documented as Latinos' elected-official story in the state, Native Americans have also achieved impressive levels of political representation in New Mexico. This community is currently represented in both chambers of the New Mexico State Legislature. Presently, there are two Native American senators out of forty-two in the New Mexico Senate and three Native American New Mexico House members out of that chamber's total membership of seventy. John Pinto, Navajo, is currently New Mexico's longest-serving state senator, now in his ninth term in that body.[4] Debra Haaland of Laguna Pueblo was unopposed for the 2014 Democratic nomination for lieutenant governor of New Mexico.

New Mexico: Red, Blue, or Purple?

New Mexico was for a long time thought of as a swing state in presidential elections, and that focused a lot of national attention on the state. In the 2000 presidential election, New Mexico was a "blue" state, though barely: Democratic presidential candidate Al Gore won the state against Republican George W. Bush by only 366 votes, the closest state margin in the country that year. Four years later, the partisan result was the reverse, "red": President George W. Bush, running for reelection, won New Mexico's popular vote over Democrat John Kerry by 5,988 votes, making New Mexico one of only three states in the nation to thus switch parties between 2000 and 2004.[5]

New Mexico's seeming "battleground," or swing, status, then—some dubbed the state "purple"—led to numerous personal visits to the state by presidential candidates and their surrogates during the 2000 and 2004 campaigns, as well as again in 2008. In that latter presidential campaign, Democrat Barack Obama made six personal trips to New Mexico, and his Republican opponent, U.S. Senator John McCain, made eight.

It was due largely to his strong Hispanic support in New Mexico that Obama was able to win the state in 2008, and by a surprisingly wide margin. The National Association of Elected and Appointed Officials reported that in the 2008 election, Hispanics cast 41 percent of all New Mexico votes, and 69 percent of them voted for Obama (with 30 percent of New Mexico Hispanics having voted for McCain), giving Obama a victory margin of 117,897 votes among New Mexico Hispanics alone in that election.[6] McCain would have won New Mexico if it had not been for Hispanic and other minority voters. National exit polls for the 2008 presidential election estimated that New Mexico non-Hispanic white voters went for McCain, 57 percent to 41 percent.[7]

The presidential election of 2012 made it evident that the 2008 blue status of New Mexico was not an anomaly. President Obama, running for a second term in 2012, was victorious in New Mexico among all racial and ethnic groups. The number of New Mexico Hispanic voters had grown since the 2008 election, and Obama won their votes by an even greater margin than before.

The Hispanic vote in New Mexico in 2012, as in other western states such as Nevada and Colorado, ensured a Democratic vote advantage that prevented Republican Mitt Romney from overall victory, and it continued New Mexico's same-as-the-nation, bellwether status. Obama won an overwhelming 77 percent of the New Mexico Hispanic vote that year, a record percentage, while Romney received just 21 percent of New Mexico Hispanic votes.[8]

The growth in the numbers of New Mexico Hispanic voters from 2008 on, coupled with their growing Democratic voting trend, meant that by the time the 2012 presidential campaign began, New Mexico had lost its battleground, or purple, status (see figure 4.1). This led to fewer presidential-candidate and surrogate visits to New Mexico than residents of the state had become used to, and, ironically, it helped put more focus on Hispanics, and voters generally, in Colorado, just to the north. Recognizing early that a 2012 Democratic victory was virtually assured in New Mexico, the Obama campaign decided to move its Hispanic campaign-outreach personnel from New Mexico to Colorado, where the vote was projected to be much tighter and where Hispanic voters could make the difference. The result was that in 2012, Colorado, like New Mexico, went blue, Democratic, due almost exclusively to an aroused and favorable Hispanic vote there.[9]

Figure 4.1. Presidential vote choice in New Mexico by race and ethnicity, 2004–2012

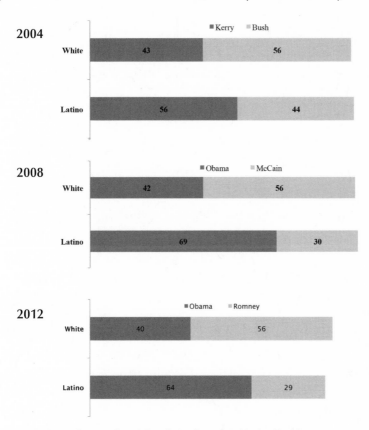

Source: U.S. Census Bureau, Current Population Survey, and Latino Decisions

Despite losing some of the national attention it got when it was regularly one of the most competitive, or swing, states in presidential elections, New Mexico has remained in the national spotlight, largely due to the state's demographic profile. New Mexico continues to be a minority-majority state, of course, and the New Mexico Hispanic population continues to increase relative to non-Hispanic whites.

The *New York Times* in 2012 carried an article headlined "New Mexico Offers Look at U.S. Elections of the Future." In it, Adrian Saenz, the Obama 2012 campaign's Hispanic vote director, was quoted as saying, "The work we do in New Mexico will inform campaigns in the future, not only about how we go out and register Hispanics, but also from a messaging standpoint—what is it that Hispanic-Americans care about."[10] With its heavily Hispanic population and a long history of Hispanic political power, New Mexico offers an excellent example of what national electoral politics may look like in the future.

Evolving New Mexico Political Culture and Partisan Politics

Over the past several decades, Hispanics have made up between 33 percent and 40 percent of all New Mexico voters.[11] In 2012 they amounted to 37 percent of the state's voters, the highest proportion of Hispanic voters in all the states.[12]

Native American voters also have more electoral influence in New Mexico than in any other state, although, of course, on a smaller scale than Hispanic voters. They amount to more than 9 percent of New Mexico's eligible voters, a percentage that is growing fast because of the relative youth of this population.[13]

New Mexico Hispanics and Native Americans have a long history of participation in state politics. Dating as far back as the 1600s, even before Mexico was an independent nation, Hispanics and Native Americans in what is now New Mexico had established their own communities with organized governments.[14] These governments were a part of the various political systems for approximately four hundred years.

This historical New Mexican racial and ethnic diversity was not always viewed positively by U.S. national officials. The territory of what is now New Mexico was annexed as a part of the United States after the U.S.-Mexican War by the Treaty of Guadalupe Hidalgo of 1848, followed by the Gadsden Purchase of 1854, but it was not until 1912 that New Mexico was finally admitted into the union. Many historians and other scholars have noted that it was New Mexico's demographic diversity that kept it from becoming a state much earlier, because the U.S. Congress was reluctant to extend statehood to a territory that was so much browner than the rest of the country.[15]

Still, New Mexico Hispanics and American Indians have not been as excluded or marginalized from political power as have so many of their counterparts in other states. Indeed, New Mexico Hispanics have in the past voted at levels somewhat comparable to New Mexico Anglos and at significantly higher levels than have Hispanics in other states.[16] All in all, a rather unique set of historical and demographic factors have helped Nuevomexicanos become, and remain, "integral and central to the politics of the state throughout its history."[17]

The combined influence of New Mexico's Hispanic and Native American communities, especially, has led to a set of policies and an overall sociopolitical climate that have generally made New Mexico more progressive than other states in the region. Such influence has also made it a state that respects cultural differences.

The original New Mexico State Constitution of 1912 provided for a fully bilingual government, with a requirement that state laws be published in both Spanish and English—a requirement that was twice later renewed, in 1931 and again in 1943. During his term as New Mexico's governor, Bill Richardson (2003–2011) issued an executive order that made undocumented immigrants eligible for New Mexico driver's licenses, and that's now regular law in New Mexico. In 2014 voters in the City of Albuquerque voted down a conservative-backed ballot referendum that would have banned abortions after twenty weeks of pregnancy. Earlier, Albuquerque voters adopted a higher minimum wage for the city than was in effect at the national level. And Santa Fe is one of the American cities that have enacted an official "living wage" law.

The Martinez Era in New Mexico Politics

Although there are many examples of progressive politics in New Mexico, it should be noted that there have also been some recent efforts toward more restrictive policies.

Susana Martinez made conservative immigration-related issues a major focus of her successful 2010 gubernatorial campaign, as well as of her first term in office.[18] The first day after she took the oath of office, Governor Martinez issued an executive order requiring state law enforcement officials to check the citizenship status of individuals they arrested. And in every legislative session during her first term, she fought hard but unsuccessfully for repeal of the law allowing undocumented immigrants to get New Mexico driver's licenses.

Martinez's immediate predecessor in the New Mexico governor's office, Bill Richardson, was a larger-than-life political figure who had previously served as a U.S. representative from New Mexico and then, successively, as the U.S. ambassador to the United Nations and as U.S. secretary of labor. He was easily elected governor of New Mexico in 2002, then reelected in 2006 by the widest margin in state history.

Following such impressive Democratic electoral successes, how was Susana Martinez, a Republican and a relatively little known district attorney in New Mexico's southern Doña Ana County, able to win the governor's office in 2010? There were a number of rather uncommon reasons. First, she was a dynamic and appealing candidate, she raised a lot of money, and she ran a smart and effective campaign. Further, Martinez is, of course, Hispanic, while her opponent in the 2010 race, Diane Denish, is not—and the political science literature has shown that Hispanic voters prefer to vote for a Hispanic candidate, particularly when he or she is viewed as being as well qualified as the opposing non-Hispanic candidate.[19] Also, Martinez seemed to run against the outgoing Governor Richardson—who by then had very low approval ratings, particularly because of various charges against him, which were later dismissed but were then being investigated by grand juries—as much as she did against Denish, her actual opponent. Martinez even challenged Richardson, a noncandidate, to a debate (which, of course, he rejected), and she continuously and effectively linked Denish, who had been Richardson's lieutenant governor for eight years, to New Mexico's struggling state economy and to allegations of political corruption and other failures during the Richardson administration—or the "Richardson-Denish administration," as Martinez repeatedly called it. Finally, 2010 was an off year, not a presidential-election year, and turnout of the Democratic voter base is typically reduced somewhat in off years.

Martinez's successful 2010 gubernatorial campaign saw her making significant inroads with New Mexico Hispanic voters. A Latino Decisions survey found that she captured 38 percent of the important New Mexico

Hispanic vote in 2010, and she remained popular throughout her first term, enjoying high approval ratings.

Elections have consequences, and the success of Martinez, as well as Republicans more widely in 2010, led to a shift in policy across multiple areas. For example, there have been changes in voting requirements in the state of late. Dianna Duran, the first Republican secretary of state elected in New Mexico since 1928, announced following her 2012 election that after cross-checking voter registration files with the New Mexico motor vehicle database, she found that there were as many as sixty-four thousand noncitizens registered to vote in New Mexico. Later, after intense public criticism of her announcement, Duran announced that her office had evidence that only 117 undocumented immigrants had actually obtained driver's licenses and registered to vote in New Mexico, with 37 of them having voted in elections between 2003 and 2010. Following a lawsuit by the New Mexico branch of the ACLU as well as pressure from other groups to force Duran to produce the results of her office's voter-fraud investigation, it was admitted that the office had found only two confirmed cases of foreign nationals having registered to vote in New Mexico, with only one individual having actually voted, and this one, without criminal intent.

Secretary of State Duran and Governor Martinez have pressed the New Mexico State Legislature to adopt a state voter-ID law that would require voters to present official photo IDs in order to vote in person. This effort has been rejected by the legislature.

But the city of Albuquerque has recently instituted its own photo-ID law for city-run elections. And although voters lacking a photo ID can still vote in Albuquerque if they sign an affidavit confirming that they are registered to vote, there is fear that even this milder law might lead to more stringent general laws in the future, laws that could have a significant effect on election outcomes and civic engagement.

During Martinez's time in office, conservative political groups have been very effective in raising and spending large amounts of political campaign money, taking advantage of the *Citizens United* U.S. Supreme Court decision that allows interest groups to spend unlimited amounts of money on campaign advertisements, as long as this spending is not directly coordinated with a campaign. The greatly increased spending in New Mexico campaigns, including campaigns for seats in the New Mexico State Legislature, has signaled a new and worrisome era in New Mexico politics in which television advertisements could take the place of grassroots campaigning.

This discussion of recent policy developments sets the stage for discussion of what the future of New Mexico politics may look like—using the best available data and considering different scenarios.

New Mexico's Political Future

There is an important distinction between the overall population and the voting-eligible population (U.S. citizens, age eighteen and above). And it should be noted again that New Mexico Hispanics and New Mexico members of other racial and ethnic minority groups are substantially younger than New Mexico non-Hispanic whites. According to the 2010 Census, the median age of New Mexico Hispanics, for example, is 31.1 years, while for New Mexico non-Hispanic whites, it's 48.2 years.[20] As figure 4.2 shows, New Mexico's Native American population is even younger than New Mexico Hispanics. This relative youth of New Mexico's minority communities suggests that, as in the rest of the nation, Hispanics and other racial and ethnic groups will eventually make up an ever more significant portion of the New Mexico voting-age population, likely surpassing the New Mexico non-Hispanic white share of the electorate in the not-so-distant future.

Demographic changes already underway—that is, particularly the growing numbers of newly voter-eligible Hispanics—are reflected in the state and national electorate, as Hispanic voter turnout is increasing with each election cycle. But the Hispanic electorate stands to grow even more because their current rates of voter-participation have yet to reach full potential. As figure 4.3 shows, actual Hispanic voting in recent elections has not paralleled Hispanic population growth.

During the 2012 New Mexico general election, only 64 percent of voting-eligible New Mexico Hispanics were registered to vote, and only 56 percent of them actually cast a ballot, compared to 71 percent of voting-eligible New Mexico non-Hispanic whites who did. These New Mexico percentages parallel

Figure 4.2 New Mexico's Population by Race, Projected to 2050

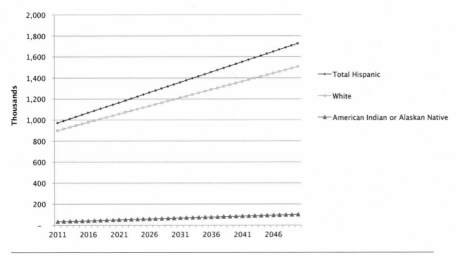

Source: U.S. Census Bureau, Population Division, Interim State Population Projections

national percentages, although New Mexico actually has a higher Hispanic voter-participation rate than most other states. But the relatively low New Mexico Hispanic voter registration and turnout in 2012 were improvements over 2008 registration and turnout: three thousand more New Mexico Latinos or Hispanics registered to vote in 2012 than in 2008, and seventeen thousand more actually voted.

Why is there such a wide gap in turnout between members of minority groups and nonminority whites? The answer has to do with one of the strongest predictors of voting and civic engagement: mobilization—that is, with whether a person is actually contacted by a party or candidate about registering or voting.[21] It is an established fact that minority communities have consistently been mobilized at a much lower rate than non-Hispanic whites.[22] That is true in New Mexico, too, as only 28.25 percent of New Mexico Hispanics said they were contacted and urged to vote in the 2012 New Mexico general election, compared to 39 percent of New Mexico non-Hispanic whites who reported that they were.[23]

Figure 4.3. Voter registration and turnout in New Mexico, Latinos and Whites, 2012

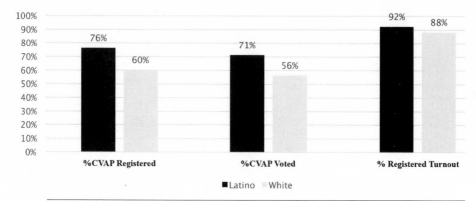

Source: U.S. Census Bureau, Current Population Survey, and Latino Decisions

Another explanation for high and low rates of political participation is the "political resource model." It identifies socioeconomic status (income, education, and age) as a strong predictor of who does or does not participate in American politics.[24] This model also accurately predicts a higher voter turnout for New Mexico non-Hispanic whites than for New Mexico members of minority racial and ethnic groups.

Fifty-five percent of New Mexico's racial and ethnic minority populations have lower incomes than the average for non-Hispanic whites. Thirty percent of all New Mexico Hispanic children live in poverty, compared to 13 percent of all New Mexico non-Hispanic white children and 14 percent of all New Mexico Asian children. New Mexico Native American children (42 percent) and African American children (33 percent) have even higher rates of poverty.[25]

Seventy-one percent of New Mexico non-Hispanic white young people complete high school, compared to only 67 percent of New Mexico Hispanic and 64 percent of New Mexico Native American young people.[26] New Mexico ranks dead last in the nation in child-health outcomes.[27] And New Mexico Hispanics have the highest teen-pregnancy rates compared to all other groups. New Mexico African Americans, Native Americans, and Hispanics have higher infant mortality rates than New Mexico non-Hispanic whites and Asians.[28]

These socioeconomic facts are sad and staggering, and they show what great challenges New Mexico faces. A reduction in New Mexico's poverty rate and level of income inequality would have a huge long-term impact on disparities in voting rates by race and ethnicity.

A vicious cycle exists: the current levels of income inequality among New Mexican families help produce serious political inequality, with those most vulnerable and most in need being least likely to be politically active and to vote and, thus, winding up with the least influence on government policies that would reduce income inequality and improve their socioeconomic status.

The 2014 New Mexico Governor's Race

The importance of various voter-turnout projections was apparent when we used them as the backdrop for our development of various scenarios of what might happen in the 2014 New Mexico governor's race.

Looking back to the 2010 gubernatorial election (see table 4.1) and assuming similar turnout rates while estimating the electorate size based on past growth rates, we were able to make reasonable predictions of what might happen.

Table 4.1. 2010 Election Results: Susana Martinez v. Diane Denish

CANDIDATE	RAW VOTES	VOTE SHARE
Denish	280,614	47%
Martinez	321,219	53%
Total	601,833	—

More specifically, to provide an idea of how things would look under various scenarios, we first manipulated the New Mexico voting-age population figures while holding other parameters constant (table 4.2).

We projected that, based on a 5 percent increase in eligible voters, a turnout

rate of 44 percent, and the same vote share as 2010, Governor Susana Martinez, running for reelection in 2014, would achieve a net gain of 53,095 votes,
winning the election handily (table 4.3).

Specifically in regard to New Mexico Hispanics, by assuming a 2 percent
increase in the total 2012 voting-eligible population, with Hispanic turnout
remaining constant (35 percent), we could say that there would be only
11,208 new Hispanic voters in 2014. Then, also assuming that Governor Martinez would capture a percentage of the total 2014 vote similar to what she got
in 2010 (38 percent), we projected that there would be a net gain of roughly
6,949 votes for the Democratic candidate. But considering that Martinez
defeated Denish in 2010 by over 40,000 votes, we could say that the incumbent governor would still win reelection in 2014, and this would be true even
with a projected intervening growth in voting by other New Mexico minority
groups similar to that for New Mexico Hispanics.

Table 4.2. 2010 Election Turnout

	CITIZEN VOTING-AGE POPULATION 2010	CITIZEN VOTING-AGE POPULATION REGISTERED	TOTAL VOTING	TURNOUT
Latinos	516,000	249,000	183,000	35%
Whites	613,000	396,000	319,000	52%

Table 4.3. 2014 gubernatorial race vote choice projections among general population

	ESTIMATED ELIGIBLE VOTERS	ESTIMATED TURNOUT	TOTAL VOTES	VOTES FOR MARTINEZ	VOTES FOR DEMOCRATIC CHALLENGER
Scenario: Republican vote share = 53%	1,431,000*	44%	629,640	333,709	289,634

* Based on a five-point increase in the total of citizens of voting age

Our projections above amount to a kind of "status quo" scenario, and under it, we projected that Martinez would win reelection rather easily in 2014, outpacing a hypothetical Democratic candidate by a relatively wide margin.

Of course, there was an early and considerable possibility that circumstances and conditions in New Mexico in 2014 could be different from those in 2010 and could, therefore, possibly yield a different election result. For example, three of the five early Democratic gubernatorial candidates vying for the 2014 Democratic nomination and the chance to challenge Governor Martinez in the general election were Hispanic: Linda Lopez, Howie Morales, and Lawrence Rael. We said that if one of those Hispanic candidates were to secure the Democratic nomination, this could decrease the percentage of the Hispanic vote that Martinez would win and potentially bring her closer to the norm for GOP gubernatorial candidates.

Another significant difference we had to consider was that in 2010 there was a major national partisan realignment in voting that produced a surge toward the GOP, resulting, for example, in the most significant shift in U.S. House of Representatives seats in over seventy years—this one from the Democrats to the Republicans. Republicans also won the majority of governors' races across the nation in 2010, at a critical time, when states were about to turn to postcensus legislative and congressional redistricting. In New Mexico in 2010, in addition to the Martinez win for governor, the GOP also picked up a handful of new seats in the New Mexico House and Senate. We had to consider that a similar national Republican surge might not be seen in 2014, that it wouldn't therefore spill over in its effect into New Mexico, and that it would thus reduce the Martinez vote in the 2014 election.

What, we asked, would be the effect of greater mobilization of Hispanics for the 2014 gubernatorial election? If we assumed that New Mexico Hispanic mobilization for 2014 would jump to 75 percent (an increase from 28.25 percent in 2010) our projections showed that Hispanic voting-eligible turnout would increase dramatically, to 50 percent, producing a total 2014 New Mexico Hispanic vote of 277,440, or 94,444 more Hispanic voters than in 2010 (table 4.4).

Under that scenario, even with a conservative estimate of a decrease in Governor Martinez's share of the 2014 New Mexico Hispanic vote from

38 percent to 35 percent, we projected that she would still get 27,564 fewer votes than in 2010, thus putting a victory over her well within the reach of any of the Democratic challengers. A more liberal projection that decreased the Martinez share of the 2014 New Mexico Hispanic vote from 38 percent to 30 percent, we said, would place the Martinez share of the New Mexico Hispanic vote more in line with that normally received by other recent statewide Republican candidates and would result in a net gain of 80,748 votes for the Democratic challenger (table 4.5). That would have made a seemingly impossible Democratic defeat of the presently popular incumbent Latina governor appear plausible.

Table 4.4. Vote share among Latinos, 2010 gubernatorial race

	TOTAL VOTES	LATINO VOTE SHARE	LATINO VOTES
Martinez	183,000	38%	69,540
Denish	183,000	62%	113,460

Source: U.S. Census Bureau, Current Population Survey 2010; exit polling data

Table 4.5. Projected vote choice for Latinos, 2014

TURNOUT	PROJECTED TOTAL VOTES	PROJECTED VOTE SHARE, REPUBLICANS	PROJECTED VOTE SHARE, DEMOCRATS	PROJECTED MARTINEZ VOTES	PROJECTED DEMOCRATIC VOTES
35%	194,208	38%	62%	73,799	120,409
50%	277,440	35%	65%	97,104	180,336
50%	277,440	30%	75%	83,232	194,208

Note: Estimated eligible Latino voters = 554,880, based on a two-point increase in the Latino voting-age population from 2012 to 2014

The November 4, 2014, New Mexico general election contest for governor actually pitted Democratic nominee Gary King, an Anglo attorney general and the son of former governor Bruce King, against the popular incumbent Hispanic Republican governor, Susana Martinez. Among the scenarios that we proposed in this chapter, the election closely resembled our "status quo" scenario, where Governor Martinez won rather easily. Among the factors that helped explain this outcome was that overall turnout was very low: approximately 512,000 voters showed up at the polls, significantly fewer than in 2010, when over 600,000 New Mexicans cast ballots. In fact, the registered voter turnout rate of 40 percent in 2014 was the lowest participation rate in decades. This helped Governor Martinez win 57 percent of the vote, the largest percentage ever for a GOP candidate. While other factors helped drive this outcome, including King running a weak campaign and a national movement toward the GOP, the governor's ability to capture a larger segment of the Hispanic vote in New Mexico was also important. Although sound polling was not done in the race, Martinez's ability to outperform expectations in northern counties with a heavy Hispanic Democratic base is a clear indicator that she likely improved her performance among Hispanic voters from 2010. This combination of factors all made for an election that did not fit any of our scenarios in which Governor Martinez would not win reelection, and in fact, led to a historic election in which the Republican Party seized control of the state legislature.

New Mexico's Political Future

Let us now turn to consideration of the important question of whether or not New Mexico has become a reliably blue state, with the days of being a battleground, or swing, state behind us.

Demographic projections make it clear that the state will become increasingly diverse over time, and New Mexico Hispanics will not only become the majority of New Mexico's voting-eligible population but also a majority of the actual voting electorate. This, coupled with the fact of New Mexico

Hispanics' record-breaking 77 percent voting support for President Obama in 2012 and his huge reelection victory, makes it tempting for one to conclude that New Mexico will not be party-competitive from now on and therefore will not, for example, receive special attention from presidential candidates and the national media every four years.

But it should be pointed out that New Mexico Hispanic voters have from time to time shown a propensity to vote for GOP candidates, and New Mexico Native American voters have sometimes relied more on their perceptions as to which candidate will be best for the pueblo or tribe than on a candidate's party label. Figure 4.1 showed that in some recent elections a pretty hefty percentage of New Mexico Hispanics have voted for the Republican presidential candidate. George W. Bush, for example, captured 44 percent of the Hispanic vote when he ran. Susana Martinez, as we've also mentioned, got 38 percent of the New Mexico Hispanic vote when she was elected in 2008. And other GOP candidates in the state have sometimes done as well.

Further, New Mexico voters have sometimes shown a propensity to make distinctions between federal- and state-level candidates, a fact that helps explain a majority of New Mexicans voting for Democratic presidential and Senate candidates and, in the same election, for Republicans in state-level races.

Latino Decisions survey data from the 2012 election indicates that Republican candidates could increase their likelihood of future New Mexico electoral success by taking a different position on immigration policy. More specifically, 21 percent of Hispanics surveyed said that they would be more likely to vote for a GOP candidate if that party took the lead in passing national, comprehensive immigration reform that included a pathway to citizenship for undocumented immigrants now in this country.[29]

Suppose, in thinking about possible Republican future electoral success in New Mexico, we begin by exploring what would happen if there were a decrease in New Mexico Hispanic turnout in the 2016 presidential election, a pessimistic but possible scenario. As noted earlier, 56 percent of voting-eligible New Mexico Hispanics actually voted in 2012, which produced 316,826 actual Hispanic votes in that election. If 2016 turnout dropped to

51 percent of those New Mexico Hispanics eligible to vote, that would result in a decrease of 17,462 New Mexico Hispanic votes (table 4.6).

But given the high 2008 and 2012 New Mexico Hispanic vote for Democrats, even a significant drop like that in Hispanic support, due, perhaps, to a different set of candidates running, would not damage the Democratic candidate sufficiently to make victory possible for the Republican candidate, if other factors remain relatively similar to those in 2012. As table 4.7 demonstrates, even if New Mexico Hispanics were to increase their support for the Republican candidate and maintain their past turnout rate, the expected future increase in the New Mexico Hispanic voting population would still imply victory for the Democratic candidate.

Table 4.6. Projected Latino electorate scenarios, New Mexico, 2016

TURNOUT SCENARIO	NUMBER OF VOTERS	CHANGE FROM 2012
51% (5-pt. decrease from 2012)	288,538	-17,462
56% (same as 2012)	316,826	+10,826
64% (state average, 2012)	362,086	+56,086
75% (mobilized scenario)	424,320	+118,320

Note: Estimated Latino eligible voters = 565,760
Source: Estimates based on U.S. Census Bureau, 2012 Election Report; University of New Mexico, Bureau of Business and Economic Research, 2012 estimates

Table 4.7. Projected vote choice for Latinos, 2016 presidential race

TURNOUT	PROJECTED TOTAL VOTES	PROJECTED VOTE SHARE, REPUBLICAN	PROJECTED VOTE SHARE, DEMOCRAT	PROJECTED VOTES, REPUBLICAN	PROJECTED VOTES, DEMOCRAT
56%	316,826	40%	60%	126,730	190,095
56%	316,826	44%	56%	139,403	177,422

Note: Estimated eligible Latino voters = 565,760, based on a four-point increase in the Latino voting-age population, 2012–2016

African Americans and Other Minorities
Pamelya Herndon

African Americans in New Mexico have been working to gain decision-making power in a state where their numbers, at the highest peak, have not exceeded 2.4 percent of the population.[1] Despite their relatively small numbers, African Americans have managed to raise their political visibility by winning statewide offices as well as positions in the New Mexico House of Representatives.[2] No African American has ever been able to win a seat representing the state in Congress.[3]

During the administration of Governor Gary Johnson (1995–2003), African Americans urged him to create a statewide Office of African American Affairs. The office was ultimately created by statute and implemented by executive order—and is still in operation.[4] Efforts to have the office converted into a state governmental department, headed by an appointed secretary who sits as a member of the governor's cabinet, have not been successful. No recent governor has been willing to support such legislation.

Consider now the plight of African American children. The New Mexico infant mortality rate among African American children is exceptionally high: 13.5 per thousand.[5] Many African American children in the fourth grade in New Mexico are reading at only one-fourth of standard proficiency. Just 39 percent of African American students who enter high school actually graduate.[6] There are no African Americans on school boards in any city in New Mexico.

Two African American men have served as members of the board of regents of the University of New Mexico, one African American woman has served on the board of regents of New Mexico Highlands University, and one African American man has served on the board of regents of New Mexico Tech.[7] Still, no African American has ever been elevated to the position of president or vice president, chancellor or vice chancellor in any New Mexico university system, nor has an African American ever been selected as dean of any university professional school, such as those for medicine, law, or nursing.

There is considerable pride around the fact that the University of New Mexico has established an Africana Studies Division. However, Africana studies (like the Office of African American Affairs in New Mexico state government) is still awaiting departmental status. Most other colleges and universities in New Mexico have only a black studies program.

AN AFRICAN AMERICAN AGENDA

As we move toward 2050, the African American community must, with other minority groups, develop a cohesive, collaborative plan to support candidates and key personnel across the state of New Mexico who will include African Americans and other minorities in critical decision-making positions. Looking toward 2050, African Americans must help bring about policy and systemic change that will ensure that African American children graduate from high school *and* attend college.

Although their voting numbers appear relatively small, the collective voting strength of New Mexican African Americans can still make a difference in a close election. For this reason, as we move toward 2050 it is important for coalition voting blocs to be established between African American communities and other minority groups, such as LGTB communities and women's groups—to ensure that all are able to reach the common goals they rightly seek.

In New Mexico the LGTB community, for example, makes up 2.9 percent of the state's population.[8] African Americans are 2.4 percent of the population. Together, these two groups can be a powerful 5.3 percent voting bloc.

More African Americans must become police officers as we move toward 2050, to help build a culture of understanding in our communities and put an end to cases like the one involving the death of Iraq War veteran Jonathan Mitchell or the shooting incident involving Oriana Farrell, the mother who was stopped for speeding in Taos, New Mexico, and fled when officers fired on her minivan with children inside.[9]

As we move toward 2050, we need African Americans appointed to civilian police oversight commissions and review boards to help develop policies and procedures that will put an end to senseless deaths in African American and other minority communities.

PROGRESS TOWARD MORE EQUALITY

New Mexico, though small in size and population, is a progressive state that can move the pendulum of progress toward greater equality for the state's African American population. This is best illustrated by looking at many of the laws recently passed in New Mexico. For example, New Mexico has adopted the Fair Pay Act for Women, giving women greater access to judicial remedies than they have through the federal government when they are not paid the same as men for doing the same job. This legislation is a step in the right direction for African American women, who earn just seventy cents for every dollar paid to men and just sixty-four cents for every dollar paid to white, non-Hispanic men.[10]

Although New Mexico has the highest rate of teen pregnancy in the country, it is also a state that passed legislation in 2012 to provide teen mothers additional time to be out of school to take care of their children without losing valuable education credits.[11] New Mexico is one of the few states that has passed a law under Title IX that requires schools to report on how they are making sports and athletic programs available for girls.[12] In New Mexico the constitutional right of same-sex couples to marry has been upheld by the state's highest court.[13] In addition, resident undocumented immigrants can get driver's licenses.[14] Undocumented students who graduate from a New Mexico high school are eligible for in-state tuition at the state's institutions of higher education.[15]

continued on next page

New Mexico has approved expanded Medicaid coverage as authorized by the federal government under the Affordable Care Act and has established a state health insurance exchange under the act. African Americans and other minorities in New Mexico will be among the greatest beneficiaries of these state developments.[16]

NEW MEXICO 2050

New Mexico has made great progress. But more must come. Why? For one reason, New Mexico is a minority-majority state: Hispanics, Native Americans, and African Americans together make up a majority of the state's population. And women are more than half of all New Mexicans. By the year 2050, we can expect to see significant effects of the Affordable Care Act in two areas: a dramatic reduction in the high rate of African American infant mortality; and the elimination of New Mexico's status as the state with the highest rate of uninsurance among women in America. With the help of a progressive state legislature, New Mexico will also increase the minimum wage in a state that now ranks forty-forth in per capita household income.[17] By the year 2050, with inclusiveness the focus of decision makers, we can ensure both de jure and de facto equality for every resident of New Mexico.

NOTES

1. U.S. Department of Commerce, 2013 Census.

2. James B. Lewis was elected as state treasurer in 2006 and reelected in 2010. African Americans elected to the New Mexico House of Representatives and their terms in office are Lenton Malry (D), 1968–1978; Eddie Corley Jr. (D), 1996–2000; Sheryl Williams Stapleton (D), 1994–present; and Jane Powdrell-Culbert (R), 2003–present.

3. James B. Lewis ran for the U.S. House of Representatives in 1990 but was defeated in the primary.

4. The Office of African American Affairs was created by statute through HB 909 (1999 Regular Legislative Session). That statute did not provide sufficient funding for the office to operate. Individuals were placed in the office by executive order so it could operate.

New Mexico 2050

We believe that it can be shown that broader civic engagement and political participation would be good for New Mexico and America. Such increases would make government more responsive to the needs of all the people, including the more vulnerable, while at the same time causing more people to feel that they have greater control over their own lives and destinies.

But, as we've seen, there is unfortunately a significant elite bias in political participation in New Mexico, as elsewhere—more highly educated New Mexicans with higher incomes being more likely to vote, donate money to

5. Center for Interdisciplinary Health and Research, University of Texas, June 2011.

6. *Mapping the Landscape of African Americans in New Mexico* (Albuquerque: UNM Center for Education Policy Research, August 2012).

7. Richard Toliver (1997–2003) and Conrad James (2013–present) served on the UNM Board of Regents. Marsha Hardeman served as chair of the New Mexico Highlands University regents in 1996. Lenton Malry served on the New Mexico Tech University Board of Regents, 1985–1991.

8. "LGBT Percentage Highest in D.C., Lowest in North Dakota," in *State of the States,* Gallup Politics, February 15, 2013.

9. "Justice for Jonathan Mitchel," *Black-butterfly7* (blog), March 17, 2014, http://blackbutterfly7.wordpress.com/2014/03/17/justice-for-jonathan-mitchell/; *New York Daily News,* December 7, 2013, www.mydailynews.com/.

10. Fair Pay Act for Women, HB 216, 2012.

11. Teen Pregnancy Rates by State, Live Science.com, February 25, 2013, http://www.livescience.com/27417-teen-pregnancy-rates-by-state.html; HB 300, 2012.

12. School Athletics Equity Act, NM Statutes Ann. §22–31–2 (2009).

13. "Appeals Court Struggles to Decode Supreme Court Message on Gay Marriage Right," *Huffington Post,* April 2014.

14. "New Mexico's Martinez Targets Driver's Licenses for Illegal Immigrants," *Washington Post,* December 18, 2013.

15. "Basic Facts about In-State Tuition," National Immigration Law Center, December 2013.

16. "New Mexico Medicaid Moving Forward in 2014," Medicaid.gov, accessed 2013, http://www.medicaid.gov/medicaid-chip-program-information/by-state/new-mexico.html.

17. U.S. Census Bureau, State and County Quick Facts, accessed February 24, 2014.

candidates, and directly contact public officials. Consequently, there is a consistent, and persistent, disconnect between the New Mexico electorate (those who regularly vote) and the wider New Mexico population, as well as a frequent disconnect between what government does and what most of the people want and need.

So we hope, and expect, that New Mexico will continue to reject the kind of legislation adopted in some other states—requiring voter IDs, shortening the number of voting days or hours, or in other ways making registration or voting more difficult—that would have the effect of shrinking political participation.

We support all registration and get-out-the-vote mobilization efforts, year-round and not just at election time, that will get more New Mexicans registered to vote and then to the polls.

We support—and expect to see in New Mexico—more efforts to mobilize voting-eligible Hispanics and other minorities. In the 2010 election, there were 330,000 New Mexico Hispanics who were eligible to vote but decided to stay home—66,000 of whom were registered to vote. A similar nonvoting pattern holds for all populations in New Mexico, but the gap is much greater for racial and ethnic minority groups. Of course, this is not a problem that is unique to New Mexico, but the challenges here are more salient, given the diversity of our population.

Our high percentage and number of nonvoters may seem to be an overwhelming problem at first glance, but there is definitely a reason for optimism if we look at the much higher rate of New Mexico Hispanics, for example, who vote if they become registered. If New Mexico invests more heavily in voter registration—as we strongly recommend and expect to see—we will get a major return on our investment.

We should realize, though, and take into account, that while we are supporting more registration and mobilization efforts, we will be up against a general wave moving away from presidential-election-driven mobilization, as New Mexico's changing demography produces less competitive statewide presidential races and, thus, fewer presidential-candidate visits, less outside money for outreach and civic engagement, and a lowering of campaign energy that would otherwise come from a tighter presidential race in the state.

In addition to expanding the scale of New Mexico voter registration and get-out-the-vote activity, raising policy issues that are especially salient or referring them to the people for popular vote can engage voters, often to a greater extent than even candidates can. The most recent example of this in New Mexico was an Albuquerque referendum that would have banned abortions after twenty weeks of pregnancy, which was defeated handily by the voters in an election that drew a higher voter turnout than had the Albuquerque mayoral race a month earlier.

Arranging for a popular vote on policy issues such as a New Mexico increase in the minimum wage or legalization of marijuana could bring more New Mexicans to the ballot box and, more importantly, get them engaged in the political process.

One policy area that proved to be influential in 2012 was immigration policy. Data from Latino Decisions indicates that immigration policy was highly salient to Hispanic voters in New Mexico, behind only the economy and jobs as the most important issue on the minds of those surveyed. Interestingly, it was found, too, that this unexpected emergence of immigration policy as a relevant issue was driven by personal connections between New Mexico Hispanics and immigrants—nearly 60 percent of New Mexico Hispanics in this survey saying that they knew an undocumented person, either a friend, family member, or coworker. Not only was immigration shown to be important to New Mexico's Hispanic population, but their policy views in this area had generally moved left over time. For example, when queried about the highly publicized driver's license issue, an overwhelming 70 percent of them said they supported driver's licenses for undocumented immigrants (with some added application requirements), while only 21 percent were opposed.[30]

We therefore recommend congressional action on creating resident status and work permits for undocumented immigrants and developing a reasonable path to citizenship, not only for Dreamers (undocumented immigrants brought here as children by their parents) but for all law-abiding, taxpaying undocumented immigrants. This action would be in line with the policy preferences of New Mexico Hispanics and could energize a large segment of the Hispanic electorate, who have grown impatient with lack of congressional action to date.

Another example of an issue that would bring more people out to vote is a proposed amendment to the New Mexico Constitution to earmark a small percentage of the annual income from the state's multibillion-dollar Land Grant Permanent Fund for early childhood education. (Chapter 2 has a full discussion of this subject.) A legislative measure aimed at referring such an amendment to the people has been stalled in the New Mexico State Legislature. If the people in the state who would stand to benefit most from this proposal were engaged in the political process, the political will would materialize to get this measure to the people and get it adopted by them.

And new investment in early childhood education would go a long way toward closing some of the major inequalities in New Mexico over time.

We use this last example specifically because it is not inherently partisan, as all New Mexicans would benefit from the adoption of this early childhood amendment. We believe that getting a wider segment of the state's population to participate in the political process would push both parties to adopt policy platforms that would make them more attractive to all elements of New Mexico's population.

Notes

1. The terms *Latino* and *Hispanic* are used interchangeably in this chapter.
2. U.S. Census Bureau, Current Population Survey: Voting Supplement, November 2012.
3. Karl Rove, "Susana Martinez," April 18, 2013, 2013 Time 100, http://time100.time.com/2013/04/18/time-100/slide/susana-martinez/.
4. "NM Native American State Elected Officials," Voter Information, New Mexico Office of the Secretary of State, http://www.sos.state.nm.us/Voter_Information/NM_Native_American_State_Elected_Officials.aspx.
5. F. Chris García, Gabriel R. Sánchez, and Christine Sierra, "Hispanos in the 2008 Election in New Mexico" (working paper, Southwest Hispanic Research Institute, University of New Mexico, 2012).
6. National Association of Latino Elected and Appointed Figures, *Latino Voters in the 2008 Presidential Election: Post-Election Survey of Latino Voters*, 2008, http://www.naleo.org/downloads/Post-Election%20Survey.pdf; see also Julia Preston, "In Big Shift, Latino Vote Was Heavily for Obama," *New York Times*, November 6, 2008, http://www.nytimes.com/2008/11/07/us/politics/07latino.html.
7. García, Sánchez, and Sierra, "Hispanos in the 2008 Election."
8. ImpreMedia/Latino Decisions, Election Eve Poll, 2012, http://www.latinodecisions.com/2012-election-eve-polls/.
9. Rob Preuhs "Colorado's Latina/Latino Gender Gap," Latino Decisions blog, September 13, 2012, http://www.latinodecisions.com/blog/2012/09/13/colorados-latinalatino-gender-gap/.

10. Fernanda Santos, "New Mexico Offers Look at U.S. Elections of the Future," *New York Times*, September 29, 2012, http://www.nytimes.com/2012/09/30/us/politics/new-mexico-gives-look-into-politics-of-future.html.

11. F. Chris García and Bianca Sapien, "Recognizing Reliability: Hispanos and the 1996 Elections in New Mexico," in *Awash in the Mainstream: Latino Politics in the 1996 Election*, ed. Rodolfo O. de la Garza and Louis DeSipio (Boulder, CO: Westview Press, 1999), 75–100; F. Chris García and Christine Marie Sierra, "New Mexico Hispanos in the 2000 General Election," in *Muted Voices: Latinos and the 2000 Elections*, ed. Rodolfo O. de la Garza and Louis DeSipio (Lanham, MD: Rowman & Littlefield, 2005), 101–29; and Christine Marie Sierra, and F. Chris García, "Hispanic Politics in a Battleground State: New Mexico in 2004," in *Beyond the Barrio: Latinos in the 2004 Elections*, ed. Rodolfo O. de la Garza, Louis DeSipio, and David L. Leal (South Bend, IN: University of Notre Dame Press, 2010), 97–130.

12. Mark Hugo-López and Paul Taylor, *Latino Voters in the 2012 Election* (Pew Hispanic Center, 2012), http://www.pewhispanic.org/files/2012/11/2012_Latino_vote_exit_poll_analysis_final_11-09.pdf.

13. Mark Trahant, "Elections 2012: Native Americans Have More Influence in New Mexico Than Any Other States," *Indian Country Today*, November 1, 2012, http://indiancountrytodaymedianetwork.com/2012/11/01/elections-2012-native-americans-have-more-influence-new-mexico-any-other-state-143397.

14. F. Chris García and Gabriel R. Sánchez, *Hispanics and the U.S. Political System: Moving into the Mainstream* (Upper Saddle River, NJ: Pearson, Prentice-Hall, 2008).

15. Laura Gómez, *Manifest Destinies: The Making of the Mexican American Race* (New York: New York University Press, 2008).

16. García and Sierra, "New Mexico Hispanos in the 2000 General Election."

17. García and Sapien, "Recognizing Reliability."

18. Gabriel Sánchez, "The State of Play In New Mexico: The Role of 2010 Winners in the 2012 Race," Latino Decisions blog, July 15, 2012, http://www.latinodecisions.com/blog/2012/07/15/the-state-of-play-in-new-mexico-the-role-of-2010-winners-in-2012-race/.

19. Matt Barreto, "Sí Se Puede! Latino Candidates and the Mobilization of Latino Voters," *American Political Science Review* 101 (2007): 425–41; Sylvia Manzano

and Gabriel R. Sánchez, "Take One for the Team: Ethnic Identity, Candidate Qualification and Co-Ethnic Voting," *Political Research Quarterly* 63 (2010): 568–80.

20. U.S. Census Bureau, Current Population Survey: Voting Supplement, November 2010.

21. Steven J. Rosenstone and John Mark Hansen, *Mobilization, Participation, and Democracy in America* (New York: Pearson, 1994).

22. J. E. Leighley, *Strength in Numbers? The Political Mobilization of Racial and Ethnic Minorities* (Princeton, NJ: Princeton University Press, 2001).

23. Lonna Atkins, Shannon Sánchez-Youngman, and Alex Adams, "Latino Descriptive Voting: Evidence in the 2010 Gubernatorial Race in New Mexico" (paper presented at the annual meeting of the Midwestern Political Science Association, April 2012).

24. See Sidney Verba, Kay Scholzman, and Henry Brady, *Voice and Equality: Civic Voluntarism in American Politics* (Boston: Harvard University Press, 1995).

25. Lisa Cacari-Stone and Deborah Boldt, *Closing the Health Disparity Gap in New Mexico: A Roadmap for Grantmaking* (Con Alma Health Foundation, May 2006), http://www.borderhealth.org/files/res_798.pdf.

26. New Mexico Public Education Department, Graduation Rates, 2012–2013.

27. Annie E Casey Foundation, *2013 Data Book: State Trends in Child Well-Being*, http://datacenter.kidscount.org/files/2013kidscountdatabook.pdf.

28. New Mexico Voices for Children, *Making Sure ALL KIDS COUNT: Disparities Among New Mexico's Children*, 2010, http://www.nmvoices.org/attachments/nmkc-disparity-rpt-12-10.pdf.

29. See ImpreMedia/Latino Decisions, Election Eve Poll, 2012, state results tables (toplines), http://www.latinodecisions.com/files/7613/5234/2212/Latino_Election_Eve_Poll_-_By_state.pdf.

30. See Gabriel R. Sánchez, "The Context of Immigration Policy in New Mexico Reflects National Trends," Latino Decisions blog, October 31, 2012, http://www.latinodecisions.com/blog/2012/10/31/the-context-of-immigration-policy-in-new-mexico-reflects-national-trends/.

Chapter 5

New Mexico Environment and Water

New Mexico Environment and Water

LAURA PASKUS AND ADRIAN OGLESBY

New Mexico Environment by Laura Paskus

As America's 1787 constitutional convention finished its work, Benjamin Franklin was asked by local citizens what kind of government the founders had produced. His answer: "A republic, if you can keep it." Similarly, when we are asked what we have here in New Mexico, we can rightly say, "A true Land of Enchantment, if we can keep it."

Can we? Will we?

Our land, air, and water quality are all facing challenges. And our water is subject to conflicting claims in a time of increasingly severe drought conditions. But there is much we can and must do if we are to meet these challenges—if we are to keep, and even improve, our Land of Enchantment.

New Mexico Land and Air and Water Quality

How many of us have traveled New Mexico—or looked up from our own back porches—and felt humbled by its landscapes? From the 13,167-foot-tall Wheeler Peak in northern New Mexico and the white sands of the southern deserts to the eastern grasslands and western badlands, every corner and canyon of the state is breathtaking in its own way.

Just as the view from each horizon is different, people see those landscapes through different lenses. For some, the beauty evokes home, history, or a visceral connection with nature. For others, those landscapes represent recreational opportunities—places to hunt, fish, hike, or bike. The state's natural resources also offer economic opportunities, whether grassy rangelands or geological formations rich with minerals or fossil fuels.

But within the past few decades, a false dichotomy has been perpetuated: the environment versus the economy. That argument has played out in a number of ways, all of which have served to alienate neighbors and citizens from one another—and have prevented New Mexico's decision makers from balancing extraction and development with environmental protection in a way that protects human and natural communities and safeguards resources for future generations.

During Governor Bill Richardson's administration (2003–2011), state employees moved forward on a number of progressive environmental regulations related to groundwater protections and greenhouse gas emissions, among others. Many of those rules have since been eliminated, despite growing concerns over drought, development, and climate change.

To the detriment of communities and the environment, issues related to water, land, and air have been politicized. Little else could be more detrimental to efforts to ensure that natural resources are conserved and protected in the coming decades. Whether the issue is oil and gas—and the drilling method known as "fracking"—or the preservation of lands from further development, one truth is clear: discussions involving natural resources and the environment must be broadened and prioritized.

We can learn from the peoples who have been in New Mexico the longest. Theresa Pasqual is Acoma Pueblo's former director of historic preservation, the first woman to hold that position. Her job was to look at all the cultural and historic resources on the pueblo's lands and determine how to manage and protect them under state laws and federal laws, including the National Environmental Policy Act. Pasqual says, "There is a finite amount of time that we can have this conversation."[1] We believe we should have begun these conversations, with all the state's many diverse populations at the table, many years ago. And the questions guiding the conversation should be: What are our values? What is our vision for the future? What are we leaving for future generations?

Even if decision makers don't consider themselves "environmentalists" or aren't interested in issues such as clean air and water or sustainable land practices, they must face some economic realities.

Today, New Mexico has the second-highest level of poverty in the nation. It's worth considering how New Mexicans would fare were water to become increasingly scarce or as oil and gas wells become tapped out and mineral resources exhausted. New Mexico's high level of poverty has persisted over decades, despite intense natural resource extraction. For example, in 2013, oil and natural gas drilling delivered more than $1.7 billion in revenue to New Mexico's general fund.[2] And according to the New Mexico Energy, Minerals, and Natural Resources Department's 2013 annual report, the mining of coal, copper, gold, industrial minerals, aggregates, other metals, molybdenum, potash, silver, and uranium together contributed more than $373 million in payroll and $43 million in state revenue.[3]

If decision makers are opposed to the conservation of natural resources for the sake of open lands and clean waters, they might consider the long-term economic wisdom of depleting the state's resources entirely in the coming decades.

It is useful to read Daniel Bergner's explanation in the *New York Times* of how natural resources exploitation of gold, in this case in Sierra Leone, can harm—or help—a nation: "The term 'resource curse' has been used by economists since the 1990s to invoke the way abundant minerals or oil can lead impoverished, misgoverned countries into worse mismanagement, civil war and more entrenched poverty. But as Paul Collier, a British economist and co-director of Oxford University's Center for the Study of African Economies, made clear to me: 'Natural-resource extraction can be a way to help the most desperate countries catch up,' if the revenue is spent on 'more productive assets such as education and infrastructure.'"[4]

Environmental challenges are all the more urgent given the fact that for more than two decades, scientists have pointed to a warming trend in New Mexico and the southwestern United States. Climate change is already here. It's time for the state's leaders to plan for a warmer—and therefore drier—future.

At the same time, decision makers should ensure that natural resources are developed responsibly—in ways that protect water, environmental resources, communities, and quality of life. They must also use some of the revenue that industry currently brings to New Mexico to initiate infrastructure changes necessary for the state's citizens to adapt to continued changes in the climate.

It's long past time for New Mexico's decision makers to determine priorities and uphold and enact reasonable regulations—or else make plans for how the state's remaining communities will survive the decades to come in a place lacking adequate water and burdened with the byproducts of unregulated development and resource extraction.

STRONG NEW MEXICO LAWS

Attorney Douglas Meiklejohn started the New Mexico Environmental Law Center more than twenty-five years ago. Over the course of five gubernatorial administrations, the center has remained steadfast in its defense of communities and the environment. And while political winds have oscillated, Meiklejohn has seen a steady improvement in attitudes of the state's citizens: "There is more awareness now about environmental issues in general and also about the need to protect resources like water," he says.[5] But a great deal of work lies still ahead. Especially if New Mexico's political leaders are going to catch up to—and truly represent—their constituents.

New Mexico Solid Waste Act

Although the Environmental Law Center initially focused on public lands, its focus later shifted toward environmental justice. That had much to do with a case in Sunland Park, New Mexico. Bordered on the east by El Paso and the south by a landfill that shares a boundary with Mexico, the community's residents are mostly poor and Spanish speaking.[6]

In the late 1980s the landfill included a medical-waste incinerator that had been built before the state had enacted air quality regulations. Residents, as well as students and employees at one of the local elementary schools, were sickened by the smells of burning flesh and plastic. Even people's laundry, hung outside to dry, was thick with the smell of burning plastic and flesh.[7]

The incinerator was eventually closed, in 1991, as a result of the New Mexico Environmental Law Center's representation of the Concerned Citizens of Sunland Park. But the victory had legs far beyond the border community. Today, New Mexico's Solid Waste Act mandates how far incinerators must be located from homes, schools, and workplaces, and new regulations govern air emissions from incinerators.

New Mexico air quality and New Mexico surface water quality are regulated under the terms of the federal Clean Air Act of 1970 (as revised in 1977 and 1990) and the federal Clean Water Act of 1972. By contrast, while the New Mexico Solid Waste Act implements the federal Resource Conservation and Recovery Act of 1976, the protections of New Mexico's law are more stringent than those provided under the relevant federal act.[8]

New Mexico Mining Act

Adopted in 1993, the New Mexico Mining Act promotes "responsible utilization and reclamation of lands affected by exploration, mining or the extraction of minerals that are vital to the welfare of New Mexico." The law applies to "hard-rock mining"—that is, extraction of minerals such as gold, silver, copper, and uranium. (The Mining Act does not apply to uranium mined by the "in situ" method of injecting water and chemicals into fissures to remove the mineral; that method of uranium mining is regulated by the U.S. Nuclear Regulatory Commission.) The New Mexico Mining Act also established the New Mexico Mining Commission, which oversees rulemaking and administrative reviews. Companies or citizens can also appeal the actions of regulators to the commission.

The New Mexico Mining Act does not implement a federal act. That, along with the fact that it's one of the most stringent hard-rock mining laws in the West, makes it crucial to protect—especially as mining companies lobby the New Mexico State Legislature to weaken it or add exemptions to it on a regular basis. During the 2013 and 2014 sessions of the legislature, for instance, amendments were unsuccessfully proposed to exempt humate mining from regulation under the New Mexico Mining Act.

New Mexico Water Quality Control Act

New Mexico's political leaders and policy makers must ensure the future of the state's water—in terms of both quantity and quality. With that in mind, two changes of attitude must occur. First, people must avoid the temptation to hope that "new" water might be discovered, drilled, piped, or developed, and instead work within the confines of scientifically developed water supply projections. Second, we must question the notion of unlimited growth, in terms of population and industry.

The federal Clean Water Act, together with New Mexico's implementation of it, governs surface waters in our state, but there are limited federal protections of *groundwater* resources. New Mexicans have been developing the state's groundwater resources since the late nineteenth century—and today, those waters supply almost 50 percent of the state's needs.[9] As of 2009, New Mexico used about 1.9 million acre-feet of groundwater annually for agricultural, municipal, and other uses, and that number continues to rise each year.[10] It is estimated that 90 percent of the water New Mexicans drink comes from groundwater.

In 1931 the New Mexico State Legislature passed the state's Groundwater Code, giving the state engineer control over the allocation of groundwater resources.[11] It wasn't until 1978, however, that the legislature passed the state's Water Quality Control Act.

For more than thirty years, enforcement of that law has protected the state's groundwater from contamination from the mining industry, the oil and gas sector, the nuclear weapons facilities in New Mexico, and concentrated animal feeding operations (CAFOs), facilities that have more than two hundred dairy cows or three hundred heifers.

COMPROMISED NEW MEXICO ENVIRONMENTAL AND AIR AND WATER QUALITY POLICY

While the New Mexico Water Quality Control Act has remained in place for more than three decades, in recent years, the administration of Governor Susana Martinez, begun in 2011, has been chipping away at its effectiveness.

In 2009 the New Mexico Legislature passed a law requiring new groundwater rules for two industries: copper mining and dairy farming. Meant to clarify pollution rules by setting certain standards, the law was negotiated between lawmakers and industry.

The following year, in 2010, during the administration of Governor Bill Richardson, the New Mexico Environment Department (NMED) promulgated a rule requiring dairies to install plastic liners to keep waste pits full of manure from contaminating water. The dairy industry appealed the rule, and when Governor Susana Martinez took office, her administration tried to block the rule from being published. After the New Mexico Supreme Court issued a rebuke, saying that no one is above the law, the state and the dairy industry reached a settlement in 2011.

Next came the New Mexico Water Control Commission's copper rule of 2013, which both the New Mexico Environmental Law Center and former New Mexico attorney general Gary King have said violates the Water Quality Control Act.

For seven months stakeholders—including representatives from agencies, the mining industry, and environmental groups—worked on a draft of the rule, which would be released by NMED and approved by the Water Quality Control Commission. Just as the rule was about to go public, NMED's senior staff pulled it back.[12] At the last minute, changes were made. Rather than prescribing and enforcing how mines must keep waste from seeping into groundwater, the new rule allowed NMED to defer to mining companies themselves on this issue.

Aside from ignoring stakeholder input and offering concessions to the mining industry, the newly written rule invalidated an earlier agreement between the state and Freeport-McMoran Copper & Gold, Inc., which owns and operates three copper mines in southwestern New Mexico. In 2010 the company and the state had reached an agreement involving the company's Tyrone Mine near Silver City. That mine includes eight open pits and 2,800 acres of waste rock and leach piles—which have polluted the water beneath. Freeport had asserted that since the water beneath the mine would never be used for drinking, it could pollute that water without fear of regulatory consequences. The state disagreed and the two parties eventually reached an agreement. In 2010 a settlement was signed: under the Water Quality Control Act, Freeport could legally pollute the water beneath the Tyrone Mine, as long as it obtained a variance—a five-year exemption to pollute a limited area—from the commission. Although the commission had granted each of the company's three requests, Freeport found the process had resulted in "excessive red tape and delays."[13]

The extent of groundwater pollution beneath the mines is significant: According to a 2012 report by the New Mexico Office of Natural Resources Trustee, groundwater pollution totals more than 20,000 acres beneath Freeport's three mines in southern New Mexico.[14]

The New Mexico Environmental Law Center and the attorney general's office both opposed the state's new rule before it was adopted, citing the proposed rule's violations of the Water Quality Control Act, but it was nevertheless adopted by the New Mexico Water Quality Control Commission at the end of 2013.

Environmental advocates and the attorney general are bracing for how the rule's adoption might affect other industries in the state. With an exception in place for copper mines, they fear it's only a matter of time before other industries and facilities in the state ask for and receive exemptions, too.

Although the copper rule is an extreme example of regulation slippage in New Mexico, it's not the only one.

Upon taking office, Governor Susana Martinez prioritized the repeal of a number of environmental regulations adopted during Governor Bill Richardson's eight years as governor, including the dairy rule, among the others already mentioned. For instance, in 2008 the Richardson administration enacted the "pit rule" to regulate the storage of waste from oil and gas drilling operations.[15] The new rule required drillers to line waste pits or to use closed-loop systems. The rule came on the heels of a state study showing that between the mid-1980s and 2003, there were about seven thousand cases of soil and water contamination from pits, and about four hundred cases of groundwater contamination. The Martinez administration repealed that rule in 2013.[16]

Similarly, in 2012 the Martinez administration overturned the earlier administration's rule requiring industry to report its greenhouse gas emissions and also replaced the statewide Green Building Code with a less stringent rule, action that is currently under appeal.

All this backsliding represents a threat to the future of the state—and cements the Martinez administration's reputation. The administration didn't just neglect to include environmental issues among its priorities. According to Meiklejohn, it has taken an active role in dismantling advances and protections made over the past four decades.

WHAT'S TO BE DONE?

New Mexico's people can go to court to fight the weakening of environmental and air and water quality protections. When New Mexico executive agencies have in the past promulgated changes that violated state or federal laws, those rules usually have been overturned in the courts. Most critically, however, concerned citizens can hold state legislators accountable. Corporations and extractive industries are not shy about lobbying legislators; nor should citizens be wary of calling or visiting their elected officials. It is necessary for New Mexicans to remain vigilant and active in the state legislature to see that existing protections are not lost and that needed new protections are enacted.

The current New Mexico drought may hold the key to progress on environmental issues. As Douglas Meiklejohn has said, "If the drought continues, there will be a continued greater awareness of the need to conserve water. I'm optimistic there will be a greater awareness to prevent groundwater pollution. After all, the more of it we pollute, the less of it we'll have to drink."[17]

New Mexicans are not powerless when their communities face environmental or health threats. Douglas Meiklejohn has said, "The first thing I would say is you can do something. I think a lot of people—although I think this is less true than it used to be—feel, 'these are forces that are beyond my control and I can't do anything about them.' That's not accurate. You can do something about them. . . . People can do things. People can organize. And people can have an impact."[18]

And some *local* progress on environmental issues offers some encouragement. For example, in 2008 the Santa Fe County Commission adopted an ordinance that placed a moratorium on oil and gas drilling in the Galisteo Basin. And Mora County adopted a Community Bill of Rights in 2013 that is aimed at protecting the county's groundwater resources from drilling impacts.

CLIMATE CHANGE

All it takes is a cursory look around New Mexico to know that climate change is already here. Since the 1960s, the growing season has lengthened by a week.[19] More than fifty of the state's native plants and animals have already been affected by climate change; some bird populations have shifted, some flowers bloom earlier.[20] In the northwestern part of the state, sand dunes are spreading as vegetation dies and their roots no longer anchor soils.[21] Conifer forests, weakened by drought and susceptible to bark beetles, are suffering die-offs.[22] Snow levels are moving higher and further north; snowpack is also melting earlier.[23]

The *Albuquerque Journal* reported in February 2014 that New Mexico is experiencing its worst drought since the 1880s, worse in severity than the terrible drought of the 1950s.[24] Not only that but temperatures today are warmer than in the 1950s. That means more surface water evaporates from lakes, reservoirs, and rivers; wild plants and crops alike require more water to survive; and soil conditions are drier. That also means that rangeland is toasted in many parts of the state, and water supplies for farms are stretched thin.

David Gutzler, a professor in the Earth and Planetary Sciences Department of the University of New Mexico, has called for a shift from political debate about the causes of climate change to a discussion about how to handle those changes. He has said, "Once we turn the political debate into a technological challenge, then we turn from things we're not so good at—which is arguing at each other—into a technological challenge, and we know we're really good at solving those."[25]

Gutzler is one of the authors of the UN Intergovernmental Panel on Climate Change's fifth assessment report, *Climate Change 2013: The Physical Science Basics*. The report's summary for policy makers notes, "Warming of the climate system is unequivocal, and since the 1950s, many of the observed changes are unprecedented over decades to millennia. The atmosphere and ocean have warmed, the amounts of snow and ice have diminished, sea level has risen, and the concentrations of greenhouse gases have increased."[26] This report repeatedly makes the case for reducing greenhouse gas emissions to address the warming of the planet. It also notes that historic and current emissions will continue to affect warming for decades.

While the U.S. Environmental Protection Agency, under the Obama administration, has pushed to enact controls on greenhouse gas emissions to mitigate future warming, it's incumbent upon New Mexico's decision makers to plan for how communities, water systems, and infrastructure will adapt to deal with the impacts of warming.

In 2005 the New Mexico State Agency Technical Work Group released a report detailing the potential effects of climate change on water resources, infrastructure, agriculture, natural systems, outdoor recreation tourism, environmental quality and health, low-income communities and communities of color, and Native American communities.[27] Prepared in response to Governor Bill Richardson's Climate Change and Greenhouse Gas Reduction Executive Order of 2005, the report was sobering.

The report's authors write that infrastructure used for flood control and drainage, air conditioning, electrical power distribution, sewage, water supply, and transportation is vulnerable to the impacts of climate change. Lower water supplies will affect infrastructure, and a potential increase in flash-flood intensity will affect flood control systems, roadways, railways, and culverts.

Warmer temperatures will lengthen the growing season, but drought will limit crop and rangeland production. Warming conditions may also affect pest populations, affecting yields and requiring farmers to devise new control strategies.

The effects on natural systems are predicted to be widespread. Aquatic systems are particularly vulnerable, and the rate of extinction is expected to increase. Species diversity will decline, and geographic ranges for wildlife and plants will continue shifting to the north and to higher elevations. Nonnative plant species are expected to spread and forests to experience more catastrophic wildfires, and alpine meadows may largely disappear from the state.

Recreational opportunities may be affected by climate change as well. Warmer winter temperatures will reduce snow sport opportunities, lower water levels in lakes and rivers will reduce opportunities for water sports, and fire hazards will restrict access to public lands for everything from picnicking to hunting. In addition, the report's authors write that "the attractiveness of our scenic vistas may be diminished by more air pollution episodes."[28]

In addition, climate change is predicted to increase air pollution; wildfires and dust storms will increase particulate air pollution. Ecosystem disruptions might also lead to outbreaks of infectious diseases, including hantavirus, plague, dengue fever, and arboviruses such as West Nile.

According to the report, the potential impacts of climate change will "disproportionally affect communities of color and low-income communities." The report also notes that traditional Native American subsistence systems are likely to be "severely impacted by climate change."[29]

A rule adopted during the Richardson administration directed the state's polluters to reduce their carbon dioxide emissions by 3 percent a year from 2010 levels. Also approved then was a separate proposal paving the way for New Mexico's participation in a cap-and-trade plan under which eleven western states and Canadian provinces have since agreed to establish a regional, market-based emission-reduction program. But that New Mexico rule has since been repealed, and New Mexico has also pulled out of the cap-and-trade plan.

Even as the Martinez administration has quashed work on climate change at the state level—and it is also now clear that climate change will not even be considered during the current work in New Mexico on development of a state water plan—some of the negative impacts predicted in the technical work group's 2005 report have already occurred.

Since the 2005 report was released, for example, New Mexico has experienced the two largest wildfires in its recorded history. During the 2011 Las Conchas fire, more than 156,000 acres in the Jemez Mountains burned. The following year the Whitewater-Baldy fire burned more than 297,000 acres of the Gila National Forest. From 2011 through 2013 communities downstream from those fires experienced serious flooding; in September 2013 communities and infrastructure across eastern and southern New Mexico were affected by severe flooding during a four-day rain event. Floods following wildfires have caused many irrigation districts and municipalities—including Albuquerque and Santa Fe—to shut down systems drawing water from the Rio Grande because of ash and debris.

Most states in the United States have climate change action plans. Some, including New York and Massachusetts, have aggressive plans for dealing with climate-warming impacts. According to the U.S. Environmental Protection Agency's website, New Mexico's Climate Change Advisory Group completed its own final report on December 1, 2006.[30] The report included a greenhouse gas inventory and sixty-nine policy recommendations, and by 2008 New Mexico was moving forward with forty of the sixty-nine recommendations. Today, a computer link to that report and to information about the advisory group doesn't even exist.[31]

Despite a lack of forward momentum on the state level, New Mexico decision makers don't have to look far for help in assessing the economic risks of climate change. In 2010 Sandia National Laboratories in Albuquerque released a report demonstrating a risk-assessment methodology for evaluating uncertain future climatic conditions. That report states, "We determine the industry-level contribution to the gross domestic product and employment impacts at the state level, as well as interstate population migration, effects on personal income, and consequences for the U.S. trade balance. We show that the mean or average risk of damage to the U.S. economy from climate change, at the national level, is on the order of $1 trillion over the next 40 years, with losses in employment equivalent to nearly 7 million full-time jobs."[32] In New Mexico, the risk of damage to the economy—if no mitigation or climate policies are undertaken or adopted—is on the order of $26 billion in gross domestic product and more than 217,000 jobs.

Addressing the impacts of climate change will be costly. Continuing to ignore them will be catastrophic—to the environment, communities, and the state's economy.

When it comes to planning for the impacts of climate change, two documents are invaluable to decision makers: the aforementioned UN Intergovernmental Panel on Climate Change's fifth assessment report and the National Climate Assessment's 2013 report on climate change in the southwestern United States.[33] The latter report notes three critical observed changes in the Southwest:

- The period since 1950 has been warmer than any period of comparable length in at least six hundred years.
- The areal extent of drought over the Southwest during 2001–2010 was the second largest observed for any decade from 1901 to 2010.
- Recent flows in the four major drainage basins of the Southwest have been lower than their twentieth-century averages. (New Mexico relies on two of those river basins, the Upper Colorado and the Rio Grande, for its water supplies.)[34]

The report also lays out projected future climatic changes. These include the following:

- Warming will continue, with longer and hotter heat waves in the summer.
- Precipitation extremes in winter will become more frequent and more intense.
- Late-season snowpack will continue to decrease.
- Declines in river flow and soil moisture will continue.
- Droughts in parts of the Southwest will become hotter, more severe, and more frequent.
- Flooding will become more frequent and intense in some seasons and some parts of the Southwest and less frequent and intense in other seasons and locations. (More frequent and/or intense precipitation extremes as well as warming trends both affect flooding.)
- Average precipitation will decrease in the southern Southwest and perhaps increase in the northern Southwest.[35]

Just as the New Mexico Agency Technical Work Group's 2005 report pointed out, the impacts from climate change will be extensive. Some of the additional recent and future effects include

- changes in geographic distributions of plant and animal species;
- changes to ecosystem functions, including the timing of seasonal events in the life cycles of species;
- changes in land cover;

- compromised water quality as surface waters are affected by scarcity or higher runoff due to precipitation intensity, flooding, and wildfire; and
- decreased reliability of energy supplies as energy demands increase in some areas.

If decision makers are unwilling to tackle the root causes of climate change—increased greenhouse gas emissions—they must accept the consequences of that inaction and begin preparing the state and its citizens to adapt to the continued impacts of climate change.

New Mexico's Changing Forests

Drive through the Four Corners region in New Mexico, or even the Jemez Mountains, and you'll notice dead and dying conifer trees. Trees stressed by severe drought were vulnerable to bark beetle infestations; other stands are gone due to wildfires since the late 1990s. Between the beetles and high-severity fires, 20 percent of the forests have been affected in New Mexico and Arizona since the late 1990s.[36]

Craig Allen, a research ecologist, came to New Mexico in 1982 to conduct research on the ecology and environmental history of southwestern landscapes. What he's seen play out over the past three decades may hold the key to the survival of New Mexico's iconic piñon-juniper woodlands. He poses this question: "Why has it been so bad here, from the standpoint of forests over the last fifteen or sixteen years?"[37]

Climate change and natural precipitation oscillations are playing a role in the loss of those forests. But what's happening also has to be viewed in tandem with land use changes and fire-suppression efforts dating back to the late nineteenth century.

In 2012 Senator Jeff Bingaman of New Mexico convened a U.S. Senate field hearing on climate change in Santa Fe.[38] Testifying at that hearing, Allen explained that prehistorically, the Southwest experienced high-frequency ground-surface fires. But the entry of the railroads and of domestic livestock into the area interrupted the continuity of grassy surface fuels. Citing Stephen J. Pyne's seminal 1982 book, *Fire in America*, Allen added,

"The suppression of surface fires by overgrazing then morphed into active fire suppression and exclusion efforts by land management agencies in the early 1900s, which has continued with ever-increasing effort and expenditure to the present." As a result of suppression, forests became increasingly dense.

In 2014, two years after those hearings, Allen said that those historic land uses helped set the stage for what's happening today: "If you have one thousand trees per acre instead of one hundred, when there's not enough water to go around, everyone weakens and the whole system is vulnerable."[39]

Allen further explains how human impacts are intersecting with natural oscillations and human-caused climate change. At the turn of the twentieth century, it was dry in New Mexico. A subsequent wet period was followed in the 1950s by another severe drought. Then it was relatively wet from the late 1970s to the 1990s, until the current drought began in the late 1990s. These cycles are natural, Allen says, pointing out that those oscillations are visible in the tree-ring record going back for centuries.

Overlaying the precipitation data with land use histories, Allen points out that fire suppression first began around 1900, during the dry spell. When the region entered a wet spell, tree growth burgeoned. Normally, natural fire regimes would have suppressed many of those saplings. Instead, they grew into adult trees. During the severe drought of the 1950s, the region saw hints of the stand-replacing crown fires that are common today. But because the forests weren't yet completely overgrown, suppression still worked. In the 1970s, when the region sloshed back into a wet phase—these phases are driven by heat patterns in the Pacific Ocean—more trees were established and the forests continued thickening. By the time the region entered another dry phase, beginning in the late 1990s, the forests were dense and overgrown. Drought stressed the forests, which also began experiencing more intense fires and insect outbreaks. And now? It's also warmer.

Drought, atop the warming driven by human-caused climate change, is exacerbating the stress on New Mexico's forests and amplifying wildfire. Today's fire season is eight weeks longer than it was thirty years ago.[40] Global warming has shortened winter: snow melts earlier in the spring, and when the snow melts, the fuels dry out—something that's happening sooner today than in the past. Not only that, but many parts of the western United States are experiencing transitions from snow to rain as cold temperatures occur later in the fall.

Allen and other climate scientists anticipate that if heat oscillations in the Pacific Ocean continue to occur as they have historically, New Mexico will soon experience a period of increased precipitation. That will put a lid on the current drought. But, he says, the cycle will swing back to dry again. In other words, today's drought offers a preview of the conditions likely to occur later in the century.[41]

That means the time for action on the forests is now. If conditions do indeed become cooler and wetter for a few years, policy makers and mangers must take advantage of that opportunity and undertake forest management practices such as prescribed fire. But, Allen says, "We better take advantage of it, because it will slosh back, and be drier—and warmer." When interviewed in early 2014, he noted that the oscillations typically occur in fifteen-year cycles. (At the time of this interview, New Mexico was in the sixteenth year of a dry cycle.) "If we haven't taken some action—doing thinning, mechanical thinning, and using fire—nature will finish the resetting job she's been working on pretty effectively here in the last fifteen years," Allen adds.[42]

When Allen talks about "resetting" the forests he's referring to the change in ecosystems currently taking place on such a drastic level in the region. As crown fires, drought, and insect infestations (all of which are intertwined) have eliminated large swaths of conifer forests, those areas are being repopulated with grasses and shrubs. This sort of resetting of a forest can happen incrementally over years, through factors such as drought, or it can occur very quickly.

The Las Conchas fire in New Mexico flared up on June 26, 2011, when high winds blew an aspen into a power line in the Jemez Mountains, in an area not far from the devastating 2000 Cerro Grande fire. In the fire's first fourteen hours, it burned more than 43,000 acres and destroyed dozens of homes. According to the Southwest Fire Science Consortium, the speed of the fire's initial spread was "astonishing."[43] For the first fourteen hours, the fire burned through one acre every 1.17 seconds.

According to Allen, fires that intense reduce an ecosystem's options to respond because so many species don't survive the instantaneous pulse of intense fire. Crown fires are indiscriminate, consuming everything in their path. Meanwhile, when forests change during a period of drought, the changes happen more slowly; the most resistant species remain and seeds still remain.

Allen points out that high-severity fires favor plant life-forms that resprout, such as grasses, herbs, and shrubs—not conifers. After intense fires, ponderosa pine stands are replaced by gamble oak and New Mexico locust, and piñon-juniper forests are replaced by wavy leaf oak, mountain mahogany, and others. And of course, all of these areas are vulnerable to the spread of invasive weeds, including cheatgrass and Russian thistle, or tumbleweed.

Although 20 percent of New Mexico and Arizona forests have already been "reset," Allen believes there is still time to act. Lacking the time and resources to treat all the necessary acres, policy makers and managers must be strategic—and interrupt the continuation of crown fire–susceptible fuels at the landscape level.

This action is important not only for forests and the species and industries they support. It's also critical for the maintenance of healthy watersheds, where surface waters originate and reservoirs are located. In addition to being dangerous to communities, intense wildfires are also expensive. The 2011 Las Conchas fire, which burned 156,593 acres, also destroyed sixty-three homes and forty-nine outbuildings. Between the fire's ignition at the end of June and September, more than two thousand people worked on the fire—which cost almost $41 million in suppression costs.[44]

Reducing fuel hazards can be consistent with restoring natural systems, says Allen. Especially if managers target the right sites. That means choosing sites carefully and paying close attention to historical fire patterns. North- and south-facing slopes burn differently, for instance. South-slope fires burn upward toward the summit. Prior to 1900 a crown fire couldn't travel more than fifteen miles because of how slopes broke up the movement of fire through forests.

Today, now that south-facing slopes are overgrown, they're similar to north-facing slopes. That's part of the reason the Las Conchas fire was able to spread so far and so fast. Breaking up that landscape mass would cause future fires to drop out of the crowns of trees and back to the ground.

The stress on New Mexico's forests is only going to increase. Decision makers should take advantage of today's preview into the future and an approaching wet cycle to take forest treatment very seriously.

BETTER STEWARDSHIP

For the people who have lived in New Mexico the longest, environmental issues are matters of the greatest urgency.

Beyond Acoma Pueblo's current land base, Theresa Pasqual, former Acoma director of historic preservation, is concerned with the pueblo ancestral or aboriginal lands, which the people of Acoma have walked for centuries and which extend from northwestern New Mexico into southwestern Colorado, southeastern Utah, and the northeastern part of Arizona—the Four Corners area.

As the Acoma people moved through the landscape, generation after generation, stories were passed down, further enforcing their connections to the landscape. Over time, Acoma people visited the same springs, gathered plants from the same places, hunted the same lands, and farmed the same crops.

That's why Pasqual has been a crucial member of the movement to protect Mount Taylor—called Kaweshtimi in Acoma Pueblo's language, Keres—from uranium mining. The 11,301-foot-tall peak is sacred to the pueblo, as well as to the Pueblo Indians of Laguna and Zuni Pueblos, the Hopi Tribe, and the Navajo Nation. It's also attractive to the uranium industry, which has proposed plans to mine in the area.

In 2008 the five tribes released a report to the government discussing their ancestral and spiritual connections to the mountain. They also requested that 400,000 acres on and surrounding the mountain be designated a "traditional cultural property" under federal and state laws. That designation does not prevent development from occurring. Rather, it gives tribes a seat at the table—the chance to have their voices heard in discussions about development.[45]

In 2008 the state's Cultural Properties Review Committee approved the request. When it was made permanent the following year, industry, local businesses, and ranchers sued. The issue wound its way through the state courts. Then, in early 2014, the New Mexico Supreme Court upheld the designation, with one exception: Cebolleta Land Grant common lands would not be included within the designation.

The entire process has been historic: the cooperation of five tribes, their decision to share knowledge considered sacred, and the power they may now be able to flex in the decision-making process.

The process also serves to demonstrate that the state's diversity of culture is a strength. Despite knowing the land intimately, indigenous people are often excluded from the decision-making process. As Pasqual explains, for indigenous people, humans aren't separate from the environment. Meanwhile, federal and state laws clearly separate humans from the environment. "We began to see policies—federal and state—that all came from the perspective of ownership, not stewardship," she says. "And the challenges we have now in the state are based in that."[46]

Looking back to the last mining boom in western New Mexico, Pasqual remembers its tail end. When she was a child, Grants, New Mexico, was booming. The town is just now starting to recover, she says, from the bust in the 1980s, when uranium prices dropped and companies pulled out of the area.

As proposals to mine uranium are considered, she doesn't want the community ripped apart again. She doesn't want to see a sacred mountain's resources destroyed. Investing in communities is wiser than allowing outside companies back in to extract resources and profits from New Mexico. The economic benefits of preservation go far beyond the immediate investment—drawing tourists and new businesses—and they don't deplete resources, she says.

"If we want visitors, why would we do things that take away from the natural beauty of the state?" Pasqual asks. "If we're trying to bring people here, why do the very things they don't want to see?"[47]

TOURISM AND ECONOMIC IMPACT

In 2011 more than 32 million visitors traveled to New Mexico. According to a 2011 analysis of the economic benefits of tourism on the state, those visitors spent $5.5 billion, which generated $7.8 billion in total business sales. More than 85,000 jobs were sustained by visitors, and tourism generated $1.2 billion in taxes, with $565 million accruing to state and local governments.[48]

The state's decision makers don't have the luxury of time to defer protection of the state's resources, not just in western New Mexico, but throughout the state. "When we talk about looking at the next fifty or one hundred years, we can't look that far ahead until we look at who we are in this state," says Pasqual. "If we can't figure out our core values in the state for what we want for our grandchildren, we're going to continue butting heads."

Having a vision for the future requires taking an honest look at what our values truly are. And that needs to happen now. "There is a finite amount of time that we can have this conversation," Pasqual says, pointing out that development is occurring at such a rate that the scales are tipping to such a point that we can't "go back."

"Tribal communities in New Mexico only have a finite amount of land to sustain them, tribal communities in New Mexico don't have the ability to move entire communities and put them someplace new," Pasqual says. "We are limited to the land we have available to us, we know we are dependent on the resources that this particular land gives us, and we know where the areas of critical concern are for us."[49]

That means New Mexicans need to start listening to one another now. Or we lose the opportunity to ensure that some of the state's natural resources are still here for future generations.

Already there are laws and processes in place, including the New Mexico State-Tribal Collaboration Act of 2009, that offer ways forward. But policy makers can't just give lip service to the act; they must incorporate tribal perspectives into policies and plans—not just to benefit tribes, but because tribal perspectives on environmental issues will benefit everyone.

Taking a look at the New Mexico State Legislature is important, too. Not only are there too few Native legislators, but there are too few Native committee leaders and task force members.

Finally, there needs to be support for the New Mexico Indian Affairs Department. When the Commission on Indian Affairs was elevated to a cabinet-level department in 2003, tribes were glad to be recognized, glad that their voices were going to be heard at the highest levels. "So why aren't they?" Pasqual asks. "We're still not all equal in the political playing field, unfortunately. And until we recognize that, a lot of these environmental issues are not going to get resolved."

Pasqual acknowledges the importance of economic development. But she knows its costs can't outweigh the benefits. And it can't go forward without people asking an important question: What kind of risk takers are we?

"There is a finite amount of water—which seems to be getting smaller and smaller every year that we talk about. There is only a finite amount of land; it's not like we're just going to generate new land. There is only a finite amount of air, and unobliterated night sky," she says. "Knowing that, shouldn't that tell us what kind of risk we need to take? If our core values are to save something for our children, shouldn't that tell us what kind of risk we're willing to take?"

For Pasqual, decision making comes down to three words: honor, respect, and stewardship. She asks the state's decision makers, "Do you have the honor to do the right thing? Are you that kind of person to honor your core values to do the honorable thing even if it's not the popular thing to do? Do you have the respect of people who have ties to the land? Are you respectful enough to really hear the voices of the people around you?"[50]

New Mexico Land and Environmental and Water Quality in 2050

The rollback of environmental protections during the Martinez administration, which began in 2011, may have devastating impacts on the future of New Mexico. At a time when New Mexico's leaders should be thinking more seriously about the protection of its groundwater, surface water, air, and land resources—and implementing tighter regulations and protections—the administration has chosen to ignore climate science, avoid planning for the future, and remove even slight protections implemented over the course of three decades, and, in particular, during the Richardson administration.

Unfortunately, this is a bipartisan issue. With a few notable exceptions, members of the state legislature have refused to take climate change, drought, mining regulation, and infrastructure planning seriously. That means it is incumbent upon citizens of New Mexico to act as good neighbors to one another. People must recognize the long-term stakes they have in their communities—and in resources such as clean water and sustainable forests—and set aside their political or historical differences and work together. Citizens must hold their legislators and elected leaders accountable—particularly when policies are being adopted that may benefit outside business interests to the detriment of citizens and communities—and dedicate themselves to asking questions, educating themselves, and setting aside the time to show up at public meetings and to call or visit elected officials. It is only by being good citizens, stewards, and neighbors that we will be truly deserving of our Land of Enchantment.

New Mexico Water Rights and Management
by Adrian Oglesby

New Mexicans are no strangers to meager water supplies; we are in our fourth period of extended drought since the late 1800s.[51] As noted earlier, recent years have been the driest of any in memory, with long precipitation-free stretches interrupted by severe and dramatic rain events. The current drought has persisted through the five years from 2009 to 2013, and 2014 has been another remarkably dry year.[52] Water rights and management involve some of the most important issues facing New Mexico—and the drought makes them even more important, and difficult.

Consider the state of New Mexico's surface water supplies today. In the spring of 2014 reservoir levels across New Mexico were dismally low, making prospects for good irrigation seasons and healthy river flows highly uncertain. El Valdo Reservoir on the Rio Chama, which stores water for both the endangered silvery minnow and the farmers on the Rio Grande between Cochiti and Bosque del Apache, was only 6 percent full.[53] The storage reservoirs for the farmers in the Lower Rio Grande, Elephant Butte and Caballo, were both less than 15 percent full.[54]

Groundwater supplies are assumed to provide security when surface supplies dwindle or are unavailable. Since the last extended drought in New Mexico, during the 1940s and 1950s, groundwater levels in all corners of the state have dropped precipitously. In Albuquerque some well levels have dropped 140 feet, the Animas Basin water table has dropped 80 feet, and around Gallup there has been a 200-foot drop in the groundwater level in just the last fifteen years.[55]

This is a crucial time in New Mexico that clearly feels very significant to many New Mexicans. There is no end of conferences, forums, and work-shops addressing various aspects of water management. Someone deeply interested in New Mexico water can find a water-related meeting to attend almost every day of the year. Yet as we struggle to better understand and manage our water, the playing field is shifting. Unfortunately, as illustrated by the regulatory rollbacks described in the environmental section of this chapter, earlier, we in New Mexico seem inclined to bury our heads in the shifting sands rather than try to adapt to our changing conditions.

One of the most apparent scenes of change is in the Jemez Mountains. Warmer temperatures have made long periods in recent years the driest ever experienced by native trees in the Jemez.[56] We've discussed how his drought has aided the spread and activity of the piñon bark beetle and twig beetle, and this has contributed to massive tree mortality in the Jemez Mountains. In 2003 alone, for example, the beetles changed the landscape of the moun-tains by killing over 2.5 million acres of piñon trees.[57] In June 2011 the cata-strophic 156,593-acre Las Conchas fire, mentioned earlier, was sparked when a tree fell on a power line near Bandelier National Monument.[58]

We have accustomed ourselves to think of natural systems as changing only within the limits we have observed over time. For example, we assign time sequences to storm events based on how often rains of such magni-tude have occurred in the past (a one-hundred-year storm in Albuquerque involves between 2.2 and 2.9 inches of rain falling within six hours).[59] However, changes in our hydrologic cycles, such as increasingly severe droughts and storm events, indicate that the historic record no longer accurately describes the sideboards of future temperature and precipitation changes.

Set aside for a moment concerns about understanding our future water supplies and contemplate our relationship to water today. While many New Mexico urban dwellers feel confident that they have a seemingly unlimited supply of water ready to gush from their taps without notice, many New Mexico rural communities do not enjoy such luxury. It is not uncommon to hear news of water being trucked into New Mexico towns and villages, such as Cloudcroft in 2013.[60] Around the same time, the Village of Magdalena lost its only water supply when the groundwater table dropped below the effective level of its well pump.[61] The residents of Las Vegas have been skirting severe water shortages for years.[62]

Small communities in New Mexico often lack adequate water infrastructure. Many people have been enticed to live in our high-mountain communities by the past performance of isolated wells sunk in fractured bedrock that eventually run dry or produce little more than a trickle of their original yields. Small communities' infrastructure problems are magnified as these communities grow. Groundwater supplies in parts of Corrales, Carlsbad, Española, Santa Fe, and Albuquerque have high levels of nitrates that have infiltrated the aquifer with rogue flows from ubiquitous septic tanks.[63] Most shocking is that many of New Mexico's most established inhabitants have no reliable local water supply. Over seventy thousand members of the Navajo Nation currently live with no running water at all.[64]

The people of New Mexico's twenty-two Native American tribes and pueblos, as well as those in the rest of New Mexico, know that we have the most beautiful rivers in the American West. Significant events and changes occur along our rivers every year, as 2013 illustrated so well.

Rio Grande

On the eastern side of the Continental Divide, the Rio Grande flows into New Mexico from Colorado's placid San Luis Valley. It then cuts deep through the lava fields of the Taos Plateau, across the massive alluvial basins of the Rio Grande Rift under Española and Albuquerque, and down to Elephant Butte Reservoir. There the water is apportioned to southern New Mexico, Texas, and Mexico.

In March 2013 President Barack Obama proclaimed almost a quarter-million acres surrounding the Rio Grande Gorge near Taos, New Mexico, to be the Rio Grande del Norte National Monument.[65] Meanwhile, in the Middle Rio Grande, water managers struggled to stretch limited surface water to meet the needs of farmers and endangered fish. News from the Lower Rio Grande in 2013 was more dramatic, as Texas filed suit against New Mexico in the U.S. Supreme Court for allegedly violating the 1938 Rio Grande Compact.

Rio Pecos

In the watershed just east of the Rio Grande, the wild and scenic headwaters of the Rio Pecos are nestled high in the Pecos Wilderness.[66] The Pecos flows from the eastern slopes of the Sangre de Cristo Mountains, through two reservoirs just below Interstate 40, and then south through farms and dairies that sit above the prolific Roswell artesian groundwater basin. After the area endured the driest three years in at least a hundred years, severe storms in September 2013 provided a miraculous reprieve, filling reservoirs on the Pecos enough to provide southern farmers their full 2014 allocation.[67]

San Juan River

Water on the western side of the Continental Divide in New Mexico flows to the Colorado River. Cutting through the red rock along the Navajo Nation reservation in the northwestern corner of New Mexico, the San Juan River is one of the largest tributaries to the mighty Colorado. Years of difficult negotiations over the division of the San Juan water between New Mexico and the Navajo Nation resulted in a 2013 settlement that provides the legal authority and funding for water to flow not only to Navajos but also to the Jicarilla Apaches and the town of Gallup.[68]

The Lower Colorado River originates in the Zuni Mountains, where there is a beautiful fish known as the Zuni bluehead sucker. In 2013 the U.S. Fish and Wildlife Service proposed to list the Zuni bluehead as an endangered species.[69] The fish occupies less than three stream miles in New Mexico, though it used to range throughout the Zuni and Lower Colorado Rivers.[70] Only a few hundred of the charismatic fish still exist, under threat from increased sediment, invasive nonnative fish, and dewatering of their streams.[71]

Canadian River

The Canadian River originates on the eastern slopes of the Sangre de Cristo Mountains in Colorado. It flows into New Mexico, where it has carved a deep and gorgeous canyon. As the largest tributary to the Arkansas River, it flows east out of New Mexico across the Texas panhandle and into Oklahoma. In 2013 the Bureau of Reclamation and the Interstate Stream Commission broke ground on a new intake system that will draw water into a proposed 151-mile pipeline that is intended to serve Canon Air Force Base and the parched towns in eastern New Mexico.

A major rationale for building this new pipeline is the dramatic mining of the Ogallala Aquifer that underlies eastern New Mexico. In some areas, the aquifer has dropped over sixty feet. It has been predicted that it may run out of water in twenty years.[72] This fear has been aggravated by the aggressive acquisition of groundwater rights in western Texas by billionaire oilman T. Boone Pickens. Pickens own the rights to pump 200,000 acre-feet per year from the Ogallala and aspires to pipe and sell that water to Dallas, 250 miles away.[73]

Gila River

The three forks of the Gila River gather in the Gila Wilderness in southwestern New Mexico. The river flows to Arizona, supporting some of New Mexico's most amazing biodiversity, small independent farming communities, and immense copper mines along the way. A lot happened along the Gila in 2013, including massive flooding that destroyed two homes and stranded campers and schoolchildren.[74] The Arizona Water Settlements Act of 2004 provides New Mexico with an opportunity to divert up to an additional 14,000 acre-feet per year from the Gila River system but also states that New Mexico will lose the opportunity to take that water if it has not declared its intent to do so by the end of 2014.

The opportunities presented by the Arizona Water Settlement Act place New Mexico at the crossroads of modern water management. The pressure to develop every drop of water possible and to prevent any water from leaving the state is a powerful motivator for politicians and traditionally minded water managers. However, the era of building big water development projects seems to be coming to an end, and it has been proposed that we should now be entering an era of rebuilding our rivers.[75]

New water for New Mexico from the Gila system will not come cheap or easy. The Gila is a powerful and dynamic river that will present significant challenges in the construction and operation of a new diversion. New Mexico will have to pay for Central Arizona Project water to be delivered to downstream users on the Gila to replace any new water taken here. Building a new diversion will likely be incredibly expensive and result in a loss of local control, increased federal regulation, reliance on the Central Arizona Project, and potentially significant environmental damage.[76]

Under the settlement act, New Mexico will receive millions of dollars that can be used to build a new diversion or to improve water supplies in other ways. During a three-year planning process that was open to all, members of local communities put forth proposals to use this money to improve existing infrastructure, fund water conservation improvements, and restore the Gila River watershed.[77] These alternatives to building a new river diversion represent a new way of thinking about our future water management.

Perhaps the future water needs of southwestern New Mexico can be met without incurring the financial and environmental costs associated with a new diversion.[78] State Senator Peter Wirth of Santa Fe has stated, "On the Gila, the list of alternatives to diversions is a forward-looking roadmap for water development and conservation in New Mexico."[79] The esteemed professor and water authority Charles Wilkinson has described this shift away from aggressive engineered control of water resources elegantly by saying, "Over the course of the past quarter century, we have moved from a dam-and-reservoir, build-at-any-cost mentality to a multifaceted approach that respects all that we need from, and love about, rivers."[80]

The path that New Mexico chooses, the big development model of the past or the softer alternatives of infrastructure improvement and watershed restoration, will set the stage for our next era of water management.

Water Law

Much of our modern water management practice is based on the needs and ideas of nineteenth-century New Mexico. New Mexico water law is founded on a few basic principles from that era. A person or entity may appropriate available water if it is put to beneficial use and not wasted. What constitutes a beneficial use is not defined in New Mexico law. Our courts, attorneys general, and state engineers have interpreted beneficial use to include domestic, agricultural, industrial, municipal, game and fish, and endangered species uses.

New Mexico water law embraces the priority doctrine. This means that in times of shortage, the first user to put a system's water to beneficial use should be the last one shut off, while the newest users will be the first to be restricted from taking water. This creates social tension, as many agricultural communities put water to use before neighboring municipalities even existed. It is not uncommon for domestic and industrial users of water to have water rights that are junior in priority to those of agricultural users. The notion of cutting off a city in order to supply water to farms is politically untenable in the minds of many elected officials.

New Mexico water law also calls for users to continually use their water or risk being accused of having abandoned or forfeited their water right. This is commonly referred to as "use it or lose it." The fear of losing a water right if it is not constantly used does nothing to promote the conservation of water. It is not uncommon to hear of water being diverted simply to preserve a water right, rather than to realize a true beneficial use.

Underlying New Mexico water law is an assumption that we should know how much water has been appropriated by each user. Our courts repeatedly use the phrase "a given quantity of water for a specified purpose."[81] However, in many parts of New Mexico, individual water use is not measured. Moreover, a majority of water rights in the state remain unadjudicated, meaning our courts have not yet confirmed the validity of the asserted rights. Enforcement of priorities and quantities of use is controversial without this important information.

The technical inability and political unwillingness to enforce the prior-appropriation doctrine in New Mexico requires the use of alternative management concepts. Our state engineers and courts have long supported alternative management agreements to allow water users to develop shortage-sharing arrangements among themselves. While these alternative management agreements do not always solve all water distribution controversies, they do give water users a stake in the mutual success of their communities and neighbors.

What Must Be Done?

We have to learn to live within our means. There will always be a desire to have more water in New Mexico. Water managers perpetually strive to find "new" sources of water. Dreams of desalinization plants, cloud seeding, and pipelines from distant lands are recurrent in New Mexico. Are these concepts practical and sustainable, or does the importation of water or the development of finite water sources create a reliance on supplies that will not be available in the future?

These questions are critical, especially given that our economic system calls for constant growth to succeed. "Water is money" is a popular refrain in New Mexico. The economic growth paradigm leads many of us to believe that development requires more water. This is not simply true. In 1995 New Mexico had a population around 1.7 million people and used almost 4.5 million acre-feet of water. Fifteen years later, with a population of over 2 million people, we now use only 3.8 million acre-feet per year.[82] Overall in the United States, water use has remained fairly constant since the late 1980s, but between the late 1980s and 2000, U.S. gross national product almost doubled.[83] For New Mexico to succeed long into the future we must learn to prosper with our available and replenishable water supplies.

NATURAL MANAGEMENT

Another way to view this issue is in terms of learning to work with our natural resources as opposed to working our water resources. Historically we have manipulated and controlled our natural environment to meet our needs. Perhaps it is possible for us to advance our understanding of natural water systems so that we can benefit from the natural functions that provide and enhance our rivers and aquifers. An interesting example of this is the shift in recent years away from purely human-centric river operations to river operations that try to harmonize the needs of people with the needs of the natural world. One such technique is referred to as "mimicking the natural hydrograph."[84]

The plants and animals that live along our rivers evolved over long periods of time in accord with the unaltered flow patterns of our rivers. Human control of rivers through damming and diverting water has changed the flow patterns so that native flora and fauna do not have the traditional resources available to them at the time they are accustomed to have them. In the Middle Rio Grande, prior to man's harnessing of the river, there was normally an extended high-water flow in the spring when the mountain snowpack melted away. Native cottonwood trees dispersed their seeds to take hold in the moist soils created by the high spring flows. As the spring flows decreased and the shallow groundwater level began to drop, the cottonwood taproots strengthened and stabilized as they followed the water down. Likewise, the endangered silvery minnow evolved to spawn during the spring high flows when their eggs could develop in the safety of the back channels and pools created by the high water.

Spring pulse flows in the Middle Rio Grande were effectively stopped by the development of dams along the Rio Grande and its tributaries. The cottonwood trees have not had a meaningful recruitment in half a century, and the silvery minnow is practically impossible to find in the river today. In response to these ecological warning signs, water managers are now struggling to re-create small pulse flows in the spring to stimulate the natural functions of the silvery minnow and cottonwoods. We are, in effect, slowly learning how to utilize our rivers according to how they function naturally rather than through the manipulated functions we impose upon them. It is apparent that further development of our understanding of the real nature of our resources will lead to more resilient river and aquifer systems.

Just as we develop our understanding of our natural systems, we must also evolve our understanding of our own natural inclinations. The old saying that "whiskey is for drinking and water is for fighting" is so worn in New Mexico that it now elicits more groans than giggles. There is a movement afoot in New Mexico to promote the notion that "water is for cooperating."[85] This is to say that the results of our attempts to resolve water and environmental issues will be based largely on the overall demeanor and attitude we adopt walking into our negotiations. We will continue to fight over water if we approach our disputes from entrenched and inflexible positions. If we adopt a spirit of neighborly concern and compassion, we can cooperate and thrive together.

We must constantly strive to create a culture of amicable dispute resolution. Current water management arrangements that work best are those that are based not just on relationships but on actual friendships among water managers and users.[86] This makes perfect sense when we view water as a multiuse resource. We do not own and capture water outright; it is rarely something we take and keep hidden away from the rest of the world. Most often, we really just get a turn to use water on its journey downstream to the next user. The water we take from the Rio Grande in New Mexico has traveled through many water systems upstream before it gets to us, just as the water we flush down our toilets and percolate through our fields ends up rejoining the river on its way to serve Texas and Mexico, below.

We should continue to honor our history of sharing water during shortages in New Mexico. *Reparto de aguas*, sharing of the water, is the centuries-old practice of equitably dividing water among users during times of drought. The acequias of New Mexico commonly practice reparto de aguas today. The imposition of the priority system of water-rights management, described earlier, has been embraced in law and concept but is seldom enforced.

The determination through adversarial court proceedings of who owns what water, and how much, has proven to be too costly, in terms of both money and time. A court case filed in 1966 seeking a legal determination of who owns water in the area north of Santa Fe is still dragging on today. Much more rapid and collegial determinations of ownership can be achieved through negotiated settlements rather than lawsuits.

Negotiated settlements are becoming the norm for the determination of water rights held by Native American tribes and communities. Besides being faster and cheaper than litigation, settlements offer the added benefit of being able to address a broad range of issues that are not dealt with in litigation.[87] For example, the settlement of the Navajo Nation's water rights in New Mexico includes plans and funding for the development of physical infrastructure to utilize the settled water rights.

SUSTAINABLE MANAGEMENT

As we advance our ability to resolve water-rights ownership disputes more quickly and affordably, we must also advance our ability to manage our water sustainably. Perhaps we can learn to lose less water. We can strive to store our water in places where more can be retained for future use. In New Mexico we spread out much of our water in hot lowland reservoirs where it dries up. We can work to lose less water to evaporation by pursuing strategies that store water either in higher-elevation reservoirs that experience less evaporation or underground in the spaces we have created by mining our aquifers.

We must also decide what we want New Mexico's water systems, both natural and man-made, to look like in the future. Will we follow the path taken in Australia of building an octopus of pipelines across multiple river basins to move the water to the population and economic centers? Should all water be shunted to Albuquerque?

Or should we try to lead people and economic development opportunities to where the water naturally occurs? By encouraging the use of water within its basin of origin, we will also be supporting the economic and social capacity of rural communities that otherwise will dry up and disappear when their water is piped away to the cities.

If we let the marketplace determine where our water goes, what will become of those uses of water not traditionally associated with high-dollar returns? Farming has long served as the backbone of New Mexico's multiple cultures. Should we allow farming to be dried up by water transfers to industrial and municipal users who can afford to pay more? With most resources these questions might ring of socialism. However, the New Mexico Constitution declares that the water not already appropriated at the time of statehood belongs to the public. How the public asserts its ownership, whether through an open market or more tightly regulated management, will have a huge impact on the future appearance of our state.

New Mexico Water Rights and Water Management in 2050

Implementation of changes in water management and law is always difficult. There always seems to be a particular interest that is adversely affected by the types of changes we discussed earlier. Such vested interests are often the most powerful. Making meaningful changes to our entrenched patterns of thinking about and using water will take great courage.

Inspiring examples support the assertion made here that improved collaboration among people and implementation of management concepts that work with nature can be accomplished with meaningful success. These practices should, and we hope will, be followed in New Mexico in the future.

The well-organized attempt to recover endangered fish in the San Juan River features a large cast of Native American and non-Native entities working together to manage the river in closer accord with its historic flow patterns. The U.S. Forest Service's Collaborative Forest Restoration Program provides funding for collaborative efforts focused on developing ecologically, economically, and socially sustainable forest and watershed management practices. The shortage-sharing agreement between the acequias on the Jemez River and the water users within Jemez Pueblo has built a sense of predictability that benefits even those who have agreed to take less water in times of shortage.

Unfortunately, there are plenty of examples of how not to proceed into the future. A lack of good communication and of common understanding of water management practices led to Texas suing New Mexico in the U.S. Supreme Court in 2013. Similarly, distrust and inflexible positions held by water managers in the Middle Rio Grande have perpetuated the threatened demise of endangered species, further aggravating water supply and management problems faced by farmers and municipalities.

This list could go on for pages, but it is more useful to focus on positive examples to help us develop a vision of New Mexico in 2050 that will inspire us to action.

The potential of who we can be and what can result by 2050, if we implement meaningful changes soon, should inspire us. For reasons like the need for sustainable long-term economic development, a majority of New Mexicans must see that failure to change our ways will likely result in catastrophe, especially as changing temperature and precipitation patterns produce a shifting playing field. Only when we recognize the consequences of failure to change will we stop wastefully mining our aquifers and exploiting our river and stream systems without maintaining them.

We can, and should, have healthy, living river systems that support strong local economies. We can envision our valleys sustainably supporting vibrant New Mexico agricultural and industrial production, sufficient to feed and support ourselves. It is exhilarating to know that by joining together and caring for our water systems, we can have a New Mexico in 2050 that will be even more resilient and beautiful than it is now.

Notes

1. Theresa Pasqual, interview by Laura Paskus, Grants, NM, March 11, 2014.

2. New Mexico Tax Research Institute, *Fiscal Impacts of Oil and Natural Gas Production in New Mexico: Preliminary Report* (Albuquerque, 2014).

3. New Mexico Energy, Minerals, and Natural Resources Department, *2013 Annual Report* (Santa Fe, 2014).

4. Daniel Bergner, "Jeffrey Wright's Gold Mine," *New York Times Magazine*, January 16, 2014, http://www.nytimes.com/2014/01/19/magazine/jeffrey-wrights-gold-mine.html?_r=0.

5. Douglas Meiklejohn, interview by Laura Paskus, Santa Fe, NM, March 3, 2014.

6. Laura Paskus, "Eco-Assault: Fresh Attacks on Environmental Regulations Threaten New Mexico's Future," *Santa Fe Reporter*, March 30, 2011, http://www.sfreporter.com/santafe/article-5992-eco-assault_.html.

7. Ibid.

8. "Resource and Recovery Act (RCRA)," U.S. Environmental Protection Agency, last modified October 30, 2013, http://www.epa.gov/agriculture/lrca.html.

9. Darcy Bushnell, *Groundwater in New Mexico* (Albuquerque: Utton Center, University of New Mexico School of Law, 2012).

10. Ibid.

11. Ibid.

12. Laura Paskus, "The Canary in the Copper Mine (Is Dead): How New Mexico's Copper Industry Wrote Its Own Rules," *Santa Fe Reporter*, May 14, 2013, http://www.sfreporter.com/santafe/article-7423-the-canary-in-the-copper-mine-%28is-dead%29.html.

13. Ibid.

14. New Mexico Office of Natural Resources Trustee, *Final Groundwater Restoration Plan for the Chino, Cobre, and Tyrone Mine Facilities* (Santa Fe, 2012).

15. "Pit Rule," New Mexico Administrative Code § 19.15.17.

16. "Regulators Repeal, Replace Pit Rule," *Santa Fe New Mexican*, June 6, 2013, http://www.santafenewmexican.com/news/local_news/article_1a277249-326e-5b85-82ef-53b4004d5a78.html.

17. Meiklejohn interview.

18. Laura Paskus, "Reasons for Hope on Earth Day in New Mexico, 2008," *Democracy for New Mexico* (blog), April 22, 2008, http://www.democracyfornewmexico.com/democracy_for_new_mexico/2008/04/guest-blog-laur.html#sthash.VepYCs1a.dpuf.

19. Dr. David Gutzler, interview by Laura Paskus, 2009.

20. Carolyn Enquist and Dave Gori, *A Climate Change Vulnerability Assessment for Biodiversity in New Mexico*, part 1, *Implications of Recent Climate Change on Conservation Priorities in New Mexico* (Washington, D.C., 2008).

21. Margaret Hiza Redsteer, Rian C. Bogle, and John M. Vogel, *Monitoring and Analysis of Sand Dune Movement and Growth on the Navajo Nation, Southwestern United States*, U.S. Geological Survey fact sheet 2011-3085 (Flagstaff, 2011), http://pubs.usgs.gov/fs/2011/3085/.

22. A. Park Williams et al., "Temperatures as a Potent Driver of Regional Forest Drought Stress and Tree Mortality," *Nature Climate Change* 3 (2013): 292–97.

23. I. T. Stewart, D. R. Cayan, and M. D. Dettinger, "Changes toward Earlier Streamflow Timing across Western North America," *Journal of Climate* 18 (2005): 1136–55.

24. John Fleck, "New Mexico in Its Worst Drought since 1880s," *Albuquerque Journal*, February 18, 2014, http://www.abqjournal.com/354854/news/new-mexicos-drought-worst-since-1880s.html.

25. Laura Paskus, "In New Mexico Climate Change Is More of the Same," KUNM, September 30, 2013, http://kunm.org/post/new-mexico-climate-change-more-same.

26. Intergovernmental Panel on Climate Change, *Climate Change 2013: The Physical Science Basics* (Cambridge, 2013), http://www.ipcc.ch/report/ar5/wg1/#. Ukn4ahCN9ZY.

27. Agency Technical Work Group, State of New Mexico, *Potential Effects of Climate Change on New Mexico* (Santa Fe, 2005), http://www.nmenv.state.nm.us/aqb/cc/Potential_Effects_Climate_Change_NM.pdf.

28. Ibid.

29. Ibid.

30. "Climate Change Action Plans," U.S. Environmental Protection Agency, last modified March 12, 2014, http://epa.gov/statelocalclimate/state/state-examples/action-plans.html#nm.

31. Ibid.

32. George Backus et al., *Executive Summary for Addressing the Near-Term Risk of Climate Uncertainty: Interdependencies among the U.S. States* (Albuquerque: Sandia National Laboratories, 2010).

33. Gregg Garfin et al., eds., *Assessment of Climate Change in the Southwest United States: A Report Prepared for the National Climate Assessment* (Washington, D.C.: 2013).

34. Ibid.

35. Ibid.

36. Williams et al., "Temperatures as a Potent Driver."

37. Craig Allen, telephone interview by Laura Paskus, March 14, 2014.

38. U.S. Senate, Committee on Energy and Natural Resources, *Impacts of Climate Change on the Intermountain West: Hearing*, 112th Cong., 2nd sess., August 17, 2012, http://www.energy.senate.gov/public/index.cfm/printed-hearings.

39. Allen interview.

40. Ibid.

41. Ibid.

42. Ibid.

43. "Las Conchas Fire, Jemez Mountains," fact sheet, Southwest Fire Science Consortium, n.d., http://swfireconsortium.org/las-conchas-field-trip-february-27-2012/.

44. Ibid.

45. Theresa Pasqual, interviews by Laura Paskus, 2009, 2013, 2014.

46. Pasqual interview.

47. Ibid.

48. Tourism Economics, *The Economic Impact of Tourism in New Mexico: 2011 Analysis*, http://nmtourism.org/resources/research.

49. Pasqual interview.

50. Pasqual interview.

51. D. S. Gutzler, "Drought in New Mexico: History, Causes and Future Prospects," in *Water Resources of the Lower Pecos Region, New Mexico: Science, Policy and a Look to the Future*, ed. P. S. Johnson, L. A. Land, L. G. Price, and F. Titus, Decision-Makers Field Guide 3 (Socorro: New Mexico Bureau of Geology and Mineral Resources, 2003).

52. Fleck, "New Mexico in Its Worst Drought."

53. USDA, Natural Resources Conservation Service, New Mexico Reservoir Storage Graph, end of February 2014, http://www.wcc.nrcs.usda.gov/cgibin/resv-graph.pl?state=NM.

54. Ibid.

55. D. Bushnell, "Groundwater," in *Water Matters!* (Albuquerque: Utton Transboundary Resources Center, 2014).

56. Ramzi Touchan et al., "Millennial Precipitation Reconstruction for the Jemez Mountains, New Mexico, Reveals Changing Drought Signal," *International Journal of Climatology* 31.6 (2011): 896–906.

57. C. D. Allen, "Interactions across Spatial Scales among Forest Dieback, Fire, and Erosion," *Ecosystems* 10 (2007): 797–808.

58. "The Las Conchas Fire," U.S. Department of the Interior, National Park Service, accessed June 5, 2012, http://www.nps.gov/band/naturescience/lasconchas.htm. See also "Fire Information," New Mexico Governor's Drought Task Force, http://www.nmdrought.state.nm.us/fire_info.html.

59. Frequently Asked Questions, Albuquerque Metropolitan Arroyo Flood Control Authority, http://www.amafca.org/FAQs/faqs.html.

60. "Turbid Times for Village Water Supply," *Ruidoso (NM) Free Press*, August 27, 2013.

61. A. Oglesby, "Drought," in *Water Matters!*

62. "Las Vegas in Water Crisis," *Albuquerque Journal*, June 11, 2011.

63. D. McQuillan, "Groundwater Contamination by Septic Tank Effluents," in *Water Quality for the Twenty-First Century* (Las Cruces: New Mexico Water Resources Research Institute, 2006), 97.

64. Hon. Tom Udall on the introduction of the Northwestern New Mexico Rural Water Projects Act, *Congressional Record* 153, pt. 7 (April 19, 2007): 9528.

65. U.S. President, proclamation, ""Establishment of the Río Grande del Norte National Monument" (March 25, 2013).

66. 65 Fed. Reg. 15891 (March 24, 2000).

67. John Fleck, "Full Reservoirs Buoy Optimism of Farmers along Pecos," *Albuquerque Journal*, November 5, 2013.

68. Supplemental Partial Final Judgment and Decree of the Water Rights of the Navajo Nation, San Juan General Stream Adjudication, November 1, 2013.

69. 78 Fed. Reg. 5351 (January 25, 2013).

70. "Zuni Bluehead Sucker *Catostomus discobolus yarrowi* ESA Status: Proposed for Listing," Wild Earth Guardians, http://www.wildearthguardians.org/site/PageServer?pagename=species_fish_Zuni_bluehead_sucker&AddInterest=1103#.Uy-Bcyhe4TM.

71. 78 Fed. Reg. 5385 (January 25, 2013).

72. John Fleck, "Why 'When the Ogallala Runs Out' Isn't the Right Way to Think about This," *Inkstain* (blog), April 9, 2013, http://www.inkstain.net/fleck/2013/04/why-when-the-ogallala-runs-out-isnt-the-right-way-to-think-about-this.

73. Charles Laurence, "US Farmers Fear the Return of the Dust Bowl," *London Telegraph*, May 4, 2014.

74. Christine Steele, ""Gila River Flooding Washing Away Houses, Leaving Debris Fields in Its Wake," *Las Cruces Sun News*, September 15, 2013.

75. Barry Nelson, "Building Rivers: A New Era of California Water Solutions," *Switchboard* (blog), March 22, 2011, http://switchboard.nrdc.org/blogs/bnelson/building_rivers_-_a_new_era_of.html.

76. Adrian Oglesby, "Implementation of the Arizona Water Settlement Act in New Mexico: An Overview of Legal Considerations," *Natural Resources Journal* 52 (2012): 215.

77. Ibid.

78. Gila Conservation Coalition, presentation to Water and Natural Resources Interim Legislative Committee, New Mexico State Legislature.

79. Senator Peter Wirth, speech at Fifty-Eighth Annual New Mexico Water Conference, November 22, 2013.

80. Charles Wilkinson, "Priorities Have Changed in Water Management," *Albuquerque Journal*, May 4, 2014.

81. E.g., Snow v. Abalos, 18 N.M. 681 (1914); New Mexico v. General Elec. Co., 32 F. Supp. 2d 1237 (2004); Worley v. U.S. Borax & Chemical Co., 78 N.M. 112 (1967).

82. Heather Balas, *Townhall on Water Planning, Development, and Use Backgrounder Report* (Albuquerque: New Mexico First, 2014), 2.

83. Peter H. Gleick and Meena Palaniappan, "Peak Water Limits to Freshwater Withdrawal and Use," *PNAS* 107.25 (June 22, 2010): 11155–62.

84. N. L. Poff et al., "The Natural Flow Regime," *BioScience* 47.11 (December 1997): 769–84.

85. John Fleck, "Cooperation Key as Drought Worsens," *Albuquerque Journal*, April 9, 2013.

86. Pat Mulroy, presentation to the Martz Conference, Getches-Wilkinson Center for Natural Resources, Energy, and the Environment, University of Colorado, 2013.

87. Elizabeth Checcio and Bonnie Colby, *Indian Water Rights: Negotiating the Future* (Tucson: Water Resources Research Center, University of Arizona, 1993).

Chapter 6

New Mexico Indian Tribes and Communities

VERONICA E. TILLER

NINE HUNDRED YEARS AGO, THE ANCESTORS OF TODAY'S PUEBLO
tribes of New Mexico moved out of their homelands in the Chaco Canyon
area of northwestern New Mexico due to severe drought conditions. Indian
historian Roxanne Dunbar-Ortiz describes the civilization they left behind:

> The famed Anasazi people of Chaco Canyon on the Colorado Plateau—
> in the present Four Corners region of Arizona, New Mexico, Colorado
> and Utah—thrived from 850 to 1250 A.D. Ancestors of the Pueblos of
> New Mexico, the Anasazi constructed more than 400 miles of roads
> radiating out from Chaco. An average of 30 feet in width, these roads
> followed straight courses, even through difficult terrain such as hills and
> rock formations. The highways connected some 75 communities.
> Around the 13th century, the [ancestral Pueblo] people abandoned the
> Chaco area and migrated, building nearly a hundred smaller agricultural
> city-states along the Rio Grande valley and its tributaries. . . . Pueblo
> trade extended as far west as the Pacific Ocean, as far east as the Great
> Plains, and as far south as Central America.[1]

Early in 2014 the prospect of climate change once again presented New Mexico's Indian tribes, along with the state itself, with starkly alternative futures. Only this time, the tribes were a very distinct minority of the state's population, and there were no longer any well-watered and uninhabited expanses where they might relocate. January 2014 was the driest January recorded for New Mexico since 1895—4 percent of normal. And 2014 is but the latest in a string of years that have left the entire state in conditions ranging from abnormally dry to extreme drought.

History and Government

The Navajos, two Apache tribes, and nineteen pueblos all made present-day New Mexico their homeland for hundreds of years before the first Europeans entered the area. These tribes existed as distinct peoples with vibrant cultures, thriving economies, and enduring means of governance. While Spanish, French, and Mexican authorities claimed varying degrees of suzerainty over New Mexico from the fifteenth to the mid-nineteenth centuries, until the United States claimed sovereignty in 1848, these tribes held actual possession of their lands and maintained political control over their territories and their peoples. The exercise of their sovereignty included engaging in defensive and offensive wars and establishing trade with each other and with non-Indians under the European powers who claimed jurisdiction over their lands by right of discovery or by conquest. The continued social, cultural, and political autonomy of these tribes is perhaps the single most constant thread that runs through New Mexico's history for the last five hundred years.[2]

Today, these tribes all play an active role in the governance of New Mexico, not only through self-governance but through their involvement in the affairs of the state and the federal government. Members of New Mexico tribes have served on public school boards, in the state legislature, as members of state regulatory bodies, and as members of federal advisory committees charged with developing regulations to implement national federal policies in housing, energy, education, the environment, and law enforcement, among other programs.

The Pueblo Tribes of New Mexico

Spanish explorers traversed present-day New Mexico as early as the 1530s, hoping to discover the kinds of riches they had found and plundered among the Aztec and Inca Empires far to the south. These ventures failed to turn up the fabled Seven Cities of Cibola but did permit the Spaniards to claim the vast expanse of the American Southwest for the Spanish crown. Francisco Vásquez de Coronado occupied the Rio Grande Valley in an extensive campaign that lasted some two years in the mid-sixteenth century and resulted in the destruction of some Pueblo villages and the complete annihilation of their people. By 1600 the Spanish were well and firmly entrenched in New Mexico, with permanent villages of their own, and were increasingly encroaching on lands occupied and farmed by the Pueblo Indians.

Although Spain recognized the Indians' right to the lands they actually occupied and tilled, their practice of exacting forced labor and tribute from the Pueblo Indians resulted in resentments that culminated in the Pueblo Revolt of 1680. Pueblo leaders met at Taos Pueblo in early 1680 and laid plans for a coordinated uprising against the Spanish, whose cruelties over the course of nearly a century were no longer tolerable. As if on signal, the Pueblo Indians rose up in the fall of 1680 and not only challenged their putative overlords but drove the Spaniards all the way back into Mexico.

In 1692 the Spaniards returned to the Middle Rio Grande Valley in sufficient strength to reassert their authority as conquerors and to impose their will by force. They maintained this role until Mexico gained its independence from Spain in 1821. During this period, Spanish authorities issued grants to land in New Mexico that have survived in some form to the present day. Many pueblos were issued grants to an area of one league in each direction from the center of the pueblo. These "Spanish land grants" were recognized by the Mexican government and later by the United States under the Treaty of Guadalupe Hidalgo of 1848.[3]

When the Mexican-American War of 1846 was concluded by the Treaty of Guadalupe Hidalgo, the United States asserted full sovereignty and federal jurisdiction over the lands ceded by Mexico, including the Indian lands, but agreed to respect the rights that had been acknowledged by

Mexico and Spain before that. This treaty by no means ended conflicting claims to Pueblo Indian lands, and when New Mexico was admitted to the union in 1912, the new state was required to disclaim any right to Indian lands within its borders. This disclaimer was soon challenged with respect to Indian lands by the novel proposition that the Pueblo people were not really Indians entitled to federal protection since they lived in settled villages. The Supreme Court of the United States rejected that argument and vindicated federal supervision and protection of Pueblo lands in the case of *United States v. Sandoval* (231 U.S. 28 [1913]).[4]

Disputes over the extent and exact boundaries of these Pueblo lands continued well into the late twentieth century, however. Today the nineteen remaining New Mexico Pueblo tribes continue to occupy the lands and villages where the Spaniards encountered them almost five hundred years ago and are governed largely by their ancient traditions, although a few of them have adopted constitutional forms of government, as authorized by U.S. federal law in 1934. The executive duties are discharged by a governor and lieutenant governor, assisted and guided by tribal councils that are either elected or appointed by traditional leaders.

Navajo Nation

While the Spanish, Mexican, and American authorities claimed to recognize the rights of Pueblo tribes to the lands they occupied and farmed, the same could not be said for the rights of the Navajo and Apache tribes within what is now New Mexico. Long before any European set foot in the Americas, the Navajo people, the Diné, defined their homeland as that territory bounded by four sacred mountains. Mount Blanca (Dawn or White Shell Mountain) near Alamosa, Colorado, defines the eastern boundary. Mount Taylor (Blue Bead Mountain), north of Laguna, New Mexico, delineates the southern boundary. The San Francisco Peaks (Abalone Shell Mountain) near Flagstaff, Arizona, mark the westernmost edge of Dinetha. Mount Hesperus (Big Mountain Sheep) in the La Plata range of the Colorado Rocky Mountains anchors the northern boundary.[5]

The Diné have been in the southwestern United States since they migrated south from western Canada around 1300 AD. The Navajos resisted Spanish and Mexican domination prior to 1848 and waged defensive wars against U.S. attempts at subjugation following the Mexican-American War. In 1864, following a literal scorched earth campaign, the U.S. military succeeded in bringing the Navajos under submission and forcibly deported them from their homeland to Bosque Redondo, near Fort Sumner, New Mexico, in the Pecos River Valley. More than two hundred Navajos perished on the "Long Walk" there, and the Bosque Redondo area was neither suitable nor adequate to sustain their numbers.

In a treaty in 1868 the United States agreed to permit the Navajos to return to a reservation of some 3.5 million acres within the area surrounded by their four sacred mountains, to have a government, and to send their children to schools that would be established for them. Over the last 150 years, the Navajo Reservation has been extended to accommodate their growing numbers so that it includes some 16 million acres in the states of Arizona, Utah, and New Mexico. The New Mexico portion includes the three "satellite" Navajo reservations of Alamo, Ramah, and Cañoncito (now known as To'hajiilee). Some 671,043 acres of the Navajo Reservation in New Mexico were subsequently allotted to individual members of the tribe and are still held in trust for them or their descendants by the federal government.

The Navajo Tribe rejected the 1934 Indian Reorganization Act, which authorized Indian tribes to adopt constitutional forms of government, and instead governed themselves by a tribal council at first elected under regulations issued by the federal Bureau of Indian Affairs (BIA). Since 2010 the Navajo Nation has been governed by a twenty-four-member tribal council, reduced from the former number of eighty-eight, which represent the 110 semiautonomous "chapter" governments throughout the reservation. Executive functions are directed by a president and vice president elected every four years. Judicial functions are carried out by a judiciary branch that is separate from the political branches of government.

Mescalero Apache Tribe

The Mescalero Apache Tribe largely escaped conflict with the Spanish and the Mexicans during their respective periods of occupation of the southwestern United States. The Mescaleros' homelands in southern New Mexico were included in the territory ceded to the United States in 1848. Hostilities ensued following the establishment of New Mexico Territory in 1850, when the U.S. Army and American settlers began to more earnestly encroach upon the Mescaleros' domain. In 1852 the Mescalero Apaches entered into a treaty that consigned them to a small reservation at Bosque Redondo. But poor conditions there led many Mescaleros to return to their homelands.

A presidential executive order in 1873 established a reservation for the Mescalero Apaches in the Sacramento Mountains, permitting their return to the heart of their aboriginal territory. Subsequent executive orders expanded the reservation, and the U.S. Army began to relocate bands of Lipan Apaches there, along with eventually some of Geronimo's Chiricahua Apaches who escaped removal to prison in Florida. Throughout most of the twentieth century, the Mescaleros were allowed to remain largely unmolested on their reservation, save for desultory efforts by the federal Office of Indian Services to turn them into farmers.[6]

The Mescalero Apaches did take advantage of the provisions of the federal Indian Reorganization Act of 1934 that authorized Indian tribes to adopt constitutional forms of government, subject to the approval by the secretary of the interior. Today the tribe is governed by a president, a vice president, and an eight-member tribal council, all elected at large. Council members serve two-year, staggered terms with elections occurring every year. The tribe's initial constitution was ratified on March 25, 1936, and revised on December 18, 1964. The tribe's laws were compiled into the Mescalero Tribal Code, which was approved on January 13, 1984.[7]

Jicarilla Apache Nation

The territory of the Jicarilla Apaches since time immemorial was northeastern New Mexico, southeastern Colorado, and the plains area of western Texas and

Oklahoma. Beginning in the sixteenth century, the Spanish gradually moved their settlements onto Jicarilla lands, bringing with them horses, livestock, and trade goods that eventually became the medium of intercultural exchange. By the mid-eighteenth century, the Jicarilla lands were well settled with Spanish villages that would later accommodate the influx of American settlers who would come from the east by way of the Santa Fe Trail. Eventually the Jicarillas became a "homeless" people living in the midst of their homeland, and their lands officially became a part of the United States in 1848.

The natural consequence of the invasion of the Jicarilla homelands was conflict, and this led to war in 1854 and 1855. The eventual military defeat of the Jicarilla Apaches might have resulted in their removal to an Indian reservation set aside for them under the by-then well-developed pattern for ending hostilities and securing peace between Indian tribes and their non-Indian neighbors. Several Indian reservations, in fact, were established for the Jicarillas in various parts of New Mexico Territory prior to 1887. The U.S. government was never wholly successful, however, in moving the Jicarillas to these reservations and out of their beloved homelands. Finally, a permanent 416,000-acre Jicarilla Apache Indian Reservation was created in the mountain fastness of northern New Mexico on February 11, 1887, by executive order.[8] The Indian Reorganization Act of 1934 inaugurated a new era for the Jicarilla Apaches, and in 1937 the Jicarilla Apache Tribe voted to accept a tribal constitution and by-laws under the provisions of the act.

Today the Jicarilla Apache government has three branches, executive, legislative, and judicial. It has a president and vice president, who are elected every four years, an eight-member legislative council, in which terms are staggered so that half of the council members are elected every two years. There is a tribal court whose judges are appointed by the president with legislative confirmation. In 1995 the Jicarilla Apache Tribe officially changed its name to the Jicarilla Apache Nation.

U.S. Federal Indian Policies and New Mexico Indians

Twenty-two federally recognized Indian tribes are primarily located in New Mexico. A small portion of the Ute Mountain Tribe's Colorado reservation lies in the far northwest corner of New Mexico. Large portions of the Navajo Reservation lie in Arizona and Utah. The Navajo tribal headquarters is in Window Rock, Arizona. Besides the significant portion of "Big Navajo" that lies in northwestern New Mexico, the three Navajo "satellite reservations" of Ramah, To'hajiilee, and Alamo all lie wholly within New Mexico. Recently, the federal government has agreed to hold in trust a parcel of land in southern New Mexico for the Fort Sill Apache Tribe of Oklahoma, leading to that tribe's claim now to be the twenty-third New Mexico Indian tribe. No Fort Sill Apaches yet live on their trust land in New Mexico.

The issuance by or on behalf of Spanish sovereigns of actual grants of land to Pueblo tribes in New Mexico created a different form of ownership than that held by other tribes who did not have such grants from Spain or Mexico. These differences created considerable confusion and disputes for many years over whether the Pueblo people were really "Indians" in the same sense as were the Navajos and Apaches; over whether the Pueblo Indians' water rights were protected at all by federal law or were even superior to any other water right by virtue of the "Pueblo water rights" that would have been recognized under Spanish law in any dispute; and whether the Pueblo Indians themselves were actually citizens of the United States by virtue of their status as citizens of New Mexico prior to 1848.

New Mexico's admission to the union in 1912 raised these and other issues regarding the status of the Pueblo people as "Indians" or "Indian tribes," as those terms are used in federal laws respecting Indians. In the case of *United States v. Sandoval* (231 U.S. 28 [1913]), mentioned earlier, the U.S. Supreme Court ruled that the power of Congress

> to regulate commerce with foreign Nations among the several States and with the Indian tribes [U.S. CONST. ART. I, Sec. 8, Cl. 3], provided the federal government with the authority and the power to legislate for the Pueblo Indians as for other tribes, notwithstanding that their land titles derived from previous sovereigns and were not set aside by the United States itself. It was not necessary for the Supreme Court to decide in the *Sandoval* case whether the Pueblo Indians were citizens of the United States by virtue of their citizenship under previous sovereigns, and the

question was soon answered with the Indian Citizenship Act of 1924, which unilaterally bestowed citizenship upon all American Indians not already citizens [43 Stat. 453 (1924)].[9]

The major federal Indian policy of the late nineteenth century that significantly shaped the future of American Indian tribes was set forth in the General Allotment Act of 1887 (24 Stat. 388 [1887]). This policy was designed to break up the communal, tribal ownership of Indian lands by issuing to individual Indians patents for small "allotments" of land, returning the so-called surplus lands to the public domain, and opening these lands to non-Indian settlement under the federal homestead laws. This allotment policy soon became a disaster for both Indian tribes and the federal government, and it was later repudiated in the Indian Reorganization Act (48 Stat. 984 [1934]). The disastrous effects of the so-called allotment policy continue to plague both tribes, who saw some 90 million acres removed from their reservation land bases, and the U.S. government, which today finds itself responsible for the administration of some 4 million separate, individual ownership interests in former tribal lands now owned largely by the Indian descendants of those original Indian "allottees." With the exception of the Navajo Nation and Laguna Pueblo, New Mexico tribes successfully resisted the allotment of their reservations and the devastating loss of reservation lands this policy visited upon other tribes throughout the country.

The next major federal policy affecting New Mexico tribes was enacted into law with the Indian Self-Determination and Education Assistance Act of 1975 (88 Stat. 2203). This law, among other things, authorized Indian tribes to contract with the federal government for the provision of services and administration of programs designed for their benefit. Tribes throughout the country, including New Mexico tribes, were soon administering programs for education, law enforcement, road construction, forestry management, housing, and many other services that previously had been carried out for them by federal employees assigned to those duties. In 2014 self-determination for Indian tribes continued to be the announced policy of the United States, offering tribes the opportunity to revise and tailor federal programs to meet their unique circumstances and needs.

The most recent and far-reaching federal Indian policy to have significant effects for New Mexico tribes has been the Indian Gaming Regulatory Act (102 Stat. 2469 [1988]), which authorized Indian tribes, in certain circumstances and subject to certain conditions, to operate gaming facilities as a means of generating revenues and strengthening tribal governments. In 2014, fourteen of New Mexico's twenty-two federally recognized tribes operated gaming enterprises in New Mexico. Under agreements required to be negotiated with the state, these tribes share a portion of their gaming revenues with the state of New Mexico. In 2011 tribal casinos contributed $68.9 million to the state treasury through revenue sharing.[10]

The Growth of Modern Tribal Economies in New Mexico

Since the introduction of the horse, sheep, goats, and cattle by the Spanish, the New Mexico tribes' economies have been agriculture based. The livestock industry has been the mainstay of the Navajo and Apache reservations since their establishment in the late 1800s. The Navajos were so successful in the growth of their herds that in the 1930s the federal government had to force them into herd reductions as a land conservation measure. From the 1940s to the 1960s, the federal government assisted the small subsistence sheep ranches with water development and soil conservation.

The Jicarilla people started their highly successful livestock industry in the 1920s but suffered heavy losses in the 1930s due to record-high snowfalls on their northern reservation. In southern New Mexico the Mescaleros and the nineteen pueblos along the Rio Grande and Rio San Jose and at the Zuni reservation were marginally successful in their livestock operations. The agricultural industry on the Apache Indian reservations was spurred on by the Indian Reorganization Act's provisions for the purchase of additional lands, the consolidation of land bases, and loans from the authorized revolving loan fund. Cattle and sheep raising thrived at least on the two Apache reservations. All the tribes experienced some windfall profits due to high demands during the World War II years. The 1950s and 1960s saw a decrease in the tribal livestock operations on all the reservations, with the exception of the Navajo Reservation, where small family operations continued.[11]

Both of the Apache tribes shifted their operations from family ranches to large-scale commercial operations, with the Mescaleros having one of the more successful operations. By the 1970s this sector had decreased tremendously, to the point where it made little difference in the overall tribal income. Today there are only small sheep and cattle operations dotting the Indian reservation landscape. In 2008,

> on the Navajo Nation, there are 511,784 sheep units of permitted live-stock which includes cattle, sheep, horses, goats, and llamas on the 17,061,885 acres of land. There are approximately eighty individual Navajo tribal ranches within the twenty-five core tribal ranches, in both New Mexico and Arizona. The majority are located in the eastern portion of the Navajo Nation in New Mexico. The Navajo Nation leases ranches out to individuals with intent of developing strategic management plans to promote range improvements in an effort to produce quality beef. There are 843 land use permits on the irrigated Fruitland, Cudei and Hogback projects in the Shiprock Agency. This does not include the numerous traditional dryland farming operations on the reservation, but this activity brings in $26,535,295 in gross receipts.[12]

If livestock provided the basis for the Navajo and Apache economies in early years, agriculture has been the foundation of the Pueblo economies since before Coronado graced the deserts and plains with his expeditionary forces. The Pueblo Indians have cultivated fields along the Rio Grande Valley for hundreds of years. In 1890, according to historian James A. Vlasich, there were 1,516 Pueblo farmers cultivating 7,921 acres on all Pueblo reservations. On these lands they grew a wide variety of fruits, vegetables, and grain and hay crops. The average size of field was 1.77 acres.[13] Government funding for water development in the West provided major assistance to Pueblo farmers. Congress appropriated funding for the Indian Irrigation Division of the Bureau of Indian Affairs as early as 1884, but the Pueblo Indians, due to their status, did not qualify for assistance until 1913. After that, this division assisted the Pueblo Indians with ditch construction and provided irrigation tools and maintenance.[14] For example, under the Pueblo Lands Compensation Act of 1933, the Pueblo Indians received $761,954 to purchase land and water rights and fund irrigation-works construction.[15] The Middle Rio Grande Conservancy District, created in 1932 for non-Indians, actually helped to increase the available agricultural lands for certain Pueblo Indians, namely, those able to afford the cost of upgrading their irrigation works and land leveling. The major activities designed to help Pueblo farmers involved the development of water projects. Despite the development of water projects on Pueblo lands, between 1900 and 1936, the area of the Pueblo Indians' crop production decreased from about 15,000 acres to 18,379.[16] The period from 1962 to 1980 saw the greatest decrease in agricultural acreage. For example, at San Felipe in 1940, 641 acres were devoted to crop production, but by 1981 it was 469 acres.[17] This virtual collapse of Pueblo agriculture contributed significantly to off-reservation employment and a rapid expansion in government employment among the Pueblo Indians, resulting in a general overall downturn in Pueblo economic productivity.

A bright spot in Indian agriculture has been the development of a large-scale commercial operation named the Navajo Indian Irrigation Project near Farmington, New Mexico. This 110,630-acre irrigated farm was created by Congress in 1956 and its construction was authorized in 1962. In 1970 the Navajo Agricultural Products Industry was established as a tribal entity to operate the project. The water was to be supplied by an annual diversion of 508,000 acre-feet of water from Navajo Reservoir, to be stored behind Navajo Dam, then moved through a total of 450 miles of canals, tunnels, and other irrigation works and structures.[18]

The Forestry Industry on New Mexico Indian Reservations

JICARILLA FORESTRY

The forestry industry on both the Jicarilla Apache and Mescalero Apache Reservations has been big business. Logging began on the Jicarilla Reservation in 1914 on about 230,000 acres and on the Mescalero Reservation in 1916 on about 175,000 acres. The first commercial harvest took place in 1914, when 1.6 million board feet was harvested for stumpage receipts in the amount of

$5,026. Timber sales peaked in 1920, when 32.4 million board feet was harvested for over $100,000 received by the tribe in stumpage payments.[19]

This great forestry natural resource provided the foundation for building the livestock economy in the 1920s through the 1940s. With proceeds from timber sales, the tribe purchased livestock for all the Jicarilla families on the reservation. There was intermittent logging between 1937 and 1986. The total volume of timber harvested between 1914 and 1971 was 395 million board feet. Between 1987 and 1994, the tribe sold over 37 million board feet, for sales in the $6 million range.[20] Unfortunately, neither the tribe nor the federal government did anything to train or employ Jicarillas in any capacity in the woods or at the sawmills. Jicarilla timber had become an export product. Outside timber companies came in to denude the lands and with no plans for replanting. As the timber industry wound down, even the railroads that had been built into Jicarilla forests to remove the timber were taken up, and nothing was left behind for subsequent infrastructure development. In 1974 the Jicarilla Apache Tribe accepted an offer of $9 million to settle claims of mismanagement of its forest lands. The tribe itself has subsequently replanted millions of conifers, and it patrols the forests to maintain a balance between forest growth and wildlife consumption of and damage to saplings.

MESCALERO FORESTRY

The Mescalero Apaches experienced a lot of down time in getting its operations off the ground, but once they got off the ground, the tribe made great strides in managing and developing its timber resources. Today, the tribe's Mescalero Forest Products enterprise contracts for direct sales of processed and unprocessed timber throughout the Southwest. The Mescalero Forest Products sawmill employed eighty people in 2006. The tribe and the BIA forestry branch jointly harvest approximately 20 million board feet of timber annually, employing model uneven-age silvicultural management to provide perpetual timber crops. In 2004 the tribe purchased the former White Sands Forest Products in Alamogordo, New Mexico. Renamed Mescalero Forest Products II, this mill produces two-by-four and two-by-six studs as well as posts and poles. It employs about eighty people. In 2006 the tribe was considering the development of a biomass cogeneration plant at the mill.[21]

NAVAJO FORESTRY

There are approximately 700,000 acres of pine-fir forest and 4.5 million acres of piñon pine on the Navajo Reservation in both New Mexico and Arizona. As of 2006, the annual sustained-yield cut hovered at 35 million board feet per year. Total forestry employment was as high as one thousand people, generating an estimated annual economic output of about $87 million. Revenues to the tribal government from timber sales and the activity of the Navajo Forest Industries amounted to about $1.5 million prior to 2000. The department has a cooperative agreement with the U.S. Forest Service to provide tribal employees with work experience within the federal organization. Navajo Forest Products Industries used to be the largest purchaser of timber from the Navajo forest. Because of cutting restrictions imposed on the Navajo corporation, the sawmill plant had to close its operations on July 25, 1994.[22]

Forest management was once the sole province of the Bureau of Indian Affairs, but in the early 1970s, under authority of the Indian Self-Determination Act, the Navajo Forestry Department took over the management of thinning operations. Since 1991 the department has contracted for all forest-management duties except for suppressing fires and some activities relating to improving forest stands. Pueblo lands in New Mexico have not provided similarly large-scale forestry operations, but Isleta Pueblo in 2007 accepted $3 million to settle forest mismanagement claims against the United States.[23]

The Tourism Industry on New Mexico Indian Reservations

The Pueblos are very active participants in the tourism economy of New Mexico. They make unique forms of silver jewelry, pottery, and woven articles. Their sales presence at plazas like the Palace of the Governors and the La Fonda Hotel in Santa Fe and at Old Town in Albuquerque serves as an iconic symbol for New Mexico's tourism in general, and the mere presence of the Indian tribes in New Mexico has become a national tourist attraction for the state. The famous and ancient villages of Acoma's Sky City and Taos Pueblo are destination attractions for international visitors. Each year the pueblos' annual feasts, from Taos to Isleta, attract thousands of visitors. This private sector tourism economy with an emphasis on artisan goods flourishes today among the Pueblo Indians. The state of New Mexico actively exploits the presence of all the Indian tribes in New Mexico through print media advertising.

Critical Issues Facing Indian Tribes in the Twenty-First Century

Population

Population growth or lack of growth will affect tribal economies, the tribal social arena, the distribution of tribal wealth and opportunities, and the continued movement to off-reservation areas. In general, population growth will occur in and around areas where there is employment and housing, where educational institutions are located, where retirement infrastructure is available, where there are amenities to attract upwardly mobile adults and affluent retirees, and where water is available to sustain population and economic growth.[24] Historically, the American Indian and Alaska Native population has increased at a much faster rate than the population of New Mexico generally.

Table 6.1 shows both the 2000 and 2010 U.S. Census figures on the population and employment and educational status for each of the twenty-two New Mexico Indian tribes.

It is not unusual for tribes to dispute census data for reasons ranging from low participation to outright errors in its collection. Collection of demographic data in support of tribal economic development, strategic planning, government proposals, feasibility studies, or evidence for a legal case is a recent phenomenon for tribes and Indian communities. More often than not, the data is not for public consumption, leaving anyone wanting specific and updated information to rely on generalized federal, state, municipal, or private business data and studies that rely primarily on U.S. Census data.

Table 6.1. New Mexico tribal census data, 2000 and 2010

TRIBE	YEAR	POPULATION	UNEMPLOYMENT RATE (%)	NUMBER IN LABOR FORCE	PER CAPITA INCOME ($)	HIGH SCHOOL GRADUATION RATE (%)	HOLDERS OF A BA DEGREE OR HIGHER (%)
Acoma	2010	3,011	17.1	1,302	11,386	85.4	6.3
	2000	2,802	7.2	932	8,749	73.0	8.5
Cochiti	2010	1,727	4.0	267	18,343	84.6	29.9
	2000	1,502	2.3	585	15,363	81.9	27.2
Isleta	2010	3,400	4.6	1,372	18,567	89.5	11.1
	2000	3,166	5.7	1,316	11,438	72.9	6.1
Jemez	2010	1,815	6.0	901	14,492	84.7	11.0
	2000	1,958	10.5	685	8,045	71.7	7.6
Jicarilla	2010	3,254	9.1	1,278	15,274	78.6	12.9
	2000	2,755	8.4	1,051	10,136	78.0	13.9
Laguna	2010	4,043	12.5	1,757	11,933	84.1	9.0
	2000	3,815	7.7	1,288	8,773	79.4	7.5
Mescalero	2010	3,613	15.3	1,414	8,806	72.4	10.7
	2000	3,156	8.6	1,076	8,118	72.6	6.4
Nambe	2010	1,611	11.8	291	15,452	84.4	24.5
	2000	1,764	2.3	670	16,543	82.7	21.0
Navajo	2010	173,667	7.0	49,605	9,948	65.8	7.1
	2000	180,462	11.2	51,363	7,269	55.9	7.3
Ohkay Owingeh (San Juan)	2010	6,309	13.6	3,043	18,034	79.3	11.1
	2000	6,748	4.6	2,951	12,083	68.8	8.5
Picuris	2010	1,886	15.4	728	16,467	76.1	15.1
	2000	1,801	4.7	692	10,970	70.3	14.6

TRIBE	YEAR	POPULATION	UNEMPLOYMENT RATE (%)	NUMBER IN LABOR FORCE	PER CAPITA INCOME ($)	HIGH SCHOOL GRADUATION RATE (%)	HOLDERS OF A BA DEGREE OR HIGHER (%)
Pojoaque	2010	3,316	8.0	1,744	26,174	87.5	26.2
	2000	2,712	1.6	1,366	17,348	81.8	23.7
Sandia	2010	4,965	9.9	2,494	15,838	73.0	11.4
	2000	4,414	3.3	1,924	12,341	67.1	9.6
San Felipe	2010	3,563	12.6	1,408	14,485	75.3	11.8
	2000	3,185	5.7	690	9,266	68.0	6.0
San Ildefonso	2010	1,752	12.9	909	26,131	89.0	21.8
	2000	1,524	4.2	731	14,848	82.9	21.7
Santa Ana	2010	621	3.0	369	15,048	88.6	9.7
	2000	487	6.4	206	9,857	85.4	2.7
Santa Clara	2010	11,021	7.4	5,557	22,182	80.3	19.9
	2000	10,658	4.8	5,015	15,336	77.5	19.8
Santo Domingo	2010	3,255	12.1	1,222	9,657	72.0	8.2
	2000	3,166	8.5	920	5,713	68.5	2.7
Taos	2010	4,384	10.7	2,878	21,721	89.1	26.2
	2000	4,492	8.8	2,318	14,222	80.5	23.3
Tesuque	2010	841	6.5	402	19,653	82.2	19.7
	2000	806	4.8	408	16,484	81.2	18.8
Zia	2010	737	10.9	376	12,372	75.9	3.8
	2000	646	5.1	258	8,689	73.9	8.9
Zuni	2010	7,891	8.8	4,473	10,081	77.0	5.6
	2000	7,758	9.5	2,698	6,976	64.4	6.8

Source: Compiled by Christina Harrison, Tiller Research Inc., 2014

A few tribes, like the Navajo Nation, collect data for reasons similar to those of any governmental agency, educational institution, or company. For example, according to the 2000 U.S. Census, there were 298,215 Navajo people residing in the United States, and 173,987 lived on the Navajo Reservation. The census did not break down the figures among the Navajos in Arizona, New Mexico, and Utah, nor did it specifically identify the number of Navajos living in the New Mexico border towns of Farmington, Gallup, and Grants. As stated in the Navajo Nation's *2000–2001 Comprehensive Economic Development Strategy Report*, the nation's unemployment rate was 44 percent, and not the 11 percent listed in the 2000 U.S. Census. Similarly, per capita income was $6,217 according to Navajo data and not $7,269 as reported in federal data.[25]

The Navajo Nation has the highest poverty rate in the United States. In 2000 the Navajo Division of Economic Development indicated that the median family income was only $20,005, while the U.S. median family income was $41,994. The average annual per capita income among Navajos was less than $7,269, while the per capita income for the state of Arizona was approximately $24,028. More than 40 percent of the Navajo families on the reservation lived below the federal poverty levels, compared with less than 16 percent of the general U.S. population, making it among the most impoverished regions in the United States. Poverty and related conditions have contributed to emigration from the Navajo Reservation. Between 1990 and 2000 the Navajo population on the reservation and trust land increased by 21.6 percent, while the population outside of these areas increased by 53.2 percent. If these disparities are not addressed, the nation predicts that by 2020, more than half of the Navajo people may be living off of the reservation.[26]

According to one educational study, between 2000 and 2005, New Mexico's population grew at an annual rate of 1.51 percent, compared to 1.88 percent for the American Indian and Alaska Native population. This disparity in population growth rates is expected to continue through 2010, although there is evidence that the gap is narrowing.[27] In the future, the population of American Indians and Alaska Natives is expected to continue to expand at a faster rate than that of New Mexicans as a group. By 2025 Native Americans in New Mexico will number about 280,000. This is an increase of about 45 percent, or about 89,000 people, over twenty-five years. New Mexico's population will grow by about 38 percent during the same time period. The American Indian and Alaska Native population, like other nonwhite race groups, will be aging.[28]

Climate Change

Climate change is one issue that all New Mexicans have no choice but to deal with. And tribes have a major stake in seeking ways and means to deal with the changing climate throughout the Southwest. The amount of land the tribes control and the natural resources on their lands puts them in the forefront of dealing with this issue. The nineteen Indian pueblos together own about 2.2 million acres, the two Apache tribes own 1.3 million acres, and the Navajo Nation lands in New Mexico total just over 4.1 million acres—for a grand total of just under 8 million acres for all tribally owned lands in New Mexico.[29]

The U.S. Environmental Protection Agency explains, "It is general knowledge that the climate of the Southwest is changing. Over the last century, the average annual temperature has increased about 1.5°F. Average annual temperature is projected to rise an additional 2.5–8°F by the end of the century."[30]

Climate change is caused predominantly by heat-trapping gases produced from the burning of fossil fuels, aided by the clearing of forests and agricultural activities. Humans almost inevitably will need to undertake measures to adapt to climate change, and here in New Mexico the impacts are already apparent in our environment, with changes in stream flows, more wildfires, lessened crop productivity, and growing water shortages.[31]

Water Resources

A recent report authored by Brian Bird and other environmentalists stated, "Warming trends in the Southwest are considered to be swifter than [in] other regions of the country and may be significantly greater than the global average. . . . The rapid increase in temperatures in this region, particularly summertime temperature, will have drastic effects on hydrology, which in turn may result in severe water supply challenges in the near future."[32]

More frequent and severe droughts will contribute to the lowering of water tables because of inadequate recharging of groundwater-based systems and reduced snowpack that leads to river-flow reductions and the dwindling of reservoirs. In turn, droughts will worsen existing competition for water resources. Contributing to this process will be rapid population growth, which will increase the competition for water resources across sectors, states, and tribes, and even between the United States and Mexico.[33] Increasing scarcity of water supplies will call for trade-offs among competing uses. Water allocations in the region, some of which were agreed upon almost a century ago, will become more difficult to carry out.

INDIAN WATER RIGHTS IN NEW MEXICO

Mark Twain is often credited with a saying common in the American West (and mentioned in chapter 5): "Whiskey is for drinking. Water is for fighting." He might well have been looking at twenty-first-century New Mexico. The twenty-two tribes in New Mexico are located within four of the state's larger water basins, including the Upper Rio Grande, which extends from the Colorado–New Mexico boundary to Elephant Butte Reservoir in south central New Mexico, and the Upper Colorado Basin, which extends into the northwestern section of New Mexico. The Rio Grande and the San Juan River provide the major sources of water to the state and to the tribes. Zuni Pueblo in the western central part of the state is located in the Lower Colorado River Basin. The Mescalero Apache Tribe in southern New Mexico lies within the Pecos River Basin. The tribes assert broad claims to water under aboriginal rights, federally reserved rights, and other water rights acquired with additions to their reservation land areas over time. In addition, they have extensive water rights under federal projects designed and built at least in part for their benefit. (There is more on all this in chapter 5.)

New Mexico's water picture is naturally constrained by its semiarid climate and scarcity of water. Competing demands by agriculture, by a burgeoning oil and gas industry increasingly dependent on water supplies for hydraulic fracturing, and by growing metropolitan areas along the state's central Rio Grande corridor have all combined to put great stresses on

New Mexico's limited water supply. Already New Mexico is importing water from the Colorado River Basin to supplement the water from the Rio Grande Basin, where more than half New Mexico's population lives. New Mexico farmers and ranchers are seeking to limit upstream depletions within the state by oil and gas producers in order to increase the amount of water available for livestock and farming operations. Generally speaking, the state's twenty-two Indian tribes have water rights that are prior in time and superior in priority to all these other competing claims. These Indian tribes will be significant players in the state's water future—which means in the state's economic and political future.

New Mexico, like most western states, follows the doctrine of "prior appropriation" in determining the rights of competing claimants to the use of surface waters of the state. Generally, under state law that means the first party to "appropriate" water for a beneficial use has a good right against all later claimants, with a priority date as of the first date the water was appropriated for that use in that place. These rights, or the priority date, can be lost if the beneficial use is not maintained or if the use is changed. The rules for forfeiture and abandonment of water rights are sometimes referred to by the shorthand axiom of "use it or lose it." In a pure prior-appropriation system, senior water rights are satisfied in full before junior rights are addressed. Consequently, in times of shortage junior water rights might be curtailed altogether in order to satisfy senior rights.[34]

New Mexico Indian tribes and their reservations are governed under federal law, however, and not the laws of New Mexico. The federal law governing the water rights of Indian tribes derives from a series of decisions by the U.S. Supreme Court. In *Winters v. United States* (207 U.S. 564 [1908]), the Supreme Court ruled that the federal government impliedly reserved sufficient waters to meet the "present and future needs" of the tribes on their reservations, with the priority date being the date the reservation was created. These "federally reserved rights" are not subject to the laws of the states in which the tribes are located, and this includes state laws regarding forfeiture and abandonment. In other words, Indian water rights are good against later claimants whether the Indians are making actual use of the water or not. More than fifty years after *Winters*, in order to determine what water was available to other claimants along the Lower Colorado River, the Supreme Court in *Arizona v. California* (373 U.S. 546 [1963]) ruled that the actual extent of Indian water rights could be determined by a formula based on the "practicably irrigable acreage" of the reservations. These two Supreme Court rulings have had a profound impact on New Mexico.

In 1952 the United States granted its consent for federally reserved water rights to be determined by state courts if the case involved a "general stream adjudication" to determine the relative rights and priorities of all water users on a stream system. In New Mexico these proceedings are conducted by the district courts. In a case that came to be known as the *Aamodt* case, which after some forty years was settled by an act of Congress in 2010, the New Mexico district court agreed that the Pueblo Indians of Nambe, Pojoaque, San Ildefonso, and Tesuque had water rights based on village (pueblo) irrigation systems that predated European contact by hundreds of years. These Pueblo water rights had been recognized by the Spanish sovereigns when New Mexico was part of New Spain and were subsequently acknowledged as preexisting rights when Mexico assumed jurisdiction from Spain and, again, when the United States asserted sovereignty under the Treaty of Guadalupe Hidalgo in 1848. The New Mexico district court declared these Pueblo water rights to include sufficient water to irrigate all acreage that was under cultivation between 1846 and passage of the Pueblo Lands Act of 1924, as well as adequate water for village domestic purposes. This gives many pueblos an effective priority date from time immemorial for extensive water rights in New Mexico, although it suggests a much more restrictive quantity than all the "practicably irrigable acreage" under the *Arizona v. California* doctrine. The 2010 *Aamodt* settlement did not address the extent of the Pueblo Indians' water rights in the absence of the settlement.[35]

As early as 1934 federal agencies were already studying ways to divert water from the Colorado River Basin in the northwestern portion of the state to the Rio Grande to provide water to population centers like Santa Fe and Albuquerque. The Navajo Nation spent much of the 1940s opposing plans to divert water from the San Juan River in the Colorado River Basin—through the Rio Chama to the Rio Grande and then to Albuquerque and on to southern New Mexico. New Mexico and the federal government proposed a major irrigation project to enable the Navajo Nation to make use of some of the San Juan River water it claimed under the Winters Doctrine.

Other states objected to any federal project to develop irrigation on the Navajo Reservation unless the tribe agreed to some limit on the amount of water it would ultimately claim. A 1955 study by the Bureau of Indian Affairs indicated that the Navajo Nation might have claim to as many as 778,000 acre-feet of water under federal law.[36] The matter was hung up for some thirty years, until 1962, when Congress authorized both the San Juan–Chama Project to divert water from the San Juan River to the Rio Grande Basin and the use of 508,000 acre-feet of water to irrigate a 110,000-acre farm to be developed on the Navajo Reservation as part of the San Juan–Chama diversion system.

The San Juan–Chama Project was later to play an important part in the settlement of other Indian water rights claims in New Mexico. The Jicarilla Apache settlement in 1992 provided the tribe with rights to 40,000 acre-feet annually and authorized use of waters from the San Juan–Chama diversion. This settlement acknowledged that the tribe might not soon make actual use of its water rights and authorized the marketing for up to ninety-nine years of the tribe's federally reserved water rights for off-reservation use, so long as that use was within the state of New Mexico. For many years the Jicarilla Apache Tribe sold a portion of its water rights to the city of Santa Fe.

The *Aamodt* settlement in 2010 provided for 6,096 acre-feet of water to be allocated among four pueblos and provided an agreement that Indians and non-Indians would share in future shortages. The Taos Pueblo settlement was approved in the same legislation as the *Aamodt* settlement (Pub. L. No. 111–291, 124 Stat. 3064 [2010]), and it also authorized Taos Pueblo to market up to 2,215 acre-feet of its water rights annually, utilizing the San Juan–Chama diversion system.[37]

In 2005 the Navajo Nation and the state of New Mexico announced an agreement on a further Navajo settlement that would hugely modify the water picture of western New Mexico. Under that agreement, the Navajo Nation would agree to the transfer of some 22,000 acre-feet of water per year from the Upper Colorado Basin, in the northwestern corner of New Mexico, to the city of Gallup, more than one hundred miles to the south.[38] The tribe would receive very significant additional irrigation development rights along the route and would be assured of significant storage rights in federal project facilities. In addition to the 508,000 acre-feet of water to be delivered to the Navajo Irrigation Project under the 1962 act, this settlement would provide up to 48,000 acre-feet for development of the Hogback Irrigation Project, 18,180 acre-feet for the Fruitland Irrigation Project, and 4,680 acre-feet to be developed from the Animas–La Plata Project. Nine years later, in early 2014, this agreement was authorized by Congress but has not become effective by ratification of the Navajo Nation Council.[39]

The water future of New Mexico will be largely affected by the resolution of Indian water rights claims in the state. Agreements that either permit or deny the marketing of these Indian water rights, whether to municipalities like Taos, Espanola, Albuquerque, Santa Fe, and Gallup or to the oil industry for production operations such as hydraulic fracturing, will largely determine where development proceeds in New Mexico. Continued shortages and prolonged droughts such as existed in 2014 may well eventually limit the amount of water available to New Mexico as a whole, and the early priority dates of the tribes among the state's water users will very likely make New Mexico's twenty-two Indian tribes even more important players in the state's future development.

Estimates of the cost of fully implementing the Indian water settlements in New Mexico reach the $90 million mark. The cost to New Mexico to meet the state's obligations under those settlements is some $100 million.[40] Future settlements and future agreements to permit marketing of these water rights will do much to permit these costs ultimately to be borne by or recouped from the real water users.

In the near future water shortages will be exacerbated by climate changes, increased population, overappropriation, and increased demands for industrial use. Changes in snowpack and timing of runoff are certain in much of the western United States but are especially grave in the southwestern and interior western U.S. river basins. The National Research Council has projected that the Rio Grande Basin faces the greatest reduction in runoff of any basin in the United States, an estimated decrease of 12 percent for every degree the temperature rises, and both the Upper and Lower Colorado River Basins will experience decreases in runoff of more than 6 percent for every one-degree rise in temperature.[41] Warmer temperatures will affect the amount of snowpack and the timing of snowmelt in the mountains of Colorado, which provide the freshwater resources that flow into the Rio Grande Valley. Future warming is projected to produce more severe droughts, with further reductions in water supplies.

IMPACTS ON FORESTS AND OTHER ECOSYSTEMS

Rising temperatures are killing forests globally, and Los Alamos National Laboratory scientists have found that "it is highly likely that the Southwest, including New Mexico, will lose the vast majority of its forests by 2050."[42]

Projected increases in drought, wildfire, invasive species, and pests, as well as changes in the geographic ranges of species, will likely threaten native forests and other ecosystems in the Southwest. Severe drought will threaten forest populations in New Mexico. According to a 2013 Bureau of Indian Affairs report on forestlands on Indian reservations, there are 2.6 million acres of forest on New Mexico Indian lands, of which 602,200 acres are commercial timberlands. The largest commercial acreages in New Mexico are found on the Jicarilla Reservation, with 583,010 acres, and on the Mescalero Reservation, with 235,000 acres.[43]

In 2000–2003 the dread combination of conditions led to significant die-off of piñon pines due to beetle infestation in the Four Corners region.[44] This scenario is not uncommon in forested areas when climate changes interact with other nonclimate stresses to cause imbalances in ecosystems. Increasing temperatures and related reductions in spring snowpack and low levels of soil moisture are projected to increase wildfires. Droughts are already part of New Mexico's climate, and human-induced climate change will likely result in more challenges for ecosystems and the forest products industry.

IMPACTS OF ENERGY DEVELOPMENT

Beyond the effects that climate change will have on our natural environment, it will also affect our lifestyles and levels of comfort in our very homes. Rising temperatures and prolonged droughts are expected to threaten the reliability of electricity and water supplies. Increased air conditioning demand during intense and longer-lasting heat waves will tax the capacity of hydroelectric power systems. The supply and distribution of electricity consequently will be affected. These impacts are expected to be compounded by the region's rapid population growth. The development of tribal energy resources in the last half century and their continued development in the future will also have a profound impact on New Mexico's future.

Tribes in New Mexico's Energy Picture

As home to the nerve center of the Manhattan Project and the site for design, testing, and construction of the world's first atomic bombs, which ended World War II, New Mexico has played a uniquely important role in America's energy history. New Mexico was also home to two of the postwar experimental nuclear detonations designed to explore peaceful applications of this new and terrifying power. The first of these was the 1961 Project Gnome near Carlsbad to test the potential for generating electricity by injecting water into rock formations superheated by a nuclear explosion. The second was the 1967 Project Gasbuggy near the Jicarilla Apache capital of Dulce, an attempt to free natural gas from tight sand formations by a nuclear detonation. Neither these nor any of the other experiments of Operation Plowshare resulted in the hoped-for beneficial results of peacetime atomic explosions.

On February 19, 2014, the *New York Times* reported on the continuing environmental contamination of Navajo communities from more than more than five hundred small, unmapped uranium mines abandoned throughout the Navajo Reservation after World War II and during the Cold War that followed.[45] At the other extreme of New Mexico's uranium experience, the *Times* reported, the Jackpile-Paguate Mine on the Laguna Reservation was the largest open-pit uranium mine in the world until it was abandoned, with no plans and no requirement for its reclamation. Only the personal intervention of New Mexico businessman Robert O. Anderson eventually led to an agreement in 1986 with the Pueblo of Laguna for reclaiming the mine site. That work was declared complete in 1995, but a 2007 review determined that radiation releases are still occurring. As of 2014 the U.S. Environmental Protection

Agency had not acted on the Pueblo Indians' request to place the mine site on the National Priority List for cleanup of the nation's "superfund" sites.[46]

World War II led to a rapid development of the extensive oil reserves in the Permian Basin of west Texas, which extends into the four counties in the southeastern corner of New Mexico. This oil boom was facilitated by new developments in geophysics, such as seismograph, torsion balance, and magnetometer surveys, along with stratigraphic mapping to guide drilling operations. Similarly, oil discoveries in the far northwestern corner of the state were exploited in the San Juan Basin, which overlies portions of all four of the states in the Four Corners region. The San Juan Basin is very rich in oil, natural gas, coal, and uranium. Oil and gas production from Jicarilla Apache and Navajo lands in the San Juan Basin have provided significant portions of tribal revenues since the 1950s.

The abundant coal reserves of the Fruitland Formation in the San Juan Basin provided the bulk of the Navajo Nation's cash revenues for many years. Revenue from coal mining on Navajo lands provided more than $50 million per year to the Navajo Nation from 1995 to 2000. In some more recent years, these revenues have exceeded $60 million. On the other hand, the future of the area's coal-fired power plants is in some doubt. The Mohave Generating Station near Laughlin, Nevada, which utilized coal from Navajo mines more than two hundred miles away, was closed in 2005. The current contract that supplies water to the Navajo Generating Station near Page, Arizona, expires in 2016. In 2010 the principal owner of the Four Corners Generating Station announced it would shut down three of the plant's five operating units. The Escalante Generating Station near Prewitt, New Mexico, is experimenting with biomass fuel, which, if successful, might significantly reduce that plant's reliance on Navajo coal. The San Juan Generating Station near Farmington provides power to more than one-half the customer base of the Public Service Company of New Mexico, which has struck an agreement with the U.S. Environmental Protection Agency to convert two of the four coal-burning units there to natural gas–powered units by 2017.[47] This might well open up new demand for natural gas from Indian lands in the area, but it will certainly affect Navajo Nation revenues from coal production. The Navajo Nation has devoted considerable effort in recent years toward developing a coal-fired power plant in which the tribe itself would have a substantial proprietary interest. The proposed Desert Rock Generating Station, however, faces considerable local opposition, U.S. Environmental Protection Agency reservations, and an uncertain future.[48]

Oil and natural gas production throughout the San Juan Basin (Jicarilla Apache and Navajo lands) in 2014 was experiencing a new boom market as a result of renewed interest in producing from a deep geological formation known as the Mancos Shale through hydraulic fracturing of the deep rock—"fracking"—by the injection of huge quantities of chemical-laced water to create and maintain greater porosity. More than 600,000 acres of individually owned Navajo lands were being eagerly reviewed for possible fracking operations. If successful, these operations will generate huge revenues for landowners during the producing period, which will be much shorter than conventional production periods. The actual, long-term effects of modern hydraulic fracturing on groundwater supplies, and on water quality, are matters of intense debate, even as fierce competition rages for leasehold rights.

Indian lands in New Mexico present the energy-owning tribes with a significant opportunities to participate in the state's energy future on a different basis than their previous status as landowners who passively received royalties provided them. The neighboring Southern Ute Tribe has used its royalty income to purchase pipelines and natural gas processing plants, as well as mineral rights in fields far removed from the reservation. Whether New Mexico tribes similarly diversify their own energy-producing potential remains to be seen.

Education

"Graduation Rates Dropping among Native American Students" read the headline on a 2014 *U.S. News and World Report* article. Relying on *Diplomas Count 2013*, an annual report released on June 6, 2013, by *Education Week*, the article reported that, unlike African American and Hispanic students, whose graduation rates were nearing record-high levels, Native American students were sliding backward. Nationwide, about 51 percent of Native American students in 2010 earned diplomas, down from 54 percent in 2008.

While these figures are national averages, they also point to serious deficiencies in educational achievement levels in the public schools throughout New Mexico's Indian country.

There are eighty-nine school districts in New Mexico, and twenty-three of them serve predominantly Native American K-12 students. Two of the largest urban school districts, Albuquerque and Rio Rancho, have a large number of Native American students who are members of tribes from other areas of the United States, as well as from New Mexico. In 2010 the *New Mexico School Directory* reported that there were 5,151 Native American students in the Albuquerque School District and 6,833 Native American students in the Rio Rancho School District.[49] Rio Grande Valley Pueblo Indian students, from Taos Pueblo in the north to Isleta Pueblo, south of Albuquerque, attend schools in the districts of Taos, Pojoaque, Española, Jemez Valley, Jemez Mountain, Santa Fe, Bernalillo, Albuquerque, and Los Lunas, which each average about 300 students per district. Students from Acoma and Laguna Pueblos attend schools in the Laguna-Acoma and Grants School Districts. Zuni Pueblo has its own school district and enrolls 1,394 students. Jicarilla Apache students number 633 and almost exclusively attend school in the Dulce Independent School District. In southern New Mexico, the Ruidoso and Tularosa Districts together enroll 622 Mescalero Apache students.[50]

The Native American community with the largest number of schools is the Navajo Nation. It serves 9,532 Native American students, the majority of whom are Navajos. The Gallup–McKinley County School District serves students from Gallup and surrounding areas of McKinley County—which, in 2010, totaled 13,840 students in thirty-six public and private elementary, middle, and high schools, 9,532 of them Native American students. The Central Consolidated School District serves students from an area that covers about 3,000 square miles in the Four Corners region, including 5,528 Native American students from the communities of Kirtland, Ojo Amarillo, Newcomb, Naschitti, and Shiprock.[51]

Public education in Cibola County is operated by Grants/Cibola County Schools, based in Grants. Attending the schools in this district are 1,461 Native students. South of Grants is the Ramah Navajo Indian Reservation, where the school system is operated by the Ramah Navajo School Board and the Ramah Navajo Chapter. An Indian-controlled contract school located in Pine Hill, New Mexico, accommodates students from elementary through high school. The Navajo community with the smallest number of schools is on the To'hajiilee Indian Reservation, west of the I-40 corridor and west of Laguna Pueblo.

The New Mexico Indian Education Act was adopted in New Mexico to "ensure equitable and culturally relevant learning environments for Native students in public schools" as well as to "develop and implement positive educational systems; enhance the educational opportunities for students; aid in the development of culturally relevant materials for use in New Mexico schools; develop strategies for ensuring the maintenance of Native languages; increase tribal involvement and control; create formal government to government relationships between the tribes and state; and increase parental involvement in schools."[52]

This act was passed in part to comply with the 2001 federal law known as No Child Left Behind, which required states to adopt standards based on assessments in reading, mathematics, and science. No Child Left Behind puts accountability for assessments squarely on the shoulders of the states, including tracking adequate yearly progress (AYP) of students in state school systems. The goal of No Child Left Behind was to have all students reach 100 percent proficiency by 2013–2014. To establish a proficiency baseline, New Mexico used the New Mexico Standards-Based Assessment, data first collected in 2004–2005. Using this data, yearly goals, or annual measurable objectives, were set to move the public schools toward the 100 percent proficiency goal.[53]

In the 2004–2005 school year the AYP data showed that Native American students in New Mexico were already handicapped with the lowest proficiency rates. According to the 2004–2005 *Indian Education Status Report*, three school districts, Zuni, Dulce, and Gallup, fell short in making AYP in math and reading. These three schools have the highest proportion of Native students, with Zuni at 99.1 percent, Dulce at 91.4 percent, and Gallup at 81.0 percent, as well as the highest proportion of students enrolled in Title I and Title VII programs.[54]

For schools receiving Title I funds, the consequence of failing to meet

AYP requirements for two consecutive years was an offer to parents of the option to send their children to another public school. This absurd option was totally unrealistic in Indian communities, which had only a few schools to choose from, many of which were probably not meeting the AYP goals either. If a school failed to meet targets for a third consecutive year, corrective action was to be taken against the school, action such as removing relevant staff or implementing new curriculum. The failing school system was also to have the option of getting outside advice from experts, extending the length of the school day, or reorganizing its internal organization. It is not known whether sanctions have been taken against the New Mexico districts that have not meet the AYP goals and standards.

School accountability reports issued annually by the New Mexico Public Education Department show whether students in a particular school or district have met the proficiency levels for math and reading during the previous school year, with data summarized by ethnic group. Percentages are assigned to students within an ethnic group to show their proficiency rates. In the school year 2010–2011, among the 4,520 American Indian high school students in the Gallup–McKinley School District, 27.48 percent were proficient in math and 72.52 percent were not; for reading, 30.92 percent were proficient and 69.08 percent were not. For Dulce, only 17.83 percent of the 307 high school students were proficient in math, while 83.82 percent were not; the reading percentages for Dulce were 28.6 percent proficient,71.33 percent not proficient.[55] In other New Mexico school districts that serve over two hundred Native American students, the proficient-to-not-proficient ratios were in a range similar to that found at the Gallup–McKinley and Dulce Independent School Districts.

Health

There is a serious health crisis—with high rates of diabetes, obesity, and related diseases—among the American Indians of New Mexico. In 2013 the New Mexico Department of Health issued *American Indian Health Equity: A Report on Racial and Ethnic Health Disparities in New Mexico.*[56] The report was designed to help organizations and agencies, such as the New Mexico

Department of Health, improve health equity in New Mexico, eliminating health disparities while ensuring care for all. Native American communities, according to this report, had disparately high rates of teen births, diabetes deaths, obesity among adults, pneumonia and influenza, chlamydia infections, HIV infections, motor vehicle deaths, homicide, and alcohol-related deaths.

According to the report, diabetes was the leading cause of death among Native Americans in New Mexico. The rate for American Indians in 2010–2012 was 72.1 deaths per 100 persons, compared to the national rate of 17.9 deaths per 100.

The adult rate for obesity was not much better than for diabetes. It was 39.2 per 100 persons for American Indians in New Mexico, compared to 22.1 for white Americans. Even more disheartening, American Indian youth in New Mexico were found to have the highest rate of obesity among all groups surveyed, at 19.4 out of 100 persons (up from 15 per 100 in 2000); for white American youth, the figure was at 8.9 per 100.

The death rate due to motor vehicles for Native Americans in New Mexico in 2010–2012 was 37.2 per 100,000, three times higher than for whites in New Mexico, as well as higher than the national rate of 11.3 per 100,000.

According to the same report, alcohol-related deaths for American Indians in New Mexico were higher than for any other group: 121.1 per 100,000 persons, as compared to 41.0 for white Americans.

Healthy People 2020, a federal government report, goes beyond the New Mexico Department of Health report to identify five areas of health disparities for American Indians: health and health care, social and community context, education, economic stability, and neighborhood and built environment.[57]

Recommendations

Climate Change and Energy

The issue looming over the future of New Mexico and the planet is climate change. Only time will tell whether the year 2014 was part of multiyear drought or the beginning of Armageddon. New Mexico tribes are not merely large landowners. The sacred mountains of the Navajos and Apaches, the Blue Lake of Taos Pueblo, the shrines in the Jemez and Manzano Mountains, and other places and aspects of religious and cultural life are inseparably bound up with the ancestral homelands of New Mexico tribes, which they have refused to abandon through five hundred years of occupation by, war with, and cooperation with non-Indians. Climate change must be addressed by Indian tribes with the same ferocity and determination that Coronado encountered almost five hundred years ago. Regarding this issue, however, all New Mexicans should be on the same side.

The Navajo Nation has developed an economy dependent on coal-fired power plants. New Mexico itself has developed an economy that is dependent on fossil fuel production. The state and the tribe share an interest in exploring clean-coal technologies, in developing all renewable forms of energy, and in bringing energy policy making back into the hands of New Mexicans. Wall Street arbitrageurs and Florida-based utility conglomerates should not be permitted to purchase New Mexico's economic and climactic future.

New Mexico should require its utilities to purchase power generated by projects like the proposed five-hundred-megawatt To'hajiilee Tribe's solar project and the Jemez Pueblo wind and geothermal projects.

When it comes to saving our planet, no longer can the federal, state, and tribal governments keep to their separate boundaries and interests and find refuge in jurisdictional limitations. Just as the Jicarilla Apaches once used money from mining their forest resources to seed a sustainable livestock operation, both the tribes and the state should agree to dedicate a portion of their current gaming revenues to developing a sustainable, renewable energy future for New Mexico.

Education

New Mexico bears a huge and primary responsibility for the education of New Mexico children, including Indian children within the state. All indications point to that responsibility not being discharged well. Numerous studies that indicate ways to improve childhood education should be adopted by both the state and the tribes in a way that requires more accountability than the federal No Child Left Behind Act.

Studies from other countries, as well as the United States, indicate that children who learn more than one language learn more, learn more quickly, continue the learning process longer, and retain more of what they learn than those in a monolingual environment. Native languages should be made part of the curriculum throughout New Mexico, utilizing fluent Native speakers along with digital-age technologies.

Tribes should demand accountability from the state's educational system in a way that does not reward underperforming teachers and administrators. The federal government should tie a state's right to benefit from tribal gaming revenues or severance taxes to actual achievement in the education of the tribe's children. Tribes should tie per capita distributions and other monetary benefits to school attendance and performance. Inattention to a critical education deficit is a slow-acting poison pill for tribal societies in the twenty-first century.

Health

New Mexico possesses incredibly detailed information about the health deficits of its various population groups. As noted, *Healthy People 2020* identifies five areas that are determinants of health—health care, social and community context, education economic stability, and neighborhood and built environment. New Mexico tribes have made enormous contributions in terms of the last of these, the built environment. Recreational facilities, schools, sports complexes, elder centers, and road and trail complexes have proliferated with the advent of gaming revenues. But the state and the tribes should now jointly devise an emergency-response plan to deal with the epidemiological aspects of diabetes, obesity, substance abuse, and prenatal care among New Mexico Indians. Indian health facilities throughout the state should be required to serve non-Indian New Mexicans in their service areas.

General

New Mexico and the Indian tribes should work together to address jointly not just global but national forces and influences that will significantly affect the state's future. Internet gaming will pose a threat to brick-and-mortar gaming facilities. New Mexico and the tribes should fashion a unified, New Mexico response to this potential development. New Mexico tribes must abandon the stepchild role and demonstrate the responsibility of eldest child and the wisdom of elder citizen that their role requires in the twenty-first century. Neither the state nor the tribes can afford the luxury of ascribing responsibility for failure to the other. We are in this together. Knowing what we know, benign neglect is active participation in a suicide pact.

New Mexico 2050

Economic Outlook

If 2014 conditions are a harbinger of a climate change of the magnitude that drove the Pueblo ancestors from Chaco Canyon, New Mexico's Indian tribes will be positioned to manage or adapt to the changed climate as well or better than most New Mexicans. They do own land that will permit food production and subsistence living longer than will be possible for their urbanized neighbors. Their forests will suffer and may even disappear. Their senior water rights will be increasingly valuable, either for use or for barter. Their energy resources will still be valuable to distant communities. Their vibrant cultures will still attract tourists to the state. Their gaming operations will be among the last commercial enterprises to close their doors, as long as they are legal under federal law.

The U.S. Geological Survey reports that the water of the Colorado River may be inadequate by 2016 to meet the full allocations of water to the seven states that share the river. New Mexico Indian tribes will enjoy claims to the available water that will be senior and superior to those of many other potential water users. Climate change will pose threats that New Mexico's Indian tribes and their non-Indian fellow New Mexicans will have to face together.

Political Outlook

New Mexico Indian tribes and communities have considerable and growing political influence in New Mexico politics and public affairs—far above what might ordinarily be expected given their relatively small share of the state's population. This is a result of two causes. First, New Mexico Indian tribes and communities have high levels of voting registration and, generally, a relatively high voter turnout as well. Second, with the advent of money-making tribal casinos in New Mexico, the tribes and communities have become a source of substantial campaign contributions to political candidates. This Indian political influence will continue, even though there may be some leveling off in the growth of casino income.

At least in presidential-election years, with high voter turnout, New Mexico has moved reliably into the Democratic column. Particularly in presidential elections, New Mexico Indian tribes and communities have themselves become reliably Democratic. There is no reason to believe that this Indian Democratic trend will not continue in the future.

General

New Mexico Indian tribes are putting their own resources to work to develop their communities. Revenues from gaming activities have financed community facilities such as libraries, health and wellness centers, elder care homes, preschool development centers, and first-responder capabilities. In northern New Mexico, it is often Indian responders who are the first available to rescue stranded snowmobilers and skiers and lost hunters. Tribes are bringing broadband services to their reservations, and some are even negotiating with the same digital-language-learning companies that the federal government uses to provide foreign-language training to diplomats and military personnel. The tribes, however, are contemplating Internet-based learning as a means of preserving their own languages for a generation that increasingly spends more time online than at their grandparents' knees.

New Mexico's tribes have for centuries been blessed with abundant resources that the larger society is only today learning fully to appreciate.

Tribal hunting programs bring millions of dollars per year into New Mexico, with hunters coming from several continents for the trophy-size big game that the tribes are managing on a sustainable basis. Literally millions of trees have been planted on reservation mountainsides where railroads were once built to service the virtual mining of forest products, with no thought to regeneration. Today, despite the devastating effects of beetle infestation, thrifty stands of mixed-species, uneven-aged reservation timber are repopulating mountains once virtually denuded. This silvicultural regime is designed to produce a sustainable forest products resource that may well be more valuable someday than New Mexico's vast coal, oil, gas, and uranium resources that have fueled the western United States for more than a century.

New Mexico tribes' renewable energy resource base will be increasingly important to the energy picture of the state. Even the current oil and gas boom based on new hydraulic fracturing techniques will not result in another one hundred years of cheap energy; those resources will be depleted in one or two generations. Incredibly dramatic changes in the economics of renewable energy production will make renewable energy resources increasingly valuable over the remaining few generations of cheap fossil fuels. New Mexico's tribes will contribute their resources to that new energy paradigm, and this time they will not be colonized but will be active developers, marketers, and masters of their own energy picture. No longer will Indian homes sit atop vast energy resources that go to heat and cool homes in San Diego while the Indian family in New Mexico travels farther and farther afield to gather firewood to stave off the bone-chilling cold of New Mexico winters. The same renewable energy that will be exported from the reservations will be available to the Indian homes whose lands provide it.

The tribes will increasingly be served and represented by members of their own communities in business, in the professions, and in the councils of the state, where Indians have already served in both chambers of the legislature. The tribes will make their contributions, their recommendations, and even their demands known more effectively as their contributions to the state's coffers, history, traditions, and future are increasingly understood by the non-Indian citizens of New Mexico.

There will be greater migration from the Indian reservation communities to urban areas, following the trend of New Mexico becoming more metropolitan than rural. Only if New Mexico tribes devote larger amounts of their revenue streams to the support of public school programs, health education for prevention of major diseases like diabetes, and social programs that address issues like domestic violence and alcoholism will there be substantial improvement in the quality of life on reservations and Indian communities, permitting their members to remain on reservations. In this respect, the state of New Mexico has to restrain itself from putting up legal barriers through its legislative powers to move the tribe's gaming dollars from tribal coffers to its own. The great strides and progress made in the last three decades in tribal economies have been possible because of their gaming revenues.

The New Mexico Indian tribes and the state of New Mexico will become active partners in improving the educational, health, and social conditions in New Mexico's Indian country. Sharing responsibility for addressing common problems will become the rule, rather than the exception. Indian health facilities, for example, will serve non-Indian patients who today have to drive past perfectly good Indian clinics to reach non-Indian facilities hours away. Similarly, Indians drive hundreds of miles from their homes in the cities to reach Indian clinics on the reservation.

In 2050 New Mexico will be a model envied by other states for recognizing the value, appreciating the contributions, and cherishing the history, traditions, and culture of the indigenous tribes that have always given the state much of its unique character. New Mexico's tribes in 2050 will be very much a part of New Mexico but will continue to maintain the ways they carried on and to speak the languages they spoke when Coronado arrived around five hundred years ago. The tribes and the state will be complementary, separate sovereigns sharing the splendor that makes New Mexico the Land of Enchantment.

Notes

1. Roxanne Dunbar-Ortiz, *An Indigenous Peoples' History of the United States* (Boston, MA: Beacon Press, 2014), 31.

2. Marta Weigle, Frances Levine, and Louise Stiver, *Telling New Mexico: A New History* (Santa Fe: Museum of New Mexico Press, 2009), 210–15.

3. Edward H. Spicer, *Cycles of Conquest: The Impact of Spain, México, and the United States on the Indians of the Southwest, 1533–1960* (Tucson: University of Arizona Press, 1962), 283–85.

4. Joe S. Sando, *Pueblo Nations* (Santa Fe, NM: Clear Light, 1992), 92–94.

5. Veronica E. Tiller, ed., *Tiller's Guide to Indian Country: Economic Profiles of American Indian Reservations* (Albuquerque: BowArrow, 2005), 326.

6. Morris E. Opler, "The Mescalero Apache," in *Handbook of North American Indians*, vol. 10, *Southwest*, ed. Alfonso Ortiz (Washington, D.C.: Smithsonian Institution, 1983), 419–39.

7. Tiller, *Tiller's Guide*, 736.

8. Veronica E. Tiller and Mary M. Velarde, *The Jicarilla Apache of Dulce* (Charleston, SC: Arcadia, 2012), 7.

9. Fred Harris and Laura Harris, "American Indians and Tribal Governments," in *Governing New Mexico*, ed. F. Chris Garcia, Paul L. Hain, Gilbert K. St. Clair, and Kim Seckler (Albuquerque: University of New Mexico Press, 2006), 193–95.

10. Mark Fogarty, "Gaming at NM Indian Casinos increased in 2011," *Albuquerque Business First*, February 27, 2013, www.bizjournals.com/albuquerque/news/2013/02/27/gaming-at-nm-casinos-increased-in-2011.html.

11. David Aberle, "Navajo Economic Development," in Ortiz, *Handbook*, vol. 10, *Southwest*, 641–58.

12. Arizona Cooperative Extension, College of Agriculture and Life Sciences, "The Navajo Nation and Extension Programs," publication AZ1470, October 2008, p. 3, http://extension.arizona.edu/sites/extension.arizona.edu/files/pubs/az1470.pdf. See also Navajo Nation data, 2000 U.S. Census, chart 1.

13. See James A. Vlasich, *Pueblo Indian Agriculture* (Albuquerque: University of New Mexico Press, 2005), 133.

14. Ibid., 135.

15. Ibid., 165.

16. Ibid., 184.

17. Ibid., 284.

18. Judith E. Jacobsen, "Navajo Indian Irrigation Project and Quantification of Navajo *Winters* Rights," *Natural Resources Journal* 32 (1992): 831–51.

19. Richard A. Bruckner, *Jicarilla Apache Forestry: A History of Timber Management, Forest Development and Forest Protection on the Jicarilla Apache Reservation, 1887–1994* (Dulce, NM: Jicarilla Agency, Branch of Forestry, 1995), 352.

20. Ibid.

21. Tiller, *Tiller's Guide*, 736.

22. Ibid., 329.

23. Joint Stipulation for Entry of Judgment, *Pueblo of Isleta v. United States*, Fed. Cl. Docket 96–166L, December 15, 2006 (Docket Entry 180-4, p.3), incorporated in Judgment, *Pueblo v. U.S.*, Docket Entry 182, December 18, 2006.

24. Adélamar Alcántara, "Implications of a Growing Population and Changing Demographics in New Mexico," in *Beyond the Year of Water: Living Within Our Water Limitations* (Las Cruces: New Mexico Water Resources Research Institute, 2007), 46.

25. Arizona Cooperative Extension, "Navajo Nation and Extension Programs," 3. See also Navajo Nation data, 2000 U.S. Census, chart 1.

26. Navajo Nation, Department of Water Resources, *Draft Water Resource Development Strategy for the Navajo Nation*, July 2011, 2, http://www. tribesandclimatechange.org/docs/tribes_357.pdf.

27. Theodore Jojola et al., *Indian Education in New Mexico, 2025* (Santa Fe: New Mexico Public Education Department, Indian Education Division, June 30, 2010), 8.

28. Ibid., 6.

29. See total land figures for the tribes in the New Mexico section of Tiller, *Tiller's Guide*, 717–74.

30. "Climate Impacts in the Southwest," U.S. Environmental Protection Agency, Climate Change Southwest, accessed March 5, 2014, http://www.epa.gov/ climatechange/impacts-adaptation/southwest.html.

31. Agency Technical Work Group, State of New Mexico, *Potential Effects of Climate Change on New Mexico* (Santa Fe, 2005), www.nmenv.state.nm.us/aqb/cc/Potential_Effects_Climate_Change_NM.pdf.

32. Bryan Bird, Mary O'Brien, and Mike Petersen, *Beaver and Climate Change Adaptation in North America* (Wild Earth Guardians, September 2011), 6, http://www.wildearthguardians.org/site/DocServer/Beaver_and_Climate_Change_Final.pdf?docID=3482.

33. "Climate Impacts in the Southwest."

34. Michael Osborn, "American Indian Water Rights," updated by Susuan Kelly, 2011, and by Darcy Bushnell, 2013, in *Water Matters!* (Albuquerque: Utton Transboundary Resources Center, 2013), 6-1–6-5, http://uttoncenter.unm.edu/projects/water-matters.php.

35. Title V, Taos Pueblo Indian Water Rights, Claims Resolution Act of 2010, Pub. L. No. 111-291, 124 Stat. 3064 at 3122.

36. Leah Glazer, *Navajo Indian Irrigation Project* (U.S. Bureau of Reclamation, 1998), 13, http://www.usbr.gov/projects/ImageServer?imgName=Doc_1305123940539.pdf.

37. Claims Resolution Act of 2010, 124 Stat. at 3122.

38. "Executive Summary," San Juan River Basin, New Mexico Navajo Nation Water Rights Settlement, April 19, 2005, http://www.ose.state.nm.us/Legal/settlements/NNWRS/index.php.

39. Northwestern New Mexico Rural Water Projects Act (Navajo-Gallup Water Supply Project/Navajo Water Rights), Pub. L. No. 111-11, 123 Stat 1376 at 1386 (2009).

40. U.S. Department of the Interior, Bureau of Reclamation, "Reclamation Managing Water in the West," http://recovery.doi.gov/press/bureaus/bureau-of-reclamation/.

41. Bird, O'Brien, and Petersen, *Beaver and Climate Change Adaptation*.

42. Susan Matlock, "Los Alamos Researcher: Dire Forecast for State's Forest," *New Mexican*, October 8, 2013.

43. U.S. Department of the Interior, Bureau of Indian Affairs, Division of Forestry, Branch of Forest Resources, *A Summary of Trust Forested Reservations, Southwest Region* (2013), 311–13.

44. "Climate Impacts in the Southwest: Impacts on Forests and Other Ecosystems," U.S. Environmental Protection Agency, Climate Change Southwest, accessed March 5, 2014, www.epa.gov/climatechange/impacts-adaptation/southwest.html#impactsecosystems.

45. Dan Frosch, "Amid Toxic Waste, a Navajo Village Could Lose Its Land," *New York Times*, February 19, 2014, http://nyti.ms/1crNjFk.

46. "NPL Site Narrative for Jackpile-Paguate Uranium Mine," U.S. Environmental Protection Agency, National Priorities List, accessed March 7, 2014, www.epa.gov/superfund/sites/npl/nar1865.htm.

47. Dan Schwartz, "PNM Files to Decommission San Juan Generating Station's Two Stacks," *Farmington (AZ) Daily Times*, December 27, 2013.

48. Laura Paskus, "The Life and Death of Desert Rock," *High Country News*, August 13, 2010, www.hcn.org/articles/the-life-and-death-of-desert-rock. See also "Desert Rock," Center for Media and Democracy, SourceWatch, accessed March 6, 2014, www.sourcewatch.org/index.php/Desert_Rock.

49. "2010SY 40th Day Enrollment by District, by Ethnicity," School Fact Sheets, New Mexico Public Education Department, www.ped.state.nm.us/it/schoolfactsheets.html.

50. Ibid.

51. U.S. Nuclear Regulatory Commission, "Description of the Affected Environment, Northwestern New Mexico Uranium Milling Region," Section 3.1.10.6: Education, in U.S. Nuclear Regulatory Commission, *Generic Environmental Impact Statement for In-Situ Leach Uranium Milling Facilities*, NUREG-1910, vol. 1, p. 3.5–76, www.nrc.gov/reading-rm/doc-collections/nuregs/staff/sr1910/v1/ch3-sec35.pdf. See also Jojola et al., *Indian Education in New Mexico*, 26–27.

52. Jojola et al., *Indian Education in New Mexico*, 1.

53. Ibid.

54. See New Mexico Public Education Department, *District Accountability Report 2011–12 for Gallup-McKinley County, District 43, Dulce Independent Schools, District 54, and Zuni Public Schools, District 39* (Santa Fe, 2012).

55. "2004–2005 Indian Education Status Report," New Mexico Public Education Department, http://sde.state.nm.us/IT/schoolFactSheets.html.

56. New Mexico Department of Health, *American Indian Health Equity: A Report on Racial and Ethnic Health Disparities in New Mexico* (Santa Fe: New Mexico Department of Health, Office of Policy and Accountability, Office of Heath Equity, October 2013), http://nmhealth.org/publication/view/report/44/.

57. *Healthy People 2020* as cited in New Mexico Department of Health, *American Indian Health Equity.*

Chapter 7

New Mexico Cultural Affairs and the Arts

V. B. PRICE

IN 2014 NEW MEXICO WAS, BY MOST ACCOUNTS, ONE OF THE poorest states in the union when it came to its economy. At the same time it was a state with vast creative and cultural resources, rich beyond reckoning with the talent and devotion to craft of many thousands of its citizens. New Mexico has perhaps more creative talent, per capita, than any other state. Albuquerque alone has some forty theater groups, a world-class lithography studio in the Tamarind Institute, one of the very few 24/7 classical music stations left in the country, hundreds of poets, including those who won the National Poetry Slam in 2005, one of the biggest, most aggressive public arts programs in the nation, and scores of painters and sculptors, including those who contributed to the brilliant One Million Bones project generated in New Mexico and displayed along the National Mall in Washington, D.C.

With the state's population having flattened out over the last five years at just about 2 million or under—or about seventeen people per square mile in the nation's fifth-largest state—that's a remarkable record.

And that is truly the tip of the iceberg. The Anderson Museum of Contemporary Art in Roswell, with its Artist in Residency Program, has regularly on display some three hundred works of art, many by New Mexicans. Some consider it one of the best fine arts museums in the West. Santa Fe's magnificent museum system, emphasizing New Mexico's creative genius, and its internationally acclaimed opera are without parallel in the country. Taos and its historic creative community still thrive. The Gallup Inter-Tribal

Indian Ceremonial has given the world a glimpse into the richness of Native American creative culture in New Mexico for well over fifty years. And the National Hispanic Cultural Center in Albuquerque celebrates the genius of indigenous Hispanic New Mexico and the Latino world.

The sad and difficult reality for many people of talent in New Mexico, however, is that despite their enormous gifts and the world-class work that they do, they belong to an economic underclass barely keeping its head above water. If creative people are not associated with colleges and universities or other cultural institutions such as museums, libraries, and cultural centers, chances are they have an intimate knowledge of poverty and no social safety net to speak of, as most creative people are self-employed.

New Mexico Income Inequality

Poverty in New Mexico is aggravated by our urban-rural political divisions and our fundamentally tolerant but conservative social attitudes that strive to shrink government and its services. The relative prosperity in Albuquerque, Santa Fe, Los Alamos, Rio Rancho, and Las Cruces, where as much as 70 percent of the state's population resides, is offset by the brutal poverty in rural farming and ranching country in New Mexico, with its threadbare little towns and hardscrabble counties, and the largely impoverished Native American reservations, all, however, with their forms of creative riches.

As of 2013 New Mexico had the greatest income disparity between the top and the bottom and the top and the middle of any state in the nation. Self-employed arts and creative workers added greatly to that disparity. If you play in one of the state's major orchestras, for instance, you're lucky to make $17,000 a year—meaning, of course, that musicians must be entrepreneurs and basically subcontractors, working for as many companies as they can find at once.

New Mexico was behind only Mississippi in having the greatest increases in income inequality between the top and the middle through the 1990s and into the twenty-first century, according to the *Washington Post*.[1] Our unemployment rate was at 6.6 percent in October 2013. Nearly 20 percent of New Mexico's population was living under the poverty level from 2008 to 2012, according to the U.S. Census Bureau, and New Mexico ranked forty-third in the country in per capita annual income in 2012. (See chapter 1 for more details about New Mexico income inequality.)

New Mexico Income Inequality and the Arts

How can we be as poor and sparsely populated as we are and still have such a relatively enormous creative and scholarly community in our state? This curious contrast has come to be a perennial matter of discussion. It could be because of what Albuquerque mayor David Rusk defined in the late 1970s as the attraction of New Mexico, what he called "psychic wages." He meant, I assume, the unparalleled beauty of our physical landscape, our small population, and the synergistic power of our multicultural traditions. But there is more to it than that, of course.

Creative people I've talked to over the years say pretty much the same thing. They do great work in this cultural and ecological context. The New Mexican sense of place, itself, generates creative energy for many of us. And it's true across the board, from our undernourished but extraordinarily accessible and informative cultural institutions to our communities of visual, literary, musical, and performance artists; the arts and humanities departments of our colleges and universities; and our large number of nonprofit arts organizations that help to create a world of music and theater that delight New Mexicans year after year.

Drought and the Worsening Economy

The arts have always had staying power. And they will need it in New Mexico in the future. With a protracted and historic drought settling into its fourteenth year in 2014, the state's rural economy seems more precarious than ever. (See chapter 5 for more details on New Mexico drought conditions and effects.)

Entire food-producing industries are endangered in southern New Mexico, including the dairy and cattle industries, not to mention the crops of pecan, chile, pistachio, and onion farmers. The drought is affecting traditional ideas

of sprawl development in urban areas as well. The lack of water and the slug-
gish housing market have come close to crippling growth in Albuquerque and
Rio Rancho's economies, upon which many individual artists, writers, and
performers depend. The general economic climate affects them as much as it
does small shopkeepers. But the economy of the arts and cultural affairs,
embodied in nonprofit arts organizations, has a substantial impact on the
state's economic well-being, though not as substantial as agriculture and the
construction industry.

Even though organized creative enterprises in New Mexico seem to be
booming, many artists, writers, musicians, dancers, and actors have, since the
Great Recession of 2007–2009, sunk ever deeper into dire economic straits,
not to mention the state's architects, whose profession almost went under after
the recession.

Because economic developers tend not to see the arts and cultural institutions as part of a state's economic engine, figures that would verify the
economic impact of the arts are not consistently collected or presented to the
public. It's not that the arts and cultural institutions could rival the oil and
gas industry or real estate speculation as sources of revenue for the state. But
the full scope of the contribution that the arts make to New Mexico's economy and quality of life remains largely unexplored. Unlike fossil fuels or
nuclear research or construction and housing development, the arts and cultural enterprises are composed of perhaps a dozen or more separate art forms
and cultural institutions. Collecting data on all of them has not yet been
mastered by the state or by leading arts organizations and arts advocates.
And information on the economic plight and ongoing struggles of creative
people is, to my knowledge, simply not being gathered.

Creative Workers

We need an overarching definition of cultural affairs and the arts in New
Mexico in order to understand the combined potential of the full spectrum
of creative talent and humanities-oriented scholarship in our state, as well as
the economic deprivation that many creative people face. I propose that this
spectrum comprises what I'd call creative workers. This group would include

nonprofit arts organization administrators and bureaucrats; museum and library professionals; cultural scholars and historic preservationists; public arts administrators; volunteers and docents at cultural institutions; literary, music, theater, and arts faculty in primary, secondary, and higher education; architects, landscape architects, and related faculty; actors, costume and set designers, makeup artists, and other workers at theatrical companies; workers in the film-making industry and related arts and crafts; dancers and dance company workers; singers, musicians, and composers in opera companies, orchestras, and other ensembles and their administrators; members of popular bands and singers of all genres; poets, fiction writers, and nonfiction writers; staff at book publishing companies and local bookstores; photographers and their suppliers; and painters, printmakers, lithographers, sculptors, and other visual artists. This doesn't mention chefs, jewelry artists, craftspeople of all kinds, and clothes designers.

In 2014 this mélange made up a vibrant community of artistic people, scholars, and administrators, a happy chaos of creativity and independence with little awareness of common interests and no overall strategies to improve their lot in the future.

This is partly due to the general invisibility of income inequality in the community of cultural workers. Those associated with universities, museums, libraries, and other institutions, or those arts administrators who run the major musical organizations, have mainstream incomes and a social safety net. Those artists, writers, and musicians who work on "spec" and are not associated with institutions have no such safety net and often struggle fruitlessly in the marketplace. Those who manage to thrive, often with multiple streams of income if they are lucky, work at teaching and performing to keep their creative enterprise alive. But the arts are not businesses. They are a calling for almost everyone involved. So, compensated adequately or not, poets continue making poems, violinists continue perfecting their technique, painters work in their studios, and museum curators continue to do double time or triple time to give their institutions exhibitions they can take pride in.

The work is what is important. And often, not because of a lack of initiative but because the market does not value what they do, creative people struggle financially even when doing their best work. Most artists, working in any medium, who are not affiliated with an institution are underpaid, under-respected, under-protected, and living, by the standards of the mainstream, an almost second-class existence. Just because many artists and writers have a calling doesn't mean they like living in penury or doing their creative and financial balancing acts without a safety net.

Arts and the Quality of Life

Even though our data is inadequate, we know from what information we have that the arts contribute a considerable amount to New Mexico's overall economy. But there is no way I know of at the moment to quantify its contribution to our overall quality of life. It doesn't take too great a leap of imagination to contemplate how dismal our world would be without music, without two-dimensional or three-dimensional design, without poets and novelists writing about their places and lives, without actors, without clothes designers, without the culinary arts in full flower or an architectural tradition that increases our enjoyment and sensitivity to the use of space. Where would the education of our children be without direct experiences of the visual and performing arts? Not to mention the curatorial genius that gives patrons of historical museums a chance to experience the past in ways that reading, as wonderful as it is, cannot capture?

The business community, of course, gets a huge freebie from the arts community. The value of that boost to business is next to impossible, under present thinking, to quantify. The best thing to say at the moment is that cities without a vibrant cultural and artistic life are dismal and depressing places and, aside from providing material necessities, would have no attractive or magnetic value with which to lure new businesses. And without the arts, local businesses would find themselves in the awkward position of trying to become "cultural and artistic" themselves in order to draw customers to them.

The Impact of the Cultural Environment and the Creative Economy

The best major study that I know of on the impact of the arts and cultural environment on New Mexico's economy was carried out by the Western

States Arts Federation. The results were published in 2005.[2] The study concerned itself exclusively with the state's "estimated 200 nonprofit arts organizations." It said that those organizations "spend more than $63 million in the New Mexico economy," employ 852 persons on a full-time basis and 1,484 persons on a part-time basis, and "underwrite more than 2,500 part-time contracted work positions in the state." In addition, nonprofit arts organizations "attract more than $6 million in contributed goods and services," are the "recipients of more than 670,936 volunteer hours," and "attract nearly 800,000 paid attendees to cultural events."

The report contended that nonprofit arts groups made free attendance and "complimentary youth services available to more than one million New Mexicans and New Mexico visitors." And it added that the groups "play a strong role in attracting out-of-state visitors to New Mexico, in some cases representing 50% of all paid admissions." Finally, the organizations "consistently funnel support for New Mexico's building industry by supporting new construction and renovation projects averaging approximately $10 million per year."

A more recent report, from 2012, describes "the state of the creative economy" in Albuquerque. The study was conducted by Creative Albuquerque, a nonprofit, with help from the Western States Arts Federation and was commissioned by the City of Albuquerque Cultural Services Department.[3] It's not possible to compare this study with the earlier one. The categories of analysis are not the same, and the target population is only Bernalillo County in the 2012 report.

But this 2012 study had this to say about sales figures: "For-profit arts generated $142,693,000 in revenue and sales in 2010, with $74,219,000 of that coming from 'individual artists' sales.'" In 2010 Albuquerque's "non-profit arts organizations and their audiences generated $91.9 million in economic activity, supported 3,674 full-time equivalent jobs, provided $87.8 million in household income to local residents, and delivered $121.6 million in state and local government revenue." The study also found that Albuquerque and Bernalillo County had a higher than average number of people "participating in cultural activities. The county has a high number of artists and arts businesses, signaling a strong but highly competitive arts sector." Arts business in the county is about twice the national average, the report asserted.

Compared to the contribution of the arts in Oklahoma City, Salt Lake City, Tucson, and Wichita, "cities routinely used to benchmark Albuquerque performance," our area, while doing well, "is not thriving when looked at in context with comparable locales." Based on these and other findings, the 2012 report laid out a three-step call to action:

- Recognize and cultivate the synergy between the business and the arts and culture communities.
- Rethink, revision, and rebrand Albuquerque to value our many assets.
- Engage specific leadership from across the community and the region to make action happen.

Where Are We Now?

The third step in the call to action above seems to be the most relevant here. In 2014 the creative community was dominated, in public at least, by non-profit arts administrators and their boards, which are composed, in part, of nonartists and businesspeople. That means that arts leadership is spread out over possibly some two hundred organizations. Because individual artists are not represented by unions or cooperative organizations of their own, a huge part of the creative community is leaderless, with the exception of a few altruistic public personalities who speak up for their art forms and some particularly aggressive nonprofit leaders and organizers.

POLITICAL LEADERSHIP

Political leadership supporting the arts appears to be submerged or muted. In the 2014 legislative session, a bill that would create a poet laureate for New Mexico, while it had a lot of backing, was referred to a study group for the next year, and that in a state with probably thousands of poets and with poet laureates in both Santa Fe and Albuquerque who have focused attention on poetry with amazing success. No state politician that I know of has staked out the arts and cultural affairs as his or her special area of interest and expertise.

ECONOMIC LEADERSHIP

The arts community needs leadership guided by artists and by those who concern themselves with the role of the arts in economic development. While some civic leaders give lip service to the economic necessity of supporting the arts, no organization that I know of actively lobbies for cultural workers, who are often small-business people involved in sales and the marketing of their talents, who work as contractors or part-time employees, or who are grantees. Creative leadership is dispersed and self-interested, competing for scant funds, following a business model rather than the model of creative guilds, which protected the welfare of their individual members.

New Mexico Department of Cultural Affairs

While there is no single organization that covers the full range of the efforts of cultural workers in our state, New Mexico Arts, part of the Department of Cultural Affairs, is the state agency that makes grants and oversees to some extent nonprofit arts organizations in the state. It has considerable reach but is nothing like a galvanizing influence to bring all the arts together to pursue common interests. The Department of Cultural Affairs oversees New Mexico's superb museum system.

The department is run by a cabinet secretary and so is highly politicized and operates, by and large, at the whim of the governor. But its constituency is statewide and includes members of all political parties, so there is a citizen-based check-and-balance system that has kept the executive branch attentive over the years to building and maintaining the state's museum system.

NEW MEXICO ARTS

New Mexico Arts itself is advised and overseen by the New Mexico Arts Commission, a body of some fifteen members who are appointed by the governor. From my experience the public has no actual awareness of the commission as an advocate for the arts.

NEW MEXICO MUSIC COMMISSION

There is also a New Mexico Music Commission, which is also appointed by the governor and works to promote the state's vast, but largely hidden, music community. Its major accomplishment at the moment is maintaining the New Mexico Music Directory, a "database of musicians and services supporting the music industry in the state." The Music Commission, while a state operation, is impoverished, without sufficient funds even to hire an executive director. So its promotional efforts are still largely invisible.

Albuquerque Public Arts Program

The City of Albuquerque's Public Arts Program, with its 817 works of art around town, is funded through a levy of 1 percent of the cost of construction projects added on. The program is a great example of what a supercharged leader can do for an enterprise, especially one like Sherri Bruggemann, who manages public arts and understands the enormous power of what 1 percent can do.

Leadership and Funding

The keys to the future are leadership and funding, along with development of an overarching esprit de corps among all artists, writers, performers, and cultural institutions and organizations. There is no such group spirit in New Mexico, though the state's small population makes it possible for such unity to flourish. The arts and cultural affairs remain either the domain of a large number of creative small-business people or of government, which supports and oversees nonprofit arts organizations and public cultural institutions. Private creative workers are not organized, as I've said, nor do they have a supportive relationship with many of the institutions that should be reaching out to them but can't do it with their current state of understaffing and underfunding.

When it comes to understanding the economic reality of the arts—both the extent to which the arts make an important contribution to the overall economy and the actual economic condition and status of cultural workers themselves—the creative community is trying to chart a course through murky waters without an adequate map. The existing surveys seem to be little more than booster signboards to be carried into funding meetings: "The Arts Matter." Of course they do.

Fragmented information gathered and disseminated without standard categories with which to compare cities, or even art forms, is but marginally useful. And existing studies say little to nothing about what might actually be needed to boost the arts and their contribution to the general welfare. No one knows, for instance, how much more of a boost to the local economy the arts could give if they and their cultural workers received tax benefits and other considerations commensurate with other economic engines in the state, such as the oil and gas industry.

FUNDING

When it comes to funding in general, it is worthwhile to note that arts organizations and individual creative entrepreneurs, along with all other cultural workers, may have an invigorating influence on the general business community and the general economy. Unhappily, this fact doesn't always translate into much economic benefit for the creative workers and arts organizations. One could say, without exaggeration, that creative workers are an exploited class, used to make other people money without reaping much reward themselves. Percent for the Arts programs are an important innovation in arts funding, but they really are, from my perspective, the only such innovation on the scene. Public funding of museums and libraries, grants and private funding for arts organizations, and the hardscrabble existence of small-business artists, writers, and performers leave all parts of the world of culture workers in a precarious economic situation, with no innovation in sight.

While creative excellence flourishes in New Mexico, it does so in a relative state of penury that mirrors, I am sure, the condition in other states but is made worse than most by New Mexico's overall condition of economic desperation and environmental hardship. And while the rest of New Mexico's economy tends to exploit the arts and creative workers, perhaps without really knowing it, the culture worker community is not organized internally, so it cannot lobby and market on its own behalf. It has no common agenda, nor a common bond, nor a sense of community among the disparate fields and institutions.

Cultural and arts workers are, in fact, a kind of subculture. They are people who share an aesthetic and an intellectual worldview that often isolate them from the rest of America's anti-intellectual and materialist culture. That they don't recognize their inherent bond as a class of creative people has as much to do with the American culture of competition as it does with the energy and focus it takes for individuals and organizations to survive in the arts. Competition among creative people is an anomalous and really fruitless idea. It just doesn't apply, except in the wonderful arena of slam poetry competitions. But slam's competitiveness is a form of drama. The bond among slam poets, and the coherence within the slam community, is more important than competition in the long run.

As with all aspects of culture, it's cooperation that offers the greatest potential for efforts to not only lobby government and fundraise in innovative ways but also to engage the mainstream culture in establishing a more respectful and less exploitative context within which to work. This is as true for artists who depend on galleries for sales at the cost of sometimes 60 percent of a sale itself as it is for writers who depend on agents who, in exchange for exorbitant cuts from sales, act as gatekeepers to weed out those they deem to have marginal financial potential in the marketplace, with little thought of literary excellence, equating success with sales.

Not only are creative workers fragmented by discipline and affiliation but their cooperative powers are undercut by geography. An esprit de corps is hard to build in a state with the fifth-largest land area in the country and very little public transportation. In-state regionalism and even regional competition is often driven as much by distance as by various chambers of commerce.

The Border Book Festival is largely a southern New Mexico phenomenon, for instance. The Santa Fe Indian Market attracts mostly northern and central New Mexicans. The Santa Fe Opera draws locally from Albuquerque and Santa Fe, and the Silver City Arts and Cultural District draws interested people from southwestern New Mexico. There is no "state fair" of arts and culture in New Mexico.

In short, the arts, and culture scene in New Mexico in 2014 is at once a world of great energy and genius; a world of economic frailty, instability, and often impoverishment; and a world that is disorganized, with no sense of common purpose or common need.

What's To Be Done?

What would it take to give cultural workers and the world of creativity that they inhabit greater financial security, greater impact on the overall economy, a wider audience for their talents, a greater opportunity to contribute to the social good, and a more intimate presence in the physical and mental landscape of New Mexico?

What would it take to give creative workers and their institutions greater political clout and freedom from virtually complete dependence on government for funding? What would it take to give individual artists some social safety net to help them while they mine the marketplace for clients and publishers in an arts economy that is still suffering from the arts and culture bubble collapsing in the 1980s, from radical changes in publishing and in the recording industry, and from the absence of corporate sponsorship and funding?

I have nine recommendations.

Find New Sources of Funding That Recognize the Value of the Arts to Other Businesses and to the General Quality of Life

To liberate arts and cultural enterprises from exclusive reliance on bare-bones, nonprofit granting sources or largely fruitless competition in a marketplace dominated by East and West Coast interests and a dying gallery and agenting system in which galleries take huge commissions and agents act as gatekeepers, the state of New Mexico could look to Percent for the Arts programs as an imaginative funding innovation. Using Percent for the Arts as a model, the state could create a constellation of small taxes and fees to support the role that the arts and cultural enterprises play in enhancing the quality of life and business potential of our state. A local tax on polluters would be a good place to start. It would relate the world of the arts with the world of environmental protection and would be built around a relationship between the New Mexico Environment Department and the Department of Cultural Affairs. For every act of environmental desecration that is fined, a percentage of the fine would go into a special fund for arts and culture in the state. The money could be earmarked for large arts projects and the New Mexico WPA for the Arts, to be discussed below. Arts organizations and individual artists could volunteer to watchdog environmental polluters, thus contributing to the fund.

This Arts and Culture Fund could also receive 0.025 percent of the gross receipts taxes from every county in the state. A tiny portion of a renewable energy tax rebate, as well as a small take of art's donations, could also contribute to a state Arts and Culture Fund.

I am sure there are many other ways to find small amounts of money that in aggregate would amount to considerable sums to add to the Arts and Culture Fund. This would all take some political doing, but arts and cultural leadership must be cultivated with vigor, on a governmental level and on nonprofit and for-profit levels. The fund could also have a management board to invest existing funds and aggressively seek new sources. With proper lobbying and financial sophistication, new funding sources are largely a matter of legislation.

Create a New Mexico Version of the WPA for the Visual, Literary, and Performing Arts

Creating a state version of the WPA's arts and culture programs could bring considerable prosperity across the board to New Mexico's creative community and its cultural workers. A New Mexico WPA could add to New Mexico's image as a bastion of cultural diversity and excellence in the arts and an oasis of scholarship on the Southwest. It could give a much-needed boost to the architecture, landscape architecture, and planning professions. It could award annual prizes for the performing arts and for major works of public architecture. A New Mexico WPA could fund an intensive effort to record, archive, and disseminate New Mexico's cultural history, which would entail a partnership between the state's museums and libraries, both public and university-affiliated. Building on the model of the New Mexico Humanities Council, the New Mexico WPA could bring literary, musical, and theatrical arts to communities large and small across the state. It could fund up-and-coming visual and literary artists and musicians around the state and produce performances and exhibitions of their work in their hometowns. It could commission original plays, operas, and ballets using New Mexico's musicians and playwrights and could help to create a group of set and costume designers, makeup artists, and lighting craftsmen that would help support New Mexico's film industry. A New Mexico WPA could bring the benefits of the arts to every area in the state and pay hundreds of cultural workers a living wage.

Make a Living Arts State Fair

Using the New Mexico WPA as a funding source and an administrative foundation, state, city, county, and tribal governments could partner with nonprofit performing arts groups and organizations; for-profit artists, craftspeople, and musicians; and other cultural workers to stage an annual Living Arts State Fair, either at the state fairgrounds or roving each year to the site of a county fair. It would combine a celebration of the arts, a marketplace, and a way for creative workers to establish relationships with other professions. It could also serve as a way to provide an audience for talented young people in public school arts programs. The state's colleges and universities, libraries, and museums, as well as professional performing groups, would have to buy into to the fair to give them intellectual authenticity. The fair would come to be a way to build a statewide arts community, and the opportunities it creates would maintain and develop relationships within the community. The fair could become one of the most practical ways to create an influential lobbying group and think tank for the arts. An arts think tank could spend the majority of its time exploring ways to infuse the arts and cultural activities ever more thoroughly into New Mexico's social fabric.

Help Found Cultural Unions, Co-ops, Credit Unions, and Bartering Services

Freelance creative workers, unaffiliated with nonprofit arts organizations, museums, libraries, or institutions of higher learning, need representation and services as well as opportunities to build a sense of solidarity. Achieving this is no easy matter. A New Mexico WPA could provide high-quality and highly visible work for many cultural workers. But more is needed to give this community of creative talent a fair deal. Why should they have such a thing in the first place? Because they contribute to the welfare and well-being of other businesses and jurisdictions in the state without being fairly compensated.

We cannot expect creative workers to enhance New Mexico's economy and reputation if they remain members of a largely impoverished and exploited class. Nongovernmental, membership-based organizations like Creative Albuquerque and Creative New Mexico need to expand their efforts and funding to create the necessary structure for a creative worker's credit union, an online bartering system for artists and performers that would exchange services as well as goods, a cultural union that would represent freelancers in all creative disciplines and provide consultation on intellectual property and contracts, and a state insurance co-op for creative workers.

The arts and culture industry in New Mexico has a relatively large community of workers. With the right advocacy and lobbying, these essential services for freelancers and institutional workers should provide a base for sustainable efforts.

Develop a New Cadre of Arts and Culture Leadership

Developing a cadre of arts and culture leaders with sufficient aesthetic clout and authority to lobby government, private funding sources, financial institutions, and others on behalf of the creative community is no mean task. And who is to do the developing? It really can't be the state, which already has its own leadership issues. Where is the pool of talent to come from? How are such people rewarded, nurtured, and sustained in their efforts?

Leaders need to have a public presence. Well-known writers, painters, musicians, conductors, film and stage directors, academic leaders, heads of libraries and museums, emeritus national politicians, and retired state legislators and governors would form the first pool to look to. But such leadership would probably have to both represent and constitute a cultural organization composed of an exclusively creative and scholarly membership and a governing board. In some ways it might resemble Think New Mexico, a relatively new organization that annually addresses vital issues that affect the arts and creative workers.

Such an organization, and the nurturing of a leadership pool, would have to be the invention of private arts advocates. It's something of a chicken-and-egg situation. But one reality is clear. The vast majority of arts advocates are working for altruistic motives, as the financial and political rewards for such efforts are negligible to nonexistent. It must also be said that it really takes only a handful of dedicated people to spur a whole community into action.

Create a New Bond among Nonprofit Cultural Institutions and For-Profit Artists and Other Creative Workers

Creating a new bond between nonprofit and governmental arts organizations, with their relatively well-paid staffs, and the world of generally underpaid and struggling for-profit artists, writers, musicians, and other performers may not seem like a necessary endeavor for the future flourishing of the arts. But if one considers that the community of creative individuals potentially make up the largest audience for government-sponsored cultural programs and nonprofit arts productions and that those organizations have natural allies in independent creative people, then it makes sense.

There's potential political and economic synergy between the two wings of the arts and culture world. Although they are perhaps separated at the moment by class and economics, altruistic collaborations, bartering of services, and pooling of talents could create friendships that would allow the arts and culture world to present a united front before government, private funders, and potential investors.

Work for a Collaboration between Creative Workers and Ecological Workers and Activists, Exploring the Natural Bond among People Sensitive to the Physical, Aesthetic, and Subjective Landscapes in Which They Live

Arts and creative workers have a natural, well-organized, and effective ally in environmental advocates and their organizations. The relationship between two populations that are sensitive to the physical, aesthetic, and subjective landscapes in which they live has great potential for being a positive influence in the world of both environmental and creative policy and decision making. Both a New Mexico WPA and a Living Arts State Fair could promote environmental causes without compromising or watering down their missions. In return, environmental organizations could add their clout to issues of aesthetic and political concern in the world of arts and culture. I'm sure that, in most cases, both groups would be concerned about the same things.

A joint environmental and creative lobby could bond with teachers, child advocates, mental health workers, and physicians and hospitals to create a system of mutual aid and service. These bonds would help heal the myopia that infects "siloed" specialists in any field and bring them all into a wider arena of vision, sympathy, and understanding.

Create a Cultural Worker's Employment and Worker-Advocacy Agency and an Agenda of Reforms

One of the most difficult ideas to get across to mainstream decision makers, and to creative workers themselves, is that creative workers form an industry, a sector of the economy with special interests, needs, and contributions of its own. Once that concept becomes clear, then a set of practical aids can be adapted from other industries to support the services that creative workers perform and to help them support themselves.

In this light, an employment and worker-advocacy agency that helped place creative people in paying jobs would be of great benefit. Not only could such an agency create and expand networks of skilled workers and potential employers, it could also supply legal services, tax and insurance help, and various guides to steering a small business though dangerous waters. It is an anathema to most artists to have to consider themselves members of the business class, but aside from the work they do to maintain themselves and their creative practice, they are required, by tax codes alone, to run their operations with at least a modicum of business skills to avoid state and federal tax penalties and to avail themselves of Social Security benefits and insurance plans.

Found a Creative Workers' Watchdog and Whistleblower Group That Protects Historic Sites, Landscapes, Works, and Viewsheds

In a future era of cooperation and coalition building, creative workers and environmentalists, historians and anthropologists could form activist watchdog and whistleblower groups to protect historic sites, landscapes, works of art, and viewsheds, and to rectify compromised museum and library budgets and the undermining of arts organizations and environmental regulations. This kind of solidarity among creative, intellectual, and environmental workers would make for a formidable political and public policy lobbying effort.

New Mexico Cultural Affairs and the Arts in 2050

Trying to see how the prescriptive program presented above might play out in the world of 2050 requires more than an exclusive focus on cultural affairs and the arts. As Arlene Goldbard writes in her inspiring book *The Culture of Possibility*, a "defining question for the future of life in the United States" is "how [can we] build a bridge from the mesmerizing comfort and diversion still possible in private life to fac[e] the overwhelming collective challenges? In the personal space of so many lives (including mine), there is scope for pleasure, for beauty and delight, for connection and freedom. Yet right beneath the surface, the evidence of distress simmers and bubbles. It is hard to encompass both realities in a single awareness, but if there is any hope of a living future, it is necessary."[4] By 2050 the bridge will have been built but will be beginning to crumble under the weight of even greater economic and social pressures brought on by a swiftly changing climate and an intractable history of denial and inaction.

Somewhere in the 2020s or before, New Mexicans and all other Americans will start to suffer from the both the social outrage of income inequality, made worse in New Mexico by deepening rural and urban conflict over water, and from an economic depression caused in large part by technological and political inflexibility in the face of climate change. Even if one believes that short-run predictions are iffy at best, especially in the quixotic world of stocks and bonds and historical prediction, it is hard to argue with the reliability of long-range trend analyses, such as those based on the fact that greenhouse gases have visibly disrupted climate trends and their "normal" oscillations over the last thirty years or so.

The climate and financial trends building in 2014 will put a considerable strain on the arts and cultural enterprises at first. The vast majority of creative workers belong to the lower-middle class or the barely-making-it aspiring class, near the bottom third of the 99 percent of the rest of us. While most environmental activists are volunteers, some who work for NGOs are better salaried than entrepreneurial artists and writers, and both artists and environmentalists have a surer base than most family farmers have, especially when competing with agribusiness in a time of prolonged drought. But as odd as it sounds, all three groups form a potential power base of the increasingly alienated and marginalized, a class of persons with skills and attitudes that are essential to survival.

A Hopeful Future Imagined

In this context, if my prescriptive regimen has come to fruition by 2050—as I believe it can—New Mexico will become known as the Arts and Culture State. Its reputation as a sort of artist's paradise and a place in which creative workers and cultural institutions are major players in the economy would help local talent from all disciplines find their way in the international and digitally interconnected art community. Imagine how New Mexico would seem to creative people in states that had not devised a social safety net for artistic freelancers.

Imagine, as I do, how amazing it would appear to artists and patrons in other states that New Mexico's creative leadership was made up of people whose skills had earned national and worldwide acclaim. Imagine how attractive it would be to anyone interested in the creative life of the mind to see New Mexico cultivating huge audiences for all disciplines of the arts and cultural enterprises, creating an atmosphere of aesthetic and scholarly vitality unparalleled in the country.

Environmentalists will become increasingly vocal and powerful as climate change progresses, while local agriculture will take on an ever more important role in producing a part of everyone's diet as a lag in the development of alternative fuels makes trucking food around the country prohibitively expensive. The alliance of artists with environmentalists and grow-local agricultural entrepreneurs would bring New Mexico a new fame for being at the forefront of positive change in the nation. And if these three allies could strike up working and mutually creative relationships with the technological community in our state to develop new approaches to irrigation and other water issues, then New Mexico would have come a very long way in neutralizing and even capitalizing on the troubles seen ahead.

New Mexico Trends

The trends I read at the moment in New Mexico are grim. And so the context that I envision for the arts in the coming years is grim as well, but not grim enough to squelch an efflorescence of creativity and problem solving. Overall, the following issues would seem to be important for the economic and political environments of 2050.

DROUGHT

Increasing drought in the West and in New Mexico will cause expensive struggles between states over ever shrinking water supplies, such as the struggle going on now between New Mexico and Texas over the Rio Grande. Drought will devastate New Mexico farmers at a time when the state needs to create and support a vibrant new grow-local, eat-local farm economy. Drought will cause a decrease in both rural and urban populations. New Mexico cities will shrink as out-of-state companies go elsewhere and the mobile graying population stays away from impoverished places that are beginning to push their capacity for growth and wealth development due to both a shortage of water and an ongoing series of revelations about how polluted New Mexico's groundwater has become, owing to years of official denial and neglect and kowtowing to the military-industrial complex. Shrinking urban arts budgets will put pressure on already strained nonprofit arts organizations and will create tragic circumstances for many artists and writers but will also catalyze the economic development programs for the arts that I have outlined.

CLIMATE CHANGE

Climate change will bring worldwide disaster, with intense and erratic weather patterns driving coastal populations on most continents to higher ground, plaguing cities with hurricane-force winds, and leaving the over-grown western part of the United States in an increasingly desperate condition of aridity. New Mexico's drought will at first seem to make it an even less attractive place to live and invest in than did the old mischaracterization of the state as "a land remote beyond compare." But New Mexico will be only one region of many experiencing global drought and aridity issues. Its well-connected creative community could come to the rescue and help problem solvers do intellectual jujitsu on climate change in dry environments and export their creative solutions elsewhere. It's not far-fetched to imagine a collaborative community of artists, scientists, technologists, and biologists creating entrepreneurial companies to dream up the components of a new Dry Age agriculture. And as New Mexico's population diminishes, perhaps by a third or more, the flight of national chain stores will create opportunities for other local arts-stimulated businesses, ranging from Internet design and "simplicity" think tanks to clothing design and manufacture.

ALTERNATIVE ENERGY

As climate catastrophes become ever more undeniably associated with green-house gases produced by the fossil fuel industry, a gradual transition to new energy sources could leave rural southern New Mexico in an excellent position.

Farming and ranching will no longer be the staple of New Mexico's rural economies. Those enterprises will not go away, but farmers and ranchers with land to
sell will convert quantities of their space to solar and wind development. This will
make New Mexico's future look brighter than it does now, but we will still be an
arid state. Our weather patterns are trending toward more dryness, but also to a
different kind of wetness. While our snowpack is shrinking, damaging our traditional sources of river water, our monsoonal rains are increasing in intensity
while perhaps decreasing in frequency. This leaves New Mexico with a legal and
creative challenge to make the best use of a new source of water, from heavy rain,
by slowing down the flooding and allowing it to infiltrate into the groundwater
and perhaps storing it in new and more efficient ways for later use. This is an
ideal opportunity for landscape architects and planners to work with rural communities and perhaps incorporate fresh ideas from other creative disciplines.

STRENGTHENING BONDS

While mainstream economic and social systems might crumble under the pressure of drought and its resulting chaos, I place my bets on the resiliency and
resourcefulness of Native American and indigenous Hispanic rural communities
that have long experience with weathering hardship. Creative workers and the
creative community in general have natural affinities with traditional communities in New Mexico, and it seems possible that those bonds will strengthen in the
mid-twenty-first century, as many creative workers themselves hail from traditional Hispanic and Native American cultures. With a new entrepreneurial and
problem-solving spirit in the state, led by the creative community, traditional
water practices might become templates for new products that tribes and villages
could also export to other arid regions.

NEW CREATIVITY

This context of new and often dire climate opportunities could spur creativity
in all sectors of New Mexican society. For some, these troubles might catalyze a
da Vinci experience, expanding their creative problem-solving gifts from one
area of expertise into other, more technical, and as yet unforeseeable forms.

New Vitality

While in general one can see New Mexico in 2050 as a dry, harsh, increasingly impoverished place, with its cities under siege and its rural economies gasping for air, it also seems possible to me—and hopeful—that a long period of transition and adjustment might be coming to a head by 2050, resulting in a new concept of economic vitality, one based on quality of life rather than on mere physical expansion. If quality of life becomes the new standard by which to judge economic and social success, then creative workers will have a vital role to play no matter what else happens.

If the problem of arts-oriented political leadership is solved early in the first half of the century, by 2050 the creative world of New Mexico will have cultivated multiple streams of income from pollution taxes that link the arts to the environmental health of the state. This means, of course, that New Mexico politicians will see clearly for themselves that the arts and cultural enterprises play a vital role in a maintaining high quality of life in the state. Said another way, they will see that creative people have empowered themselves to keep the aesthetic spirit of New Mexico alive and well in very difficult times. It will also mean that New Mexico's leadership will link the economic and social drag of pollution and desecration of natural landscape to the collapse of prosperity in our cities and in our major tourist destinations as we transition into an economy that does not doubt its arid conditions. Leaders will have come to see the arts and cultural enterprises as the central, if not dominant, contributor to the health of an economy based on quality of life, not expansive growth.

With the creation of a New Mexico version of the WPA, the state's towns and cities will see writers and historians collecting oral histories and writing local histories. Painters and sculptors will create public art that communities large and small can use to promote themselves as destinations and that local people can make use of in their own quest for identity and sense of place. Architects and landscape architects will work around the state to help communities solve land-based issues and inefficiencies and infelicities in their built environments. Archives and libraries will be built around efforts to explore modern New Mexico history, including the interaction of marginalized populations with world-class technology and the military-industrial complex. If new funding sources made up of many tiny bites out of large tax bases hold up, then I can envision virtually every locality in the state having its own arts and culture cadre working to serve its needs.

It's possible that each town and village in the state could develop its own local history programs and produce history tabloids. With sufficient funds, local libraries could be reinvigorated and restaffed, serving local needs and becoming repositories for local history and culture. We could see historic church renovations and creative enhancements at all our public schools. Each town could count on the regular appearance of multiple performing arts groups, including dance groups, performance groups, and chamber orchestras.

Great singing and dancing, great music and acting, great poetry and its performance could be everywhere in the state. We could see a renaissance in locally written and produced theater and opera productions that has salaried work for all manner of craftspeople, set designers, costumers, and makeup artists.

The New Mexico WPA could increase the quality of life of hundreds of thousands of people in New Mexico. It could also show the world that, while we may have stringent environmental regulations and rigorous water-rationing laws and strategies, we are also a place that values the subjective health, curiosity, and intellectual pleasures of its citizens. New Mexico could become a place that attracts smart people and people who refuse to be defeated, depressed, or disempowered by the seemingly intractable situations of the moment. And if the New Mexico WPA could generate an annual Living Arts State Fair into which all the state's creative energy could be poured, both in a sense of solidarity and in a sense of community service, and that creative people of all disciplines and levels of success, even the most famous, worked to create, the place could be jumping with vitality, high spirits, and the optimism that comes with success. It could also draw crowds from out of state, with the economic benefits of that influx.

With solidarity in the creative community enhanced by communication across disciplines and through efforts to soften class distinctions and reduce income inequality between nonprofit and governmental workers and struggling freelancers through a creative workers' credit union that focused on microlending and other economic devices, the creative community will be in a better position to help infuse the general culture with a sense of optimism in the future. Solidarity among creative workers will give the industry and the community a chance to explore possible solutions to environmental and social problems and perhaps sidestep old intellectual stalemates among opposing forces in various technical and social specialties. It's not impossible to see a future in which water and energy planners, say, hire artists, actors, and historians to help them think outside the box in order to solve persistent problems. By 2050 it's entirely possible that brain power, the ability to think and imagine our way out of troubles and into solutions, might well be New Mexico's greatest asset, especially if it's accompanied by the image of New Mexico as an arts paradise and a haven for brainy, forward-thinking entrepreneurs.

New Leadership

All this depends, of course, on leadership within the creative community. I foresee that at some point before 2050 New Mexico's more famous writers, artists, scholars, and performers will take on the challenge of community leadership, not only lending their fame and the power of their influence to further the ends of the creative workforce but also acting as pioneers in the interweaving of the creative process with scientific and environmental problem solving. When the worlds of policy making and business see the positive impact of a creative community infusing itself into society as a whole, making contributions across disciplines and interests, politics could look different in New Mexico. It would be influenced not solely by big money but also by those forces of ingenuity and imagination that help to create new worlds. In 2050 creative workers, emboldened to some degree by increased employment opportunities and a new esprit de corps, will quicken and empower the intellectual and aesthetic life of New Mexico, just when the arts, scholarship, and the prowess of the imagination are needed the most. And in concert with environmental and social activists and the grow local, eat local movement, the creative community will help to make it harder and harder to use New Mexico and its people as a sacrifice zone for mining companies, the military, and corporate entities that take little or no responsibility for their waste and its proper disposal.

New Hope

All in all, 2050 could be a hard year, but not appreciably harder than the first years of the twenty-first century have been. The difficulties of the future could be made more palatable by a growing sense of hopefulness engendered by the altruism and optimism of creative workers acting in concert with those who value social, natural, and cultural health, without putting profits first. If things go as I hope, 2050 might see the creative world having reached a threshold of considerable influence and beginning to chart a fresh course of social sustenance and partnership. We might even see New Mexico become a refuge for other creative talent in the country, migrating from big population areas that have not created a friendly economic and social environment for the arts and cultural institutions. The economic disadvantages of New Mexico's drought could be overridden to some extent by the state's growing reputation as a state with a high quality of life, with a fascinating and inspiring mix of creative and cultural riches that have ceased to be add-ons and have come to be seen as integral to our way of life. By joining forces and affiliating, in sympathy and camaraderie, with Native American and traditional Hispanic communities and alternative technology entrepreneurs, the creative world could stimulate problem-solving experimentation throughout the state. This connectedness and engagement would mark the fruition of efforts to create a sense of solidarity among creative people working in the arts and culture industry by providing struggling freelancers with socially and creatively relevant work and devising means to fund something of a social safety net for such creative workers. By forging alliances with like-minded groups of people sensitive to the environment and to needs of the future and creating highly visible and community-oriented arts events and institutions that would involve as many creative people as possible and provide residents of the state, urban and rural, with access to vastly expanded arts events and cultural services, New Mexico could become the arts and culture capital of the American West.

Could the creative community become a catalyst for a new economic model built on the aim of advancing quality of life? Could the creative community help to stimulate the kind of innovative thinking that helps disseminate its sense of liberty, craft, and conscience to other problems solvers in the state? With committed leadership, there's a good chance that it might. After statehood, New Mexico learned that its multicultural uniqueness and the stunning beauty of its landscape, along with the creative genius that was drawn to them, had intrinsic value. In the past, one might argue, that value was exploited for the tourist trade.

By 2050 it's quite possible, however, that these values will have come full circle and have transcended their tourist roots to create a state of aesthetic and creative grace that is an ideal location not only for the arts but for the ingenious leaps in science and technology that could make a new future possible.

Notes

1. Niraj Chokshi, "Population Growth in New Mexico Is Approaching Zero—and Other Bad Signs," *GovBeat* (blog), January 17, 2014, http://www.washingtonpost.com/blogs/govbeat/wp/2014/01/17/population-growth-in-new-mexico-is-approaching-zero-and-other-bad-signs/.

2. Dinah Zeiger, *New Mexico Arts: Nurturing the State's Economy* (Denver: Western States Arts Federation, January 2005), http://www.nmarts.org/pdf/westaf-econ-impact-report-jan05.pdf.

3. Creative Albuquerque, *Albuquerque 2012: The State of the Creative Economy*, http://www.cabq.gov/urban-enhancement-trust-fund/documents/copy_of_ABQ_Creative_Economy_2012.pdf.

4. Arlene Goldbard, *The Culture of Possibility: Art, Artists, & the Future* (Richmond, CA: Waterlight Press, 2013), 122.

Chapter 8

New Mexico Transportation and Planning

AARON SUSSMAN

WHERE WE LIVE, HOW WE LIVE, AND HOW WE TRAVEL ARE DEEPLY
intertwined. When imagining life in 2050, it is tempting to picture a future of
advanced technology that bears little resemblance to our present. What is more
likely is a series of shifts, many of them subtle, that will not necessarily reinvent
how we travel or how we live but will affect the shape of communities in New
Mexico and the ways we reach our destinations.

This is to say that there may be not *one* dramatically different transportation future but many, driven by changing population distribution patterns and the associated economic activity. Where we live affects the
transportation options at our disposal and, conversely, how we prefer to
travel affects the types of places we choose to live in. Yet within the context
of our choices there are larger trends at play. New Mexico has historically
been a rural state, but in many ways it is becoming more urban as population gravitates to the larger towns and cities. While Albuquerque will not
exactly become another San Francisco or New York in terms of size or
density, at a minimum more New Mexicans may lead an urban or urban-
adjacent lifestyle in the coming decades.

New Mexico's transportation future will be shaped by these population
trends, but regardless of where within the state New Mexicans live, private
vehicles are sure to play a role well into the future. The high amount of driving and long distances traveled by New Mexicans every day speaks to the role
that cars play for New Mexico residents. However, transportation needs vary

269

considerably across the state, and planning for private vehicles and investing in highways alone is not sufficient to meet future needs. For example, mass transit options in Albuquerque may be critical for attracting and retaining workers and making the city a competitive place to do business. Meanwhile, a rail connection to northwest New Mexico and expansion of the roadway network east of Farmington are keys to facilitating development and supporting economic opportunities. In parts of the state where natural resource extraction is occurring, there is heavy reliance on freight trucks, which can place a disproportionate burden on the roads and requires increased infrastructure and maintenance investments. Along the border, freight travel is expected to surge as the Santa Teresa intermodal facility is developed, and roadway connections to Mexico may also prove to be critical investments.

A number of challenges need to be confronted. Funding limitations mean that attention is increasingly turned to maintaining infrastructure in a "state of good repair."[1] Uneven growth will make the provision of services and repair of roads in some parts of the state increasingly difficult. The large amount of freight traffic expected to pass through New Mexico will have a significant impact on the state's roadways. New Mexico also possesses one of the nation's poorer driver-safety records, with a traffic fatality rate 27 percent higher than the nation's overall.[2]

At the same time, there are opportunities. The transportation system can be leveraged for economic development, as with private rail infrastructure for the distribution of goods and the ports of entry along the southern border for trade with Mexico. New Mexico is experiencing changing travel patterns and growing interest in alternative transit modes that can support more sustainable development patterns. The state's congestion levels and travel times are also relatively modest by national standards (although there are more than a few key bottlenecks in major urban areas, there is no Los Angeles–style rush hour traffic to contend with), meaning there is time for policy makers to be creative and proactive as they prepare for the future.

This chapter will address some of the overarching trends that will inform transportation investments and public policy decisions in the decades to come. In particular, it will consider the state's demographic conditions, changing travel patterns, and the question of financing the transportation systems of the future. This will require an analysis of transportation behavior in New Mexico today but must also rely on national research to understand how preferences in housing and transportation are evolving and to consider what those trends mean for the state. The reality is that transportation patterns are indeed changing and New Mexico must be ready to adapt.

Demographics: Population and Housing

To understand New Mexico's transportation future, it is important to examine the demographic forces that will shape where New Mexicans live and what type of lifestyles they will pursue. Despite the recent impacts of the Great Recession, New Mexico has been and is projected to be a rapidly growing state. Over the sixty-year span from 1950 to 2010, New Mexico grew by almost 1.9 percent per year and nearly tripled in population. The Albuquerque metropolitan statistical area grew even faster, at a rate of 2.6 percent per year, resulting in nearly four times as many residents.

High levels of growth continued through the 2000s, until economic conditions changed and abruptly altered migration patterns and population growth rates. Population growth fell to less than 1 percent per year from 2010 to 2013.[3] For the first time on record, in 2012 the state experienced negative net migration as more residents left the state than moved in.[4] However, this short-term trend is not expected to continue. New Mexico is projected to remain an appealing place for migrants and retirees, and the population is expected to grow considerably.

The most recent available state-level population projections, developed by the Geospatial Population Studies Group at the University of New Mexico's Bureau of Business and Economic Research, consider conditions only through the year 2040. Nevertheless, they provide insights into the changing population dynamics expected in New Mexico in the coming decades. According to those estimates, despite the impacts of the recession and limited short-term population gain, New Mexico's statewide population is expected to grow by 37 percent between 2010 and 2040, amounting to about 760,000 new residents, for a total population of more than 2.8 million.[5] By contrast, the overall U.S. population is expected to grow by 23 percent through 2040.

Table 8.1. New Mexico historical population growth

	NEW MEXICO		ALBUQUERQUE MSA	
Year	Population	Annual average growth rate (%)	Population	Annual average growth rate (%)
1950	681,187	—	188,604	—
1960	951,023	3.4	321,982	5.5
1970	1,017,055	0.7	379,095	1.6
1980	1,303,302	2.5	523,105	3.3
1990	1,515,069	1.5	599,416	1.4
2000	1,819,046	1.8	729,649	2.0
2010	2,059,179	1.2	887,077	2.0

Source: U.S. Census Bureau

The form that growth and population change take will be highly varied across the state (see table 8.2). While some counties are projected to grow considerably, others are likely to lose population. New Mexico will also become increasingly "gray" as retirees move into the state and birthrates slowly but steadily fall. The disproportionate share of senior citizens in the population has wide-ranging implications, not least of which is the need to ensure safe transportation options and access to critical services.

Changing Population Dynamics

URBANIZATION AND HIGH-GROWTH LOCATIONS

While the Geospatial Population Studies Group projects that New Mexico will grow far faster than the United States overall, the state's population will be increasingly concentrated and growth will be anything but evenly distributed. The fastest-growing portion of the state will be the Interstate 25/Rail Runner corridor, following the path of the commuter rail from Belen to Albuquerque to Santa Fe and comprising Valencia, Bernalillo, Sandoval, and Santa Fe Counties. This agglomeration will grow by 67 percent, meaning that two-thirds of the state's population growth is projected

Table 8.2. Population by county and rates of change, 2010–2040

	2010	2040	CHANGE 2010–2040	
			#	%
New Mexico	2,065,826	2,827,692	761,866	36.90
County				
Bernalillo	664,636	970,371	305,735	46.0
Sandoval	132,434	265,607	133,173	100.6
Dona Ana	210,536	299,088	88,552	42.1
Lea	64,727	110,661	45,934	71.0
San Juan	130,170	175,678	45,508	35.0
Santa Fe	144,532	184,832	40,300	27.9
Valencia	76,735	106,830	30,095	39.2
Chaves	65,783	83,263	17,480	26.6
Curry	48,941	60,395	11,454	23.4
Eddy	53,829	65,258	11,429	21.2
Luna	25,095	35,595	10,500	41.8
Roosevelt	20,040	27,912	7,872	39.3
Taos	32,937	40,062	7,125	21.6
Cibola	27,213	32,090	4,877	17.9
Torrance	16,383	19,801	3,418	20.9
Otero	64,275	66,841	2,566	4.0
Union	4,549	5,977	1,428	31.4
Lincoln	20,497	21,888	1,391	6.8
Sierra	11,988	12,737	749	6.2
Catron	3,725	4,012	287	7.7
Guadalupe	4,687	4,760	73	1.6
Harding	695	607	-88	-12.7
De Baca	2,022	1,803	-219	-10.8
McKinley	71,802	71,580	-222	-0.3
Quay	9,041	8,805	-236	-2.6
Grant	29,371	29,102	-269	-0.9
Rio Arriba	40,371	40,008	-363	-0.9
Mora	4,881	4,423	-458	-9.4
Hidalgo	4,894	4,403	-491	-10.0
Los Alamos	18,026	17,210	-816	-4.5
Socorro	17,866	16,857	-1,009	-5.6
Colfax	13,752	12,642	-1,110	-8.1
San Miguel	29,393	26,594	-2,799	-9.5

Source: University of New Mexico, Bureau of Business and Economic Research GPS 2010–2040 projections

to occur in just these four counties in central New Mexico (see table 8.3). The disproportionate growth also means the Albuquerque–Santa Fe corridor will become increasingly influential within the state—politically, culturally, and economically.

Other locations that are projected to gain population include Doña Ana County, home to Las Cruces, which is likely to benefit from growing populations and improving economic conditions along the U.S.-Mexico border; San Juan County and the growing Farmington metropolitan area; and Lea County, home to Hobbs and growing natural resource extraction industries. In fact, between 2012 and 2013, Hobbs was one of the fastest-growing towns in the county, adding about 1,900 residents for a 3 percent year-to-year increase.[6]

The concentration of population in urban areas has been unfolding in New

Table 8.3. Projected disproportion in population growth

	2010	2040	CHANGE 2010–2040 #	CHANGE 2010–2040 %
New Mexico	2,065,826	2,827,692	761,866	36.90
County				
Bernalillo	664,636	970,371	305,735	46.0
Sandoval	132,434	265,607	133,173	100.6
Dona Ana	210,536	299,088	88,552	42.1
Lea	64,727	110,661	45,934	71.0
San Juan	130,170	175,678	45,508	35.0
Santa Fe	144,532	184,832	40,300	27.9
Valencia	76,735	106,830	30,095	39.2
Chaves	65,783	83,263	17,480	26.6
Curry	48,941	60,395	11,454	23.4
Eddy	53,829	65,258	11,429	21.2
Luna	25,095	35,595	10,500	41.8

Source: University of New Mexico, Bureau of Business and Economic Research GPS 2010–2040 projections

Mexico for some time. The seven counties that are considered by the U.S. Census Bureau to be part of metropolitan statistical areas (MSAs) grew from 63 percent of the state in 2000 to 66.6 percent by 2010. Those seven counties—Bernalillo, Doña Ana, San Juan, Sandoval, Santa Fe, Valencia, and Torrance—will make up 71.5 percent of New Mexico's population in 2040.[7] Considering the MSAs understates the reality that most of the state's growth will occur in and around a few cities. Only seven counties will have more than one hundred thousand residents, and only one county will have more than three hundred thousand. A full one-third of the state will live in Bernalillo County.

Likely to have just as much influence on the greater Las Cruces area as the trend toward urbanization are the fates of neighboring El Paso and Ciudad Juárez and the growing economic activity along the U.S.-Mexico border. El Paso now hosts more than thirty-four thousand military personnel and another forty-five thousand family members and civilian contractors at Fort Bliss. The city is projected to grow by more than 335,000 between 2010 and 2040, and while much of the growth will occur to the east of the city and near Fort Bliss, some of it will indeed spill into New Mexico and draw the cities of El Paso and Las Cruces closer together.[8] Meanwhile, Mexico's economy is growing and Juárez is no longer one of the most dangerous cities in the world, with homicides dropping from more than three thousand in 2010 to less than five hundred in 2013.[9] Juárez itself is expected to add two hundred thousand new residents in the next two decades.[10]

Growing economic activity along the border region, and around the Santa Teresa border crossing in particular, will also help create a major center for population and industry in southern New Mexico. Major happenings include Union Pacific's new intermodal freight facility in the town of Santa Teresa, which began operations in 2014, and a proposed 70,000-acre binational campus that would leverage the easy access to rail and truck freight for distribution across North America. As a result, the border-crossing outpost of San Jerónimo, Chihuahua, which today contains a major Foxconn electronics plant with five thousand employees but no population to speak of, is expected to add thousands of residents and additional jobs in the next couple of decades.[11] The state of Chihuahua and the Mexican national government are investing heavily in infrastructure to support these initiatives, which may include rerouting northbound rail freight from El Paso to Santa Teresa.[12] The result of all of this activity is that southern New Mexico, the El Paso area, and Juárez and northern Chihuahua will be increasingly interconnected economically and Las Cruces will in many ways be more connected to the cities to the south than to the rest of New Mexico.

In short, New Mexico is experiencing an urbanizing trend that will lead to the majority of the state's population being clustered in just a few areas. Projections do not necessarily indicate the rise of densely populated urban areas across the state, instead pointing to the rise of a series of regional population centers—think Las Cruces, Farmington, and Hobbs—and one true major metropolitan area, with nearly 1 million residents in the city of Albuquerque and around 1.5 million in the corridor from Belen to Santa Fe.[13]

RURAL POPULATION LOSS

At the same time that populations are gravitating toward urban centers, a full third of New Mexico counties are projected to lose population in the coming decades (see table 8.4). This continues a trend that can be observed in the 2000 and 2010 Censuses, in which nearly half of all New Mexico counties lost population. From 2012 to 2013, twenty-two of the state's thirty-three counties lost population.[14] None of the counties projected to lose population are particularly large, and in many cases, the population losses are small in absolute numbers; in only three cases is the loss greater than one thousand residents, and the largest loss is in San Miguel County, where the population is projected to fall by less than three thousand over thirty years. But these figures represent an important trend, as much culturally as in demographic terms.[15]

In New Mexico, as in many places around the country, the economics of ranching and farming are becoming more difficult, prompting younger generations to move to cities for job opportunities. The resulting drop in the tax base in rural areas will make it increasingly challenging to provide services such as public schools, police, sanitation, and medical care. Inherent in the pattern of urbanization is that such a trend runs counter to traditional New Mexican identity. If trends hold true, fewer people will be able to make a

Table 8.4. Projected population losses by county

County	2010	2040	CHANGE 2010–2040 #	%
Harding	695	607	-88	-12.7
De Baca	2,022	1,803	-219	-10.8
Hidalgo	4,894	4,403	-491	-10.0
San Miguel	29,393	26,594	-2,799	-9.5
Mora	4,881	4,423	-458	-9.4
Colfax	13,752	12,642	-1,110	-8.1
Socorro	17,866	16,857	-1,009	-5.6
Los Alamos	18,026	17,210	-816	-4.5
Quay	9,041	8,805	-236	-2.6
Grant	29,371	29,102	-269	-0.9
Rio Arriba	40,371	40,008	-363	-0.9

Source: University of New Mexico, Bureau of Business and Economic Research GPS 2010–2040 projections

living in the rural settings that their parents and grandparents called home. As a result, some traditions and agricultural history may be lost. From a more practical standpoint, inhabitants of rural communities that are losing population will also find themselves farther away from basic needs, thus reinforcing the impulse among younger and more mobile populations to move to more urbanized areas.

At the same time, there are benefits that come with a more urban lifestyle. Economic activity has been gravitating to cities at the national level for some time. From a public sector perspective, it is generally more efficient to provide services to residents in urban settings. This is particularly true for providing transportation options and mass transit in particular, which is disproportionately costly in more rural settings because of low ridership and long distances between destinations. Urban living is also comparably more environmentally friendly when one considers per capita energy consumption and transportation-related emissions.[16] This may be small consolation for many New Mexico residents whose identities are tied to rural lifestyles.

GROWTH OF NEW MEXICO'S SENIOR CITIZEN POPULATION

In addition to the general urbanizing trend and the hollowing-out of some rural areas in New Mexico, the major population challenge facing the state is the disproportionate growth of certain age groups. In particular, New Mexico faces a rapidly growing senior citizen population due to a combination of increased life expectancy, falling birthrates, and the attractiveness of New Mexico as a place to retire. New Mexico's senior population is expected to grow by 131 percent by 2040, with the absolute number increasing from 273,000 in 2010 to more than 630,000 seniors statewide.

New Mexico is hardly alone in facing an increasing senior population, but the change here will be more dramatic than in the nation overall. The U.S. population is projected to grow from 308.7 million in 2010 to 399.8 million residents by 2050, of which almost 84 million, or 21 percent, will be over the age of sixty-five, compared to 13 percent in 2010.[17] While not exactly facing the "gray tsunami" of places like Japan or China, New Mexico is on track to exceed the 2050 national share of senior citizens (that is, 21 percent) ten years ahead of the United States overall (that is, more than 22 percent by 2040).[18]

The increased number of senior citizens also means that other age groups will make up a smaller share of the New Mexico population. For example, although the youth population—those under the age of sixteen—will increase as an absolute number, there will be more senior citizens than youths, and youths will decrease as a share of the total population.[19] One way to think about this dynamic is to consider the dependency ratio: the percentage of people outside of the labor force compared to those of working age, considered to be sixteen to sixty-four years of age. In 2010 the dependency ratio was 35:65, meaning there were almost two workers for every one dependent. In 2040 the ratio is projected to climb to 42:58, meaning there will be fewer than three workers for every two dependents. Although workers are starting to delay retirement until later in life, it is quite likely that the labor force will shrink over time. Such a shift will affect not only the industries in which jobs will be available but also overall transportation needs, as senior citizens make fewer peak-period commuting trips but engage in more dispersed travel across the day.

Much like the distribution of residents overall within New Mexico, the distribution of senior citizens within the state is critical and worth considering (see figures 8.1 and 8.2). The largest counties and those experiencing the greatest growth will maintain a healthy population distribution and a strong labor force. Bernalillo, Chaves, Doña Ana, Lea, and San Juan Counties are among the locations where the share of senior citizen will be 20 percent or lower. However, six counties—Taos, Harding, Catron, Santa Fe, Colfax, and Lincoln Counties—are projected to have more than 30 percent of their residents age sixty-five years or older (see table 8.5). In Catron and Harding Counties, the percentage of people of working age is actually expected to be smaller than the combined set of residents under the age of sixteen and over sixty-five. Most critically, many of the counties that are expected to lose population are also expected to see increases in the share of senior citizens. Such a combination of forces could mean fewer workers, fewer people to operate stores and teach in schools, and fewer children to attend them. And if current trends persist, many rural New Mexicans will find themselves increasingly isolated from services.

Figure 8.1. Population by age group, 2010

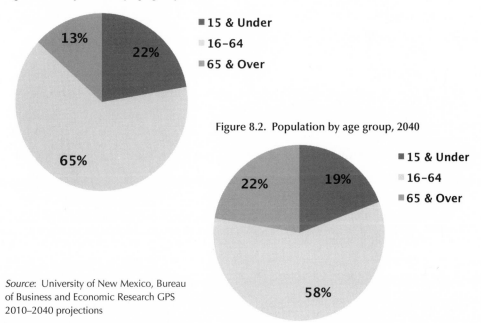

Figure 8.2. Population by age group, 2040

Source: University of New Mexico, Bureau of Business and Economic Research GPS 2010–2040 projections

Table 8.5. Projected county population distributions by age (percentages)

	2010 POPULATION			2040 POPULATION		
County	15 & under	16–64	65 & over	15 & under	16–64	65 & over
Taos	18	65	17	13	50	36
Harding	12	59	29	16	48	36
Catron	13	59	28	19	47	34
Santa Fe	19	66	15	14	53	33
Colfax	18	62	20	17	52	31
Lincoln	16	62	22	19	51	30
Mora	19	63	19	18	52	30
De Baca	20	57	23	19	53	28
Los Alamos	21	64	15	20	54	27
Sierra	14	55	31	22	52	26
Hidalgo	22	61	17	18	56	26
Socorro	21	65	14	20	54	26
Rio Arriba	22	64	14	21	54	26
Valencia	23	64	13	19	56	25

Source: University of New Mexico, Bureau of Business and Economic Research GPS 2010–2040 projections

It is important to be clear that projections do not mean that communities are destined to fade away. Population projections and the birthrates and migration patterns that drive them are not set in stone; rather, they are subject to change and are constantly being revised. Nor do the projections destine New Mexico to any particular fate. But they do crystallize a series of challenges that New Mexico can be expected to face and for which the state must be prepared.

Housing Preference and Urban Living

Changing economic conditions, housing preferences, and lifestyle demands across the country make the projected population shifts in New Mexico increasingly likely. Among seniors, for example, there appears to be a growing desire to downsize their homes and have easy access to medical care.[20] A recent study concluded, "Many baby boomers, who no longer need multi-room houses and backyards (because their children have moved out), have begun moving to homes that are smaller and in locations that have easily-accessible societal amenities."[21] It is likely that more and more seniors will find it easier to meet their lifestyle needs in urban settings, and there will certainly be greater demand for senior-friendly housing and services that cater to this expanding group.[22]

An even greater influence on urban migration patterns, housing stocks, lifestyles, and therefore transportation choices will come from the 80 to 90 million millennials in the United States, including more than six hundred thousand in New Mexico.[23] In fact, there are more millennials today than baby boomers, many of whom are just beginning to enter professional life. Perhaps somewhat fittingly, millennials will be in or approaching the senior citizen category by 2050 and their preferences and habits will strongly shape cities and communities in the coming decades.

This influence begins with a desire for active street life and convenient access to the amenities that major metropolitan areas have to offer. While plenty of millennials will seek a life in rural and suburban areas, as their parents did, they demonstrate a far stronger preference for urban environments than previous generations. According to a 2013 Urban Land Institute survey, 76 percent of millennials place high value on walkability in communities and 59 percent prefer a range of housing choices in their communities. High numbers of millennials indicate they are likely to move in the next five years, which is consistent with their preference for smaller-scale rental options and good access to jobs and services.[24] In a separate 2011 survey, 77 percent of millennials stated they planned to live in urban core areas.[25]

While New Mexico–specific data on housing preferences is not as robust as at the national level, the preference by millennials for an urban lifestyle is certainly consistent with the state's migration patterns. As Leigh Gallagher notes in *The End of the Suburbs*, "If even a fraction of the 77 percent of Millennials prefers urban areas, as the studies show, and they act on those preferences, it will have an enormous impact on conventional subdivision-style suburbs."[26] The same can be said for rural portions of New Mexico. If younger generations leave rural communities at anywhere near the rates identified in national surveys and trends, the effects on traditional New Mexico communities could be dramatic.

NEW HOUSING DEMANDS

Of course, housing preferences are often contradictory and do not always lend themselves to clear policy objectives. For example, there is a strongly stated preference among all generations for walkable neighborhoods with a mix of shops and businesses, and individuals claim to be willing to sacrifice yard size for shorter commutes. At the same time, many Americans want large homes, easy parking access, and above all, privacy.[27] The takeaway would seem to be that available housing options do not align well with changing demands, and there is a need for a larger range of housing options than is currently available. This is especially true when one considers the demographic trends. Nationwide, there will be more than 20 million new households without children in the next two decades, forming an increasing share of total households. The percentage of single-person households will also increase. As a result, rural and suburban housing options designed for larger families simply will not make sense to many people who live alone or have small families, and as much as 40 percent of new housing demand will be for multifamily or attached housing, which is most frequently found in urban settings. Even demand for small-lot single-family housing is expected to be greater than for large-lot housing options.[28]

It is difficult to say for certain to what degree these trends will play out locally. New Mexico's housing stock features a smaller proportion of multifamily housing units than most states, but mobile and manufactured homes make up a higher share of overall housing. The slow growth of the Albuquerque metro-area housing market, for instance, may be interpreted as evidence that New Mexico runs counter to national trends. What is more, average rents in Albuquerque are low and have increased at a lower rate than the costs of construction, meaning that developers find it difficult to produce viable market-rate products.[29] Nevertheless, it is important to remember that these national housing trends appear to be long-term and reinforce a movement toward urban areas and an increasing number of smaller, denser housing environments. And as we shall see, the changing preferences in housing go along with rapidly changing travel behavior and growing acceptance of alternative modes of transportation, indicating that urban migration and housing preference are not just about urban lifestyles—they are about transportation decisions too.

Emerging Trends in Transportation: New Mexico and the United States

New Mexico is a car-loving and car-dependent state. It is a place synonymous with Route 66, wide-open spaces, and long distances between towns. The automobile is not only essential in most parts of the state but also ingrained in the culture. The result, not surprisingly, is a place where people do an awful lot of driving. Along with the sixth-lowest population density of any state, New Mexico has the sixth-highest number of miles traveled by car per capita annually.[30] And it is a state where 90 percent of residents commute by private vehicle, mostly while traveling alone.[31]

Yet changes in transportation patterns both nationally and locally indicate the ways New Mexicans will travel in the years ahead. While private vehicles are currently and are likely to remain the dominant travel mode for the foreseeable future—although the types of vehicles we drive may change dramatically by 2050—other modes of travel are quickly emerging, and reliance on private vehicles as the only mode of travel is decreasing.

U.S. Transportation Trends

Since Americans do most of their traveling by car, the clearest indicator of changing travel behavior is the sheer amount of driving taking place on a year-to-year basis. Nationwide, from 1970 to 2007, vehicle miles traveled (VMT) grew by 2.7 percent annually, far faster than the rate of population growth (see figure 8.3). At its peak in 2007, total annual VMT surpassed three trillion miles. This coincided with great amounts of roadway expansion, as the United States built more than three hundred thousand lane miles of public roads over the same thirty-seven-year span.[32] However, from 2007 to 2012, U.S. annual VMT dropped by a total of slightly more than 3 percent. Perhaps even more strikingly, the total amount of personal driving—measured in VMT per capita—peaked in 2004. Since then, national VMT per capita has fallen almost 9 percent, decreasing from more than 9,300 to less than 8,500 miles per year. Total miles driven per licensed driver fell by an even larger amount, from a peak of 13,700 to less than 12,500 miles per year.[33] The major question became, was this drop a function of the Great Recession and a decline in economic activity, as initially assumed, or the beginning of a new and important trend?

Recent studies published by the University of Michigan Transportation Research Institute disentangle the trends in vehicle usage in light of the Great Recession. The results indicate that Americans are not only driving shorter distances each day on average but their relationship with vehicles appears to be

Figure 8.3. Annual total VMT (millions), United States, 1970–2012

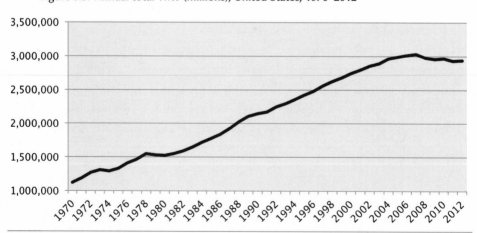

Source: Federal Highway Administration

changing. In addition to per capita VMT, rates of vehicle ownership per person, per household, and per licensed driver all peaked in 2005 or 2006, years *before* the Great Recession, and have gone down ever since.[34] This is an important shift because vehicle ownership rates had long risen at rates higher than population growth. It is clear from the data that cars are not going away, but it is also important to point out that the total number of drivers and vehicles are now increasing at decreasing rates, meaning each year there are fewer new drivers.[35]

The changes are being felt most acutely in U.S. cities. VMT has decreased since the mid-2000s in three-quarters of large urban areas. At the same time, most urban areas are witnessing an increase in the number of zero-car households and an increase in the percentage of workers commuting by transit and bicycle.[36] While the dominant mode in all but a few U.S. cities is personal vehicles, and the relatively small percentages do not indicate a complete paradigm shift in transportation preferences, the numbers do reflect meaningful changes in traveler behavior and are consistent with stated preferences for more urban lifestyles and housing options.[37]

New Mexico Transportation Trends

New Mexico has a tendency to think of itself as unique and as a place where national trends do not apply. But it is important to note that these trends are taking place in the state of New Mexico as well; even in this car-loving state, the ever-increasing levels of driving that had been predicted to continue seem to be a thing of the past. As in the nation at large, peak driving in New Mexico took place in 2007. From 2007 to 2012, total VMT dropped by 5 percent and per capita VMT statewide fell by more than 9 percent, from a peak of thirty-seven miles to around thirty-three miles per day. This followed several decades in which the overall amount of driving by New Mexicans grew by 3.3 percent per year. This still means that New Mexicans drive among the greatest distances in the country, but the modification in driving behavior is striking nonetheless.[38]

The clearest trends can be observed in the Albuquerque metropolitan area, where VMT per capita grew from around thirteen miles to a peak of more than twenty-four miles per day in 2004, decreasing every year thereafter. By 2012 per

Figure 8.4. Daily VMT per capita, Albuquerque Metropolitan Area, 1970–2010

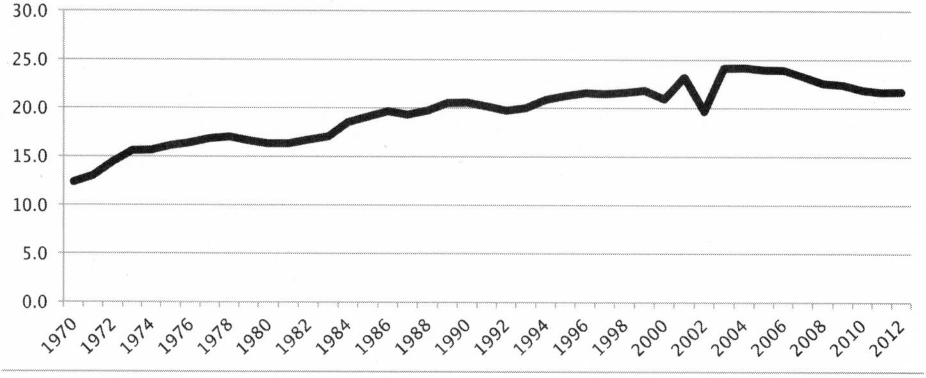

Source: Mid-Region Council of Governments, Albuquerque

capita VMT had fallen by 10 percent from its peak see figure 8.4). Making the decreases in driving even more surprising is the fact that Bernalillo County grew by 12 percent from 2004 to 2012, and much of the new housing development in the 2000s followed patterns of sprawl that moved residents farther away from their destinations. While fuel prices and economic conditions clearly had an impact, the biggest reason for the decrease in driving seems to be that New Mexicans, like Americans in general, started *deciding* to drive less.[39]

TRANSIT

At the same time that VMT has been decreasing, mass transit usage has been surging across New Mexico. Statewide transit usage increased by 85 percent from 2005 to 2012—again far outpacing the population growth rate, which was 7 percent over that span—as the state went from less than 10 million transit trips per year to more than 18 million (see figure 8.5).[40] Even ridership in rural areas increased dramatically, up 132 percent from 2005 to 2012.[41] According to the *Statewide Public Transportation Plan*, demand in rural areas is expected to continue growing by about 1.4 percent annually.[42] Perhaps most critically, transit usage started increasing at high rates before the Great Recession, suggesting transit is not merely an option of last resort.

Figure 8.5. Growth in transit ridership, 2005–2012

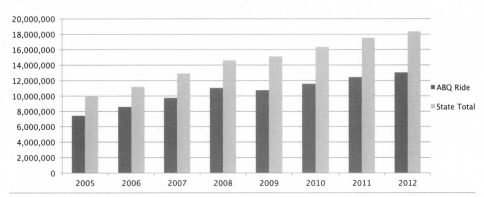

Source: Mid-Region Council of Governments, Albuquerque, and New Mexico Department of Transportation fact sheets

The growth is particularly pronounced in the Albuquerque metropolitan area, where not only did transit usage grow by 81 percent from 2005 to 2012, but transit passenger miles—the distance traveled by all users on transit and a metric equivalent to VMT—grew by 369 percent from 2005 to 2012, among the highest rates in the country.[43] The New Mexico Rail Runner Express, which began service from Belen to Bernalillo in 2006 and extended to Santa Fe in late 2008, accounts for much of the increase in transit passenger miles traveled. After some early surges and minor drops in ridership associated with schedule changes and fare increases, the service now carries about four thousand riders a day, averaging forty miles per trip.[44] Although initially controversial, the Rail Runner is proving to be an investment that not only reduces demand for freeway travel between the state's capital and its largest city but also connects the region in a new way for tourists and residents alike.

Meanwhile, ridership for ABQ Ride, the City of Albuquerque's transit service, essentially doubled in the span of a decade (see figure 8.5). This was the result of key innovations and policy choices that speak to the role that transit can play in New Mexico moving forward. The first major innovation was the introduction of Rapid Ride services: high-frequency, high-capacity buses with limited stops (that is, about every mile rather than every few blocks) to ensure faster travel times. The second innovation was a state legislature–supported policy that enabled all University of New Mexico (UNM) and Central New Mexico Community College students, staff, and faculty to utilize ABQ Ride free of charge. The policy has been tremendously important in generating new riders and reducing parking demand along Central Avenue and around the UNM main campus. Although a high percentage of transit users are students and persons with low incomes and limited access to private vehicles, as a result of these policies, the general trend is toward a more diverse ridership. There also remains tremendous room for growth in commuter, tourist, and recreational trips.[45]

What is also clear is that different models are appropriate in different places. Los Alamos's Atomic City Transit went from being operated by a non-profit to being a city-run system, free of fares. As a result, the city of twelve thousand generates nearly half a million transit trips per year (see table 8.6). There has also been growth in smaller communities, such as Alamogordo, in Grant County, and among rural services, as well as park-and-ride services operated by the New Mexico Department of Transportation, which provide services between jurisdictions rather than within communities. In more urbanized places such as Santa Fe and Farmington, service expansion has resulted in important increases in usage. Las Cruces raised fares in 2009 and saw an initial decrease in ridership but has since seen increases in ridership of more than 5 percent per year. More recently Las Cruces invested heavily in a downtown intermodal transit facility and now sees transit as an important component of downtown revitalization.

CHANGING TRAVEL PREFERENCES

Transit services in New Mexico have their limits, and it is important to be clear that, while ridership is up, there are few places where transit can go beyond providing basic access and serving populations with minimal resources. Only 1.1 percent of New Mexico residents and 2.1 percent of Albuquerque residents commute to work by transit, compared to 0.8 percent and 1.7 percent, respectively, in 2000.[46] While Michael Sivak of the University of Michigan and others raise the specter of "peak motorization" or "peak car" usage, the changes to trends in vehicle miles traveled and vehicle ownership are similarly modest

Table 8.6. Annual transit trip growth, by city

TRANSIT PROVIDER	TRANSIT GROWTH, 2005–2012 (%)
Los Alamos–Atomic City Transit	816
Grant County/SWRTD	343
Farmington Red Apple	213
Alamogordo Ztrans	193
Rural Services	132
Santa Fe Trails	85
ABQ Ride	75
NMDOT Park & Ride	35
Roswell Pecos Trails	14
Las Cruces Road Runner	13
Statewide total	85

Source: New Mexico Department of Transportation fact sheets

and do not constitute a complete, universal shift away from automobiles. Nevertheless, the demand for transit is clearly growing and a growing body of evidence suggests travel patterns are fundamentally changing.

Traveler-behavior studies and stated-preference surveys indicate we are indeed witnessing the beginning of a trend away from dependence on single-occupancy vehicles, with the most dramatic changes being observed among younger generations. Results from the most recent National Household Travel Survey indicate that sixteen-to-thirty-four-year-olds took 24 percent more bicycle trips and 16 percent more walking trips and traveled 40 percent more miles on public transit in 2009 than in 2001.[47] In fact, millennials are three times more likely to use transit than other generations, and 60 percent of the additional ten billion transit-passenger miles traveled were traveled by sixteen-to-thirty-four-year-olds.[48] Meanwhile, per capita VMT among this age group decreased by nearly a quarter (10,300 to 7,900 miles) between 2001 and 2009, a function of fewer and shorter trips and a greater share of trips made via alternative modes of transportation, while the percentage of millennials without a driver's license grew from 21 percent to 26 percent.[49]

A study from U.S. PIRG and the Frontier Group contends that the trends toward reduced driving and increased urban-style living are long-term, particularly as technological advances make communication easier, make some trips unnecessary, and make public transit and shared transportation (that is, carshare or bikeshare programs) more accessible and easier to use. The study even asserts that among urban millennials, "public transportation is more compatible with a lifestyle based on mobility and peer-to-peer connectivity."[50] Similarly, a survey by the National Association of Realtors showed that eighteen-to-twenty-nine-year-olds placed the highest value on having social amenities within walking distance and on proximity to transit.[51] Millennials also are most likely to intentionally reduce their driving in order to protect the environment.[52] This is happening regardless of income. In households with income over $70,000, public transit, biking, and walking trips all increased dramatically in the last decade, and "young people who have jobs today drive less than young people who had jobs before the recession."[53]

Early results from the Mid-Region Travel Survey, a comprehensive study of household travel behavior in the Albuquerque metro area, indicate that generational differences observed at a national scale hold true in New Mexico as well. In fact, people aged sixteen to thirty-one travel 39 percent fewer miles in an average day than those aged thirty-two to forty-nine and 12 percent less than those aged fifty to sixty-seven. Some of the difference can be attributed to a lifestyle free of children, but the presence or absence of children does not appear to be the only factor at play.[54]

While public transit is not something that will work in all parts of New Mexico, providing a wider range of transportation options and connections is a realistic goal. Not only is there an emerging market for it among urban residents and millennials in particular, but there will be growing numbers of senior citizens who rely on transit as a safe means of travel. For rural residents and senior citizens in particular, a transit system that provides connections to urban areas for shopping opportunities and access to medical services is a crucial first step. Such service may be less frequent but should be regular and predictable. For example, the Rail Runner is heavily utilized by Valencia

County residents, who lack nearby medical services but can travel by bus relatively easily from the downtown Albuquerque station to nearby clinics and hospitals. Similarly, services provided by the New Mexico Department of Transportation (NMDOT) and the regional transit districts provide round-trip, daily rural-to-urban connections, and the City of Las Cruces is opening an intermodal transit center in 2014 that will serve as a hub for local services and a terminal point for regional services to Alamogordo and El Paso.[55] Fully developed transit systems will not emerge in all New Mexico towns and cities, but it is realistic to expect the development of basic access between communities, accompanied by more complete networks within major urban areas.

The growth of transit services across the state, and in Albuquerque in particular, speaks to a future of transportation in New Mexico that is more diverse in terms of options available to residents. Planners across New Mexico are thus grappling with how best to provide a range of services that are safe, effective, and efficient. For instance, new emphasis is being placed on Complete Streets and Main Streets investments, which are designed to bring transportation down to a more pedestrian scale.[56] The question then becomes, what do these trends mean in terms of transportation infrastructure investments in the coming decades? This question is inextricably linked with the issue of funding such investments. To begin to address these questions we must begin with the role that individual travel, and driving in particular, plays in funding transportation infrastructure and how technological advances affect the traditional approach to paying for the infrastructure we need.

Transportation Financing

Meeting evolving transportation needs not only requires long-term planning and creative thinking, it also requires something more basic: money. With the exception of rail freight, transportation infrastructure is generally a public investment supported by a recurring flow of revenue to maintain it. Those public infrastructure needs are ever expanding, and funding is in increasingly short supply. A significant portion of the state's roads and bridges are nearing the end of their life cycles, while the main source of federal and state funding, the gasoline tax, has not been raised in decades and is not tied to inflation, meaning it is losing more of its purchasing power every year.[57] In addition, New Mexico has the eighth-lowest gas-tax rate in the country.[58] This creates a situation in which infrastructure must be replaced but the state does not have the revenues to undertake these projects.

In its most recent annual report card, the American Society of Civil Engineers gave the state of New Mexico a grade of C overall, including a C for roads, a C- for bridges, and a C+ for transit.[59] These grades actually put the state ahead of the nation, which received a D overall. Yet the state faces more than its share of challenges. The report succinctly concludes that "the main difficulty New Mexico faces is the shortage of funding: New Mexico must find more resources for its road improvement and maintenance. A long-term and comprehensive solution is needed, not merely a one-time measure."[60]

The budget for NMDOT is about $835 million, about half of which is federal dollars from the Highway Trust Fund, with the other half coming from the State Road Fund, which is supported by a combination of state gas-tax revenue and various fees.[61] A significant portion of the federal dollars pay the debt service on previously constructed major capital projects, and almost all of the state-generated dollars "fund routine maintenance functions across each District."[62] Yet 44 percent of the more than 68,000 miles of public roads are in "poor or mediocre" condition, while 8 percent of bridges are considered "structurally deficient" and 9 percent are "functionally obsolete," meaning they no longer meet highway design standards.[63] The condition of the New Mexico's infrastructure has real consequences. Not only can poor roadway conditions affect safety, but according to TRIP, a transportation research organization, "driving on rough roads costs the typical New Mexico urban motorist an average of $458 annually in extra vehicle operating costs—a total of $439 million annually for all drivers statewide."[64] The funding that remains is simply insufficient. The current annual need for construction projects is approximately $450 million, with an additional $150 million needed for bridge construction. Meeting these combined construction needs would consume more than two-thirds of the NMDOT budget, and the agency "estimates that its current level of funding is only enough to address about 20 percent of its projected needs."[65]

Proper infrastructure offers essential support for economic activity by allowing workers to access jobs and goods to be moved to market. In New Mexico's extractive industries, the heavy freight trucks required to transport natural resources can play havoc on the state's roads. In 2013 TRIP identified the projects that would have the greatest economic impact across New Mexico. Many of the projects identified are in rural areas with low traffic volumes, especially compared to arterial roads in Albuquerque, Santa Fe, or Las Cruces. But such facilities are critical for trade and the growing extractive industries. For example, growing commerce along the Mexico border and the opening of the Santa Teresa intermodal facility will generate high levels of freight travel across southern New Mexico, with five hundred to eight hundred trucks departing the "inland port" facility in the near term. It is unclear whether the roadways serving the site can adequately handle that level of demand or withstand the pounding such activity will incur.[66] It is clear, however, that under the current system, sufficient funding cannot be generated to address all of the state's needs.

The Fate of the Gas Tax

The essential problem in addressing transportation shortcomings in New Mexico is revenue generation. The gas tax provides resources for the National Highway Trust Fund and is a major source of local revenue for NMDOT, which receives more than $380 million per year from the State Road Fund. Yet a revenue system that relies on the gasoline tax becomes even less sustainable over time; the Highway Trust Fund loses more money each year, and recent predictions indicate that by 2021 the highway account will be nearly $100 billion in the red and the mass transit account will have a $30 billion shortfall.[67]

The need for additional revenue is made more acute by the fact that VMT per capita is falling nationally and locally and vehicles are becoming increasingly efficient. Out of justified environmental concerns, emissions rates and fuel efficiency have been improved through regulation of the Corporate Average Fuel Efficiency (CAFE) standards, which reflect the fleet-wide average fuel economy standards for each automaker for passenger vehicles (that is, cars and light trucks). CAFE standards currently require vehicles to get at least 25 miles per gallon and are set to rise to 35.5 miles per gallon by 2016 and 54.5 miles per gallon by 2025. Such a move will make it more affordable to operate vehicles and will reduce oil dependency. However, the move will make gas-tax revenue increasingly insufficient for maintenance needs.[68] Fuel-efficient vehicles such as hybrids generate less revenue on a per mile basis than standard vehicles, while electric vehicles, which are likely to form an increasing share of the fleet mix in coming decades, generate no revenue whatsoever for roadway maintenance.

The growing insolvency of the Highway Trust Fund is an established problem that is made worse by the fact that the New Mexico and federal gasoline taxes were last raised in 1993. New Mexico is one of thirty-six states that utilize a fixed-rate gasoline tax, in which the same rate is applied every year, regardless of the cost of fuel or the rate of inflation. Despite more than two decades of rising maintenance costs, the gas tax rates remain at 18.9 cents per gallon at the state level and 18.4 cents per gallon at the national level. A 2011 report by the Institute on Taxation and Economic Policy (ITEP) concluded that by not indexing state-level gasoline taxes to inflation, states forgo a combined $10 billion annually in purchasing power, and that that loss of revenue is a "major contributor to the $130 billion that the ASCE [American Society of Civil Engineers] estimates is lost each year due to vehicle repairs and travel time delays caused by deficiencies in America's transportation systems."[69] The ITEP report also provides a comprehensive assessment of how decisions about the structure of the gas tax affect individual states. ITEP found that, since 1994, New Mexico has experienced a 54 percent decrease in the cost-adjusted tax rate, or the purchasing power of its gas-tax revenue, the second-highest rate after Alaska. The study concluded that New Mexico would need to raise its gas tax by 20.1 cents per gallon, from 18.9 to 40.0 cents, in order to generate the same level of revenues as in 1993. Not doing so results in annual lost revenue of more than $170 million.[70]

ITEP has provided one of many independent proposals to increase the gas tax and tie future increases to the consumer price index or some other measure. At the federal level, increasing funding for transportation and addressing the deficit in the National Highway Trust Fund are subjects frequently addressed by commissions, but so far with little change in policy. The 2008 National Surface Transportation Policy and Revenue Study Commission's

Transportation for Tomorrow report proposed raising the gas tax a total of forty cents over a period of less than ten years.[71] One year later, the National Surface Transportation Infrastructure Finance Commission recommended a short-term gas-tax increase and some form of user fee in the long term.[72] In 2010, in the midst of a deficit debate, the National Commission on Fiscal Responsibility and Reform, known popularly as the Simpson-Bowles Commission, recommended raising the federal gas tax by fifteen cents per gallon.

The idea of raising the gas tax is such a nonstarter, however, that the proposed 2014 transportation authorization bill seeks a 50 percent increase in annual funding through the closing of corporate tax loopholes without addressing the sustainability of the Highway Trust Fund.[73] While the proposed bill makes a laudable effort to improve the nation's transportation infrastructure, it does not address the underlying Highway Trust Fund problems.

In the state of New Mexico, various House Memorials have considered sustainable funding strategies, but no meaningful legislation has resulted at the state level either. A 2010 analysis, in particular, called for an increase in vehicle registration and transaction fees, an increase in the gasoline tax and in the diesel tax by ten cents per gallon, and improved compliance with the weight-distance and trip taxes applied to freight trucks.[74]

A VMT Tax as a Transportation Financing Alternative

Addressing the shortfall in revenue is an immense challenge. Even increases in the gas tax, few of which have been proposed, are not likely to solve the long-term transportation funding challenges. However, there will come a time, sooner rather than later, when New Mexico will need to move away from the gas tax as the primary means of transportation funding.

The most likely replacement is a mileage-based user fee, also referred to as a vehicle-miles-traveled tax, or VMT tax.[75] Under a VMT tax, drivers are charged a fee based on the number of miles they drive, making a VMT tax a true pay-as-you-go system. To introduce such a system would require a significant up-front investment to equip each vehicle with the technology required to monitor driving, such as standard GPS devices, and discussions of such programs are frequently met with concerns over privacy.

Yet a move to a VMT tax is only a matter of time, and the sooner the system is embraced in New Mexico the better. Formal studies, such as one performed by the Center for Urban Transportation Research, increasingly reach the conclusion that a VMT tax is the only logical transportation funding solution over the long term.[76] Some U.S. government–sanctioned studies agree, including the report of the 2009 National Surface Transportation Infrastructure Finance Commission, which identified a mileage-based user fee as a viable alternative to the gas tax.

Support for some form of user fee extends to organizations such as the Reason Foundation, a libertarian and free-market-oriented think tank generally opposed to government largesse and higher taxes. Part of the Reason Foundation's rationale is that driving and private vehicles are not in any danger of being replaced, and roadway maintenance will be a critical long-term investment need.[77] The Reason Foundation also contends that a VMT tax would be a fairer approach than the current system: fees would apply to all users and would be proportionate to actual roadway use. Since fuel is still a cost, incentives for efficiency would remain, yet a VMT tax would generate funds required for maintenance at necessary levels.[78]

It is worth noting that leading economists, such as Edward Glaeser, favor a VMT tax as a means of managing congestion.[79] Currently, users do not bear the true costs of using roadways and there are no incentives for them to restrict their road use. Whereas traditional roadway solutions to congestion (new roads and new lanes) actually create incentives to drive by improving the efficiency of vehicle travel and thereby reducing the cost of driving for the individual, a VMT tax encourages smarter transportation decisions and is likely to lower traffic volumes and shift trips to other modes in the same manner that roadway-pricing programs do in some European and Asian cities.[80]

However, any transition in transportation financing is likely to take some time. Oregon has been the first state to experiment with a VMT tax through a series of pilot projects. The most comprehensive version will take place in 2015, when five thousand volunteers will pay a use fee of 1.5 cents per mile while being reimbursed for the 30-cent-per-gallon gas tax. To develop public understanding of the program and counter the most prominent concerns that the government may track individual movements, the project will provide a range of mileage-reporting options and rely on a private vendor for data collection.[81] Findings from earlier pilot programs have indicated that not only was a greater amount of revenue collected through the mileage fee than would have been collected through the gas tax, but Portland, Oregon, commuters altered their behavior and reduced travel during the evening peak period by 10 percent.[82] Although there is no timetable for widespread implementation, the Oregon experiments have inspired state departments of transportation around the country to begin investigating such programs in their own states.[83]

In New Mexico, policy makers must be prepared to assess how a VMT tax would affect different users and trip types. In a state with high levels of driving and in which long-distance trips are required for travel between rural communities, a fee-per-mile system could disproportionately affect parts of the state that are already expected to lose population and face tough economic conditions. Such a system could also negatively affect the tourism industry and visitation to national parks and monuments. In short, additional revenue is required, but policy makers must strive for a balance between equitable fees and sustainable funding.

Future Transportation Modes and Investments

In urban settings in particular, a greater variety of transportation options and lifestyles will emerge, yet the most likely scenario for New Mexico's transportation future is that cars will remain the dominant mode for most residents. Three primary factors are at play in the continued reliance on private vehicles. First, there are tremendous sunk costs in roadway infrastructure that make converting to other modes, such as rail, unlikely. Second, historical development and land use patterns, while changing, require many individuals to use private vehicles to access basic services. Finally, improved oil extraction techniques that support gas-powered vehicles and the emerging electric-vehicle industry mean that resource limitations will not be a factor pushing Americans away from driving.

In the near term, stricter CAFE standards will result in hybrid vehicles forming a greater share of the fleet mix. For example, Toyota expects 30 percent or more of its sales in 2016 to be hybrid vehicles.[84] But if entrepreneur

Elon Musk is to be believed, hybrids are merely a transitional technology and everything shy of rockets—what he considers essentially a "100 percent conversion"—will be electric powered in the not too distant future.[85] Such a transition is not guaranteed, and even the more aggressive estimates indicate that the electric-vehicle share of the vehicle fleet will only be around 50 percent by 2050, about 150 million vehicles.[86] This means that gas-powered automobiles will continue to have a huge role, although many or even the majority of those nonelectric vehicles will be hybrids. Of course, the continued reliance on private vehicles, regardless of power source, assumes a sustainable, long-term means of building and maintaining roads.

A transition to electric vehicles will also create the need for new types of infrastructure to power such vehicles. Whether the onus to develop electric-vehicle charging stations eventually falls on government agencies, utility companies, or the private sector remains to be seen.[87] At the very least, there will be a need for things like standardization in charging-facility design in order to make the provision of such facilities easier. Indeed, the increasing production of electric vehicles and their growing affordability indicate that New Mexico must prepare for the coming wave and anticipate the resulting energy infrastructure needs. With thoughtful planning, New Mexico could be at the forefront of the electric-vehicle revolution because of the state's vast potential for energy generation, which could power a network of electric-vehicle charging stations.

Having cleaner energy sources will not change the level of congestion that comes with growth and continued reliance on private vehicles. The personal discomfort people feel sitting on congested roadways; the growing preference for proximity of home, work, and services; and the desire to engage in more active forms of transportation are therefore the most likely catalysts for changing transportation behavior, particularly in urban settings. As a result, households and families may continue to move away from owning multiple cars and rely on a variety of transportation options.

Lifestyle changes may also lead to dramatically different trip types. Greater desire for mixed-use and walkable communities may inspire the return of more neighborhood-oriented retail and restaurants that require shorter trips and decreased reliance on private vehicles. While no New Mexican city will ever be the most walkable place in America, there are likely to be an increasing number of neighborhoods and corridors within Albuquerque, Santa Fe, and Las Cruces that are conducive to more urban lifestyles and increased pedestrian activity. Similarly, the state's distances are too vast and the roads too broad and unfriendly for bicycling to be a dominant mode. But an increasing number of roads that are overbuilt in terms of capacity—that is, there are more lanes than required to carry the daily traffic volumes now or in the future—will be downscaled and made bicycle-friendly to allow a greater number of trips to be taken without a private vehicle. Formal car-sharing services normally associated with major cities may play a role in more urbanized parts of Albuquerque and Las Cruces, as some residents choose to forgo owning cars but still desire vehicle access for some trips.

Transportation plans across New Mexico must also recognize that attempting to build out of congestion by constructing new roads and lanes is neither feasible nor affordable.[88] From a public policy perspective, transitioning to a world with increasing needs but diminished resources will require creative solutions and a willingness to support trial and error. Instead of emphasizing new roads and more lanes, planners and engineers are increasingly considering the movement of people, rather than cars, and thinking about multimodal transportation systems. That is, they are viewing vehicle, transit, bicycle, and pedestrian activities as an interconnected set of transportation networks rather than as modes to be treated in isolation. Greater attention will also be paid to the innovative use of technology to improve safety and travel conditions and get the most use out of existing infrastructure. New infrastructure in many cases may not be infrastructure at all, but technology that enables more efficient vehicle travel without adding new roadway capacity. Integrated signals and adaptive traffic-signal controls are being widely implemented, including at a citywide level in Los Angeles, and such technology was recently introduced along Albuquerque's Alameda Boulevard with great success. Likewise, communications technology may take many driving decisions out of the hands of individuals, including driverless cars and vehicle sensors that make crashes far less common.

There is also the acknowledgement among cities such as Albuquerque, Santa Fe, and Las Cruces that transit will have to play a bigger role. The transportation policy board for the Mid-Region Council of Governments went so far as to set mode-share goals in the *2035 Metropolitan Transportation Plan* for 20 percent of trips along the Albuquerque area's river crossings to be taken by transit; the levels of congestion along these roads are projected to be debilitating, and no new lanes or bridges have been proposed.[89] The board also set aside a pool of resources from the federal transportation funds distributed through the Transportation Improvement Fund for projects that support transit service across the Rio Grande.[90] Although transit-commuting shares at the city and state level are relatively low, achieving such a mode share in targeted locations is a goal within reach. There are a number of corridors in Albuquerque where transit service is frequent and ridership is high. Given the trends described here, it is not unrealistic to envision the share of all trips taken by transit growing to double digits and to foresee transit service becoming reliable and wide-reaching enough that it offers a meaningful option for commuters or for kids to travel to school.

The question is how serious policy makers are about creating transit options over time and investing in necessary vehicles, station areas, and the provision of service. A number of such investments are already being considered across New Mexico. The Rio Metro Regional Transit District, which operates the Rail Runner and other regional transit connections in Valencia, Bernalillo, and Sandoval Counties, is finalizing two bus rapid transit (BRT) studies, while Albuquerque is actively pursuing BRT service along Central Avenue, a corridor that currently carries more than eighteen thousand riders per day. This series of BRT options could form a regional high-capacity transit network that complements the Rail Runner and local routes to provide frequent and quality service over a large portion of the metropolitan area.

While less certain of implementation, commuter rail between Las Cruces and El Paso is also being considered. Although the $800 million price tag is rather daunting, there is interest from the policy boards for the metropolitan planning organizations in both El Paso and Las Cruces, and deep connections between the two cities make the investment a logical one. In addition to the shared family networks across the border region, the economies of these cities are increasingly interconnected, and there are more commuters between the two cities than between Santa Fe and Albuquerque.[91] Although there is less external tourism in the corridor, the service would provide appealing access for southern New Mexico residents to a regional center with shopping, recreational opportunities, and amenities such as a zoo and a major airport, as well as access to Ciudad Juárez.

For its part, El Paso is investing heavily in a BRT system and making a concerted effort to decrease dependence on single-occupancy vehicles. The result will be a high level of mobility for visitors to El Paso, as well as for El Pasoans. Meanwhile, in the fall of 2014 Doña Ana County residents will vote on a ballot measure to levy a gross receipts tax to fund regional transit services, which at some point could conceivably include commuter rail.

Other rail options are even less certain, though still plausible. The brief national excitement over high-speed rail has subsided, and it is hard to envision the funding becoming available—or sufficient market demand arising—to connect Albuquerque with other cities, other than as an intermediate stop between Denver and El Paso/Juárez. Calls for extending the Rail Runner to other communities speak to the desire for improved transportation options across the state and the value of implementing a quality service, but the costs would be prohibitive compared to the number of potential users, and development of the service would require both a tremendous amount of political will and dramatic changes in funding priorities at the state level.

Ironically, the funding options for public transit may be brighter than for roadways. While there is little will to raise the gas tax, voters across the country regularly impose sales and other taxes on themselves to support transit services. In 2012 and 2013, 75 percent of transit referendums nationwide passed.[92] Such revenue sources are crucial, since funding for major capital projects is limited. Regional Transit Districts (RTDs) were first formed in New Mexico in the mid-2000s for the purpose of funding and operating the Rail Runner and other regional services; they allow communities that value transit to impose a gross receipts tax to support it. RTDs also receive federal funds and offer a means of both generating needed revenue and pursuing regionally significant projects that transcend jurisdictional boundaries.[93] Thus far, two RTDs—Rio Metro and North Central—have self-imposed gross receipts taxes.[94] The South Central RTD will bring a ballot measure before voters in fall 2014.

Recommendations

I have examined changing population distribution, lifestyle preferences, and traveler behavior and how these factors will shape New Mexico communities in the coming decades. I have also discussed the ability to meet New Mexico's infrastructure demands under the current financing system. But there are a number of other factors, including water and economic conditions, which are discussed elsewhere in this book, that are fundamentally tied to how New Mexicans will live, where New Mexicans will call home, and what sort of transportation options will be available. Developing policies that ensure the sustainability of natural resources and creating livable places where people want to be requires integrating various disciplines and planning efforts. Too often, policy decisions are made without considering the full range of impacts. This includes where schools and hospitals are located, whether the utility or transportation infrastructure exists to support new developments, whether certain transportation investments incur even greater maintenance costs over time, and whether land use decisions lead to development in places where there is complete dependence on private vehicles, burdening households with high transportation costs.

While metropolitan planning organizations project population and employment growth, they do not have land use authority in New Mexico. This leads to a regional transportation planning process that is in many ways reactive to jurisdictional land use decisions. In response, metropolitan planning organizations are moving toward demonstrating the consequences—positive and negative—of different development patterns and creating incentives for federal dollars to be spent in certain ways, although federal dollars are only a small portion of the funds available within each region for project implementation.

There are other limitations on the current planning structures. Water planning is conducted at the state and regional levels but is not always well integrated into municipal or county-level efforts and can be divorced from land use planning decisions. Economic development revolves around recruiting individual businesses, sometimes creating competition between communities and failing to consider regional or statewide economic programs.

Similarly, state planning statutes are antiquated and provide little direction to planners on best practices or twenty-first-century needs.

While there are state-level agencies to support housing, transportation, water resource management, and economic development, there is not a structural means of coordinating between planning agencies and integrating decision making to ensure that public dollars are spent in a way that maximizes benefits and that long-term policy decisions can be effectively implemented. I recommend the creation of an agency to examine growth patterns across the state and infrastructure needs across regions. This state-level planning agency could be modeled after one in the state of Maryland, where the office is headed by a cabinet-level secretary.[95] The agency could build on the transportation planning efforts already conducted by metropolitan planning organizations and rural planning organizations and identify strategic statewide investments, not just in transportation but in water and energy infrastructure that transcend regional boundaries as well. The key would be integration, both vertically, from the local to the regional level, and horizontally, between state-level agencies.

A state-level planning agency existed in New Mexico in the 1970s, but because it lacked a clear mission other than resource mapping, responsibilities were eventually spread around to other agencies. Nevertheless, the need for interagency coordination has been recognized over time and roundtable agency working groups have been formed to bring departments together. An institutionalized entity for sharing information and integrating agency plans would ensure that such efforts are more successful in the future.

On a more immediate level, there are large portions of the state where municipalities, counties, and regional agencies lack the staff and resources to properly address the challenges they face in their communities. A state-level agency could provide planning support for these communities on an as-needed basis. There is, of course, a danger in creating an additional level of bureaucracy. Where regional planning efforts have been more successful, a state-level agency could risk creating unnecessary hurdles. A system would need to be devised to delegate responsibilities to agencies that have greater capacity and that could provide local assistance more immediately.

Of particular importance may be the social and economic health of rural communities. If New Mexico is serious about the survival of small towns and rural communities, many of which already feature disproportionately high senior populations and some of which are projected to experience population loss, a concerted effort will have to be made to ensure access to basic services. This could mean bringing medical care to seniors or bringing seniors to medical care in the form of a public transportation model that is friendly to senior citizens and focuses on access to urban areas. From there, increasingly robust transit services could make trips within New Mexico cities convenient and affordable. Either way, it is about more than medical coverage, it is a transportation issue that needs to be well coordinated.

- **Institute a mileage-based user fee.** Replace the state gas tax with a VMT tax to ensure a sustainable and equitable means of generating revenue to maintain the state's transportation infrastructure. The transition to electric and fuel-efficient vehicles makes such a shift increasingly urgent.
- **Plan for a range of transportation and housing options.** Cars may still be king, but they will not remain almighty, especially in cities. Investing in a range of transportation modes and creating conditions for transit-oriented development and other housing targeted to seniors and young professionals will be critical to meeting the needs and demands of New Mexico residents in future decades.
- **Confront realities of urban population gain and rural population loss.** Considering how to best meet needs and allocate resources in a changing demographic environment is a large undertaking with complex implications for the state's traditional identity.
- **Establish a state planning agency.** A statewide agency that plans for growth across regions and coordinates decisions about transportation, water resources, economic development, and energy needs.

New Mexico 2050

Given the pressures and changing patterns concerning where New Mexicans will live in the future, their housing needs and desires, and the means by which they travel, important policy decisions must be made to ensure a sustainable transportation future for the state of New Mexico. The recommendations in this chapter provide a starting point that could serve to move the state in a positive direction in the years ahead.

Notes

1. This change in emphasis can be seen in documents such as the New Mexico Department of Transportation's *State Rail Plan*. The *Statewide Multi-Modal Long-Range Transportation Plan*, to be completed in 2015, is also prioritizing maintenance of existing infrastructure.

2. According to the National Highway Traffic Safety Administration, New Mexico ranks tenth nationally in traffic fatalities per capita. Remarkably, this is substantially better than the traffic fatality rate in previous years.

3. Niraj Chokshi, "Population Growth in New Mexico Is Approaching Zero— and Other Bad Signs," *GovBeat* (blog), *Washington Post*, January 17, 2014, http://www.washingtonpost.com/blogs/govbeat/wp/2014/01/17/population-growth-in-new-mexico-is-approaching-zero-and-other-bad-signs/.

4. American Community Survey, 2012 State to State Migration Flows.

5. It is important to note that the most recent Geospatial Population Studies Group projections are based on the 2010 Census, with updated data on fertility rates and migration, both of which were affected by the Great Recession. As a result, the numbers given here are more conservative in their outlook than previous projections.

6. Dennis Domrzalski, "Oil Boom Brings More People to Southeastern NM," *Albuquerque Business First*, March 27, 2014, http://www.bizjournals.com/albuquerque/news/2014/03/27/oil-boom-brings-more-people-to-southeastern-nm.html. Growth in Hobbs was greater than in New Mexico overall (the state added only about 1,750 residents), meaning that if not for Hobbs the state would have lost population in 2013.

7. Census-defined metropolitan statistical areas refer to the county or counties surrounding urbanized areas of more than fifty thousand residents. There are four MSAs in New Mexico, surrounding the cities of Albuquerque, Farmington, Las Cruces, and Santa Fe. For Farmington, Las Cruces, and Santa Fe, the MSA comprises the county in which the city is located—San Juan, Doña Ana, and Santa Fe Counties, respectively. The Albuquerque MSA comprises Bernalillo, Sandoval, Valencia, and (somewhat oddly) Torrance Counties, resulting in a geographically large, culturally diverse grouping that contains far more rural than urban lands.

8. El Paso Metropolitan Planning Organization, *Horizon 2040 Metropolitan Transportation Plan*, October 4, 2013, 2.

9. Lauren Villagran, "Santa Teresa Is Catching Fire," *Albuquerque Journal*, April 14, 2014.

10. El Consejo Nacional de Población, Proyecciones de la Población 2010–2050.

11. Kevin Robinson-Avila and Lauren Villagran, "Juárez on the Rebound," *Albuquerque Journal*, March 9, 2014.

12. "Anuncia duarte inversion de 450 mdd en infraestructura San Jerónimo-Santa Teresa," *La Opción de Chihuahua*, August 9, 2013, http://laopcion.com.mx/noticia/1307; "San Jerónimo es ruta alterna para sacar el tren de Juárez, dice César Duarte," *El Diario Edición Juárez*, April 1, 2014, http://diario.mx/Local/2014–04–01_44017d5f/san-jeronimo-es-ruta-alterna-para-sacar-el-tren-de-juarez-dice-cesar-duarte/.

13. Accommodating urban population growth is challenging, and urban planning strategies are also evolving. While some places still shy away from regulation—for example, neither fast-growing San Juan County nor Lea County has zoning ordinances—other jurisdictions, such as Santa Fe County, are pursuing policies that concentrate development in locations where the infrastructure already exists to support it. Las Cruces has adopted a "smart code" for its downtown to integrate walkable urban conditions and allow for targeted density. Similarly, Albuquerque is about to undertake a major rethinking of its comprehensive plan and implement a unified development ordinance to streamline the development process and allow more infill and transit-oriented development.

14. Domrzalski, "Oil Boom Brings More People to Southeastern NM."

15. The loss of population in more rural areas is not a new trend. Grant, Hidalgo, Colfax, McKinley, Quay, Rio Arriba, and Sierra Counties all lost population in the ten-year span between the 2000 and 2010 Censuses.

16. David Owen, *Green Metropolis: Why Living Smaller, Living Closer, and Driving Less Are the Keys to Sustainability* (New York: Riverhead Books, 2009).

17. U.S. Census Bureau, 2012 National Population Projections.

18. This is actually a global trend, and U.S. demographics are much healthier than those of nearly all other industrialized nations. That is, the United States has more robust birthrates and generally more open immigration policies than other nations, meaning that the United States is expected to gain population rather than shrink in coming decades, and it will maintain a healthy workforce. The median age in the United States—which is thirty-seven today—will be much lower than that in most other industrialized nations; in 2050 the U.S. median age will be forty-one, compared to fifty-three in Japan and South Korea, fifty-one in Germany, and forty-six in China. In many Western European nations, there will be nearly as many dependents, or people out of the workforce, as those participating in the labor force. Declining birthrates and rapidly aging populations mean that countries like Japan, Germany, and Russia are expected to lose more than 10 percent of their overall populations, while China is expected to grow only slightly, and only after reversing its one-child-only policy. UN Department of Economic and Social Affairs, World Population Prospects: The 2012 Revision, http://esa.un.org/unpd/wpp/index.htm.

19. In 2010 there were about 460,000 residents under the age of sixteen in New Mexico. By 2040 the youth population will be about 546,000, for a growth rate of 18.5 percent.

20. Public Policy Institute, *Aging in Place: A State Survey of Livability Policies and Practices*, December 2011.

21. U.S. PIRG and Frontier Group, *Transportation and the New Generation*, April 2012, p. 13.

22. Damon Scott, "La Vida Llena to Build $50 Million Rio Rancho Community," *Albuquerque Business First*, February 19, 2014, http://www.bizjournals.com/albuquerque/news/2014/02/19/50-million-project-coming-to-rio-rancho.html.

While a growing number of senior housing developments are emerging in the Albuquerque area, according to one senior-living provider, "There is more demand than supply for senior living."

23. For the purposes of this chapter, millennials refers to those born between 1980 and 2000.

24. Urban Land Institute, *America in 2013: A ULI Survey of Views on Housing, Transportation, and Community*. The desire to be close to destinations was shared by the majority of respondents. For example, 61 percent of the respondents in the ULI survey indicated "they would prefer a smaller home with a shorter commute over a larger home with longer commute." However, millennials favor these conditions at a higher rate and appear more willing to act upon those preferences.

25. 2011 Robert Charles Lesser and Company survey cited in Leigh Gallagher, *The End of the Suburbs* (New York: Portfolio/Penguin, 2013), 157.

26. Ibid.

27. National Association of Realtors, National Community Preference Survey, October 2013.

28. Arthur C. Nelson in Gallagher, *End of the Suburbs*, 159.

29. Richard Metcalf, "Malaise Grips ABQ Apartment Market," *Albuquerque Journal*, November 11, 2013.

30. Even the state's largest city has a relatively low population density. In 2012 Albuquerque had 2,959 persons per square mile. By comparison, Los Angeles has 7,545 persons per square mile, while the figures for both Denver and Houston are over 3,600. Cities similar in size to Albuquerque, such as El Paso and Tucson, have lower population densities, at 2,543 and 2,794 persons per square mile, respectively.

31. American Community Survey, 2012 Three-Year Estimates. In New Mexico 79.2 percent of commuting trips are made by solo drivers, while 10.6 percent are carpool trips. Other southwestern states, such as Arizona and Texas, have comparable commuting rates, in which approximately 90 percent of all workers (solo and carpoolers) commute by private vehicle. In Colorado 85 percent of workers commute by private vehicle, while in California and Oregon the rates are 84.5 percent and 82 percent, respectively. While New Mexico does not rank particularly high in terms of drivers or vehicles per capita, this may be explained in part by the high number of unregistered drivers.

32. U.S. Department of Transportation, Research and Innovative Technology Division, "System Mileage Within the United States."

33. Michael Sivak, *Has Motorization in the U.S. Peaked?*, part 2, *Use of Light-Duty Vehicles* (University of Michigan Transportation Research Institute, July 2013), 9. Sivak studies light-duty vehicles, which he uses as a proxy for personal driving. Federal Highway Administration data show that total driving, which includes commercial driving, peaked slightly later, but has followed similar trends.

34. Ibid., 7. The number of vehicles per licensed driver fell from a peak of 0.79 vehicles in 2006 to 0.75 in 2011. Similarly, vehicles per household dropped from a peak of 2.05 in 2005 to 1.95 in 2011. While the Great Recession, which officially began in December 2007, "is responsible for some of the reduction in driving," a study concludes that economic conditions were "only part" of the shift. Frontier Group and U.S. PIRG, *Transportation in Transition*, December 2010.

35. Sivak, *Has Motorization in the U.S. Peaked?*, 4. As a result of the Great Recession, there were actually 2.6 million fewer registered vehicles in 2008 than in 2011; however, that trend is expected to reverse as the U.S. economy recovers.

36. Frontier Group and U.S. PIRG, *Transportation in Transition.*

37. Urban Land Institute, *America in 2013*; National Association of Realtors, National Community Preference Survey.

38. U.S. Department of Transportation, Research and Innovative Technology Division, State Transportation Statistics 2012.

39. A number of factors are at play in the decrease in overall driving. One cited reason is the increase in the number of people who telecommute to work, but that change is modest. Sivak, *Has Motorization in the U.S. Peaked?*, 9. Sivak cites U.S. Census Bureau data that indicate telecommuting grew from 3.3 percent of all commuters in 2000 to 4.3 percent in 2010. The greatest factor in the overall shift in transportation patterns in future decades, however, will be simple change in consumer preference.

40. Reliable statewide transit data beginning with the year 2005 was made available to the author. The Mid-Region Council of Governments maintains transit use data for the Albuquerque metropolitan area beginning with the year 2000.

41. New Mexico Department of Transportation, Transit and Rail Bureau fact sheets, 2005–2012.

42. New Mexico Department of Transportation, *New Mexico Statewide Public Transportation Plan*, October 2010, 45.

43. Frontier Group and U.S. PIRG, *Transportation in Transition*, 24–25.

44. Data on ridership and passenger miles traveled provided directly by Rio Metro Regional Transit District. Data is also available through the Federal Transit Administration National Transit Database.

45. In addition to the increase in transit usage, in the years since the 2000 Census, Albuquerque has witnessed modest increases in the percentage of workers who commute by bike or work at home and in the number of households with zero vehicles. At the same time the proportion of workers who commuted by car decreased. Comparison of 2000 Census figures and the 2008–2012 American Community Survey shows a 1.1 percent decrease in the proportion of workers who commuted by car; a 0.2 percent increase in workers who commuted by bike; a 0.6 percent increase in workers who worked from home; and a 1.2 percent increase in households with zero vehicles.

46. 2000 Census; American Community Survey, 2012 Three-Year Estimates. Census data capture only commuting trips and do not reflect overall transit usage rates.

47. National Household Travel Survey, 2001, 2009.

48. Urban Land Institute, *America in 2013*; Frontier Group and U.S. PIRG, *Transportation and the New Generation*, 10.

49. Frontier Group and U.S. PIRG, *Transportation and the New Generation*, 3. Some policies and external factors contribute to lower driving levels among younger drivers, including higher costs of driving, the impacts of the Great Recession, and tougher restrictions, such as graduated driver's licenses. But the lower rates also reflect growing apathy toward driving and reinforce the assertion that "America's current transportation policy—dominated by road building—is fundamentally out-of-step with the transportation patterns and expressed preferences of growing numbers of Americans." Ibid.

50. Ibid.

51. National Association of Realtors survey quoted in ibid., 17–18.

52. Ibid., 25.

53. Ibid., 26.

54. Draft results from the Mid-Region Travel Survey, conducted in 2013–2014 by the Mid-Region Council of Governments.

55. Steve Ramirez, "Intermodal Transit Center Readies to Open," *Las Cruces Sun-News*, October 11, 2013, http://www.lcsun-news.com/las_cruces-news/ci_24293337/intermodal-transit-center-readies-open.

56. According to Smart Growth America, Complete Streets policies "ensure that transportation planners and engineers consistently design and operate the entire roadway with all users in mind—including bicyclists, public transportation vehicles and riders, and pedestrians of all ages and abilities." Smart Growth America, National Complete Streets Coalition, http://www.smartgrowthamerica.org/complete-streets.

57. American Society of Civil Engineers, *America's Infrastructure Report Card 2013: New Mexico*, 94, http://www.infrastructurereportcard.org/new_mexico/new-mexico-overview/.

58. Tax Foundation, State Gasoline Tax Rates, 2009–2013, March 21, 2013, http://taxfoundation.org/article/state-gasoline-tax-rates-2009-2013.

59. American Society of Civil Engineers, *America's Infrastructure Report Card*.

60. Ibid., 99.

61. New Mexico Department of Transportation, "State Road Fund Forecast Update," presented to the Revenue Stabilization and Tax Policy Committee, New Mexico State Legislature, September 23, 2013.

62. New Mexico Department of Transportation, *2013 Annual Report*, 5. About $160 million goes to debt service for the Governor Richardson's Investment Partnership and Citizens' Highway Advisory Taskforce programs.

63. U.S. Department of Transportation, Research and Innovative Technology Division, State Transportation Statistics 2012. While not necessarily inspiring confidence, the condition of bridges in New Mexico is not nearly as dire as in most other states.

64. TRIP, *New Mexico Transportation by the Numbers: Meeting the State's Need for Safe and Efficient Mobility*, January 2014, 3.

65. American Society of Civil Engineers, *America's Infrastructure Report Card*. While counties and municipalities pay for road construction and maintenance through a combination of general obligation bonds, local tax revenue, and

state resources, they too find themselves unable to keep up with maintenance demands. According to the American Society of Civil Engineers report, "Albuquerque has 1,170 lane miles in poor and very poor condition, which would take $240 million to mill and inlay."

66. Brook Stockberger, "BIA: New Road Needed in Santa Teresa to Handle 'Tsunami' of Truck Traffic," *Las Cruces Sun-News*, March 9, 2014, http://www. lcsun-news.com/las_cruces-news/ci_25308314/bia-new-road-needed-santa-teresa-handle-tsunami.

67. Irwin Dawid, "The Highway Trust Fund Challenge: Policy Reform and Increasing Revenue," Planetizen, November 6, 2011, http://www.planetizen. com/node/52261. The growing gap between revenues and annual expenditures is made up for at the national level through loans from the general fund to the Highway Trust Fund.

68. The National Highway Traffic Safety Administration stated in August 2012 that the new CAFE standards will save consumers $1.7 trillion and twelve billion barrels of oil. Efficiency increases for freight trucks will also have a dramatic impact on air quality. "Obama Administration Finalizes Historic 54.5 mpg Fuel Efficiency Standards," press release, August 28, 2012, http:// www.nhtsa.gov/About+NHTSA/Press+Releases/2012/tion+Finalizes+Historic+ 54.5+mpg+Fuel+Efficiency+Standards.

69. Institute on Taxation and Economic Policy, *Building a Better Gas Tax: How to Fix One of State Government's Least Sustainable Revenue Sources*, December 2011, 11.

70. Ibid., 12. Similarly, the New Mexico diesel fuel tax was last increased in 2004, resulting in an additional $22.2 million in lost annual revenue (15). Therefore, according to ITEP, a total of $193 million per year in additional revenue would have been generated if gas taxes were tied to inflation (18).

71. Irwin Dawid, "National Transportation Commission Calls for 40 Cent Gas Tax Increase," Planetizen, January 17, 2008, http://www.planetizen.com/ node/29338.

72. Irwin Dawid, "Raise the Gas Tax AND Switch to VMT Fee, Says Commission," Planetizen, March 2, 2009, http://www.planetizen.com/ node/37628.

73. Michael D. Shear and Coral Davenport, "To Pay for Infrastructure Repairs, Obama Seeks Tax Changes," *New York Times*, February 26, 2014.

74. Cambridge Systematics and NMDOT, *House Memorial 5: Sustainable Funding Strategies*, March 2010, report prepared for 2013 House Memorial on Raising Revenue for Transportation Infrastructure.

75. Some states have moved to privatize a greater percentage of roads or to charge more fees in the form of tolls. But not all roads can be tolled, and the combination of lower levels of driving and free, if less direct, alternative routes make this approach to revenue generation less than perfect.

76. Center for Transportation Research, University of South Florida, *Florida MPOAC Transportation Revenue Study*, July 2012.

77. In particular, the Reason Foundation questions whether current trends among millennials will really inform long-term travel patterns and asserts that not only do senior citizens drive more today than in the past, but improved technology and safety features, potentially including driverless cars, will ensure high levels of driving among older generations into the future. Robert Poole, "Public Works Financing: How Much Will Americans Drive in the Future," June 5, 2013, Reason Foundation, http://reason.org/news/printer/how-much-will-americans-drive-in-th.

78. Adrian Moore, "Mileage-Based User Fees and Sustainable Transportation" (presentation at the Association of Metropolitan Planning Organizations Annual Conference, Portland, OR, October 22–25, 2013).

79. Edward Glaeser, *Triumph of the City* (New York: Penguin Books, 2001). Gilles Duranton and Matthew Turner indicate that user fees are the only effective means of reducing congestion. Gilles Duranton and Matthew A. Turner, "The Fundamental Law of Road Congestion: Evidence from U.S. Cities," *American Economic Review* 101.6 (October 2011): 2616–52.

80. Congestion pricing programs in London, Stockholm, Singapore, and other cities have been introduced to reduce driving in central cities and to encourage use of other modes of transportation. Such programs are most effective when they control access to particular locations with high demand, but they are less appropriate at a large scale.

81. Ben O'Neil, "Oregon Phases in Country's First Pay-Per-Mile Program," *Next City*, July 11, 2013, http://nextcity.org/daily/entry/oregon-phases-in-countrys-first-ever-pay-per-mile-program-vmt-tax.

82. Oregon Department of Transportation, *Road Usage Charge Pilot Program: Preliminary Findings*, February 2013, 5; Steve Scauzillo, "As Highway Fund Goes Broke, Southern California Planners Advocate Drivers Pay a Vehicle Miles Fee," *San Gabriel Valley Tribune*, March 27, 2014 http://www.sgvtribune.com/government-and-politics/20140327/as-highway-fund-goes-broke-southern-california-planners-advocate-drivers-pay-a-vehicle-miles-fee.

83. Scauzillo, "As Highway Fund Goes Broke"; "Mileage Tax Proposal," WLOS.com, April 2014, http://wlos.com/shared/news/features/top-stories/stories/wlos_mileage-tax-proposal-15722.shtml.

84. Steve Diehlman, "Japanese Automakers Ready for 2016 CAFE Standards," *Automobile*, October 30, 2009, http://www.automobilemag.com/features/news/japanese-automakers-ready-for-2016-cafe-standards-2066/.

85. Elon Musk, interview by Fareed Zakaria, *GPS*, CNN, November 24, 2013, transcript, http://transcripts.cnn.com/TRANSCRIPTS/1311/24/fzgps.01.html.

86. Rocky Mountain Institute, U.S. Projected Electric Vehicle Stocks, 2010–2050, http://www.rmi.org/RFGraph-US_projected_electric_vehicle_stocks.

87. For more on the expanded role for the state and local jurisdictions in supporting the conversion to electric vehicles, see the Rocky Mountain Institute's Get Ready Project, http://www.rmi.org/project_get_ready.

88. Mid-Region Council of Governments, *2035 Metropolitan Transportation Plan*, Ex-1. The Las Cruces Metropolitan Planning Organization's *Transport 2040* plan identifies as one of its transportation principles, "Maintain and improve the existing transportation system first and foremost" (86).

89. The goals state that 10 percent of river crossing trips are to be completed by transit by 2025 and 20 percent by 2035. The current share of trips across the Rio Grande made by transit is less than 2 percent, although that includes all trips along Interstate 40. Central Avenue has a transit mode share across the river of around 8 percent.

90. Federal funds for transportation projects in metropolitan areas are managed by metropolitan planning organizations through the Transportation Improvement Program (TIP).

91. U.S. Census, Journey to Work Data, 2006–2010. Travel between the cities is augmented by the policy that allows residents of eight southern New Mexico counties to attend the University of Texas–El Paso and pay in-state tuition rates, while West Texas residents can attend New Mexico State for the same rate as New Mexico residents.

92. Center for Transportation Excellence, www.ctfe.org.

93. A similar model exists in Texas with Regional Mobility Authorities, which are sanctioned by the state to implement significant regional projects. The *Statewide Public Transit Plan* identifies RTDs as a potential means of introducing new services that cannot be fully funded at the state level.

94. In 2008 voters in Bernalillo, Valencia, and Sandoval Counties (part of the Rio Metro RTD) and voters in Santa Fe, Los Alamos, Rio Arriba, and Taos Counties (part of the North Central RTD) all voted to fund the Rail Runner and other regional transit services.

95. The Maryland state planning office places particular emphasis on smart growth policies and the regional impacts of land use decisions. The agency offers technical assistance to municipalities and counties and is responsible for a range of data collection and analysis. See "Our Work," Maryland Department of Planning, http://planning.maryland.gov/OurWork/ourwork.shtml.

Epilogue

FRED HARRIS

THE BOOK IS FINISHED. THAT'S IT. THAT'S OUR STORY.

That's our ode to New Mexico. That's our list of this proud state's great assets, as well as some of its worrisome liabilities.

These are the marching orders for those of us who want New Mexico to become an even greater Land of Enchantment.

And I've come to believe that New Mexico's official flag salute points the way: "I salute the flag of the state of New Mexico, the Zia symbol of perfect friendship among united cultures."

We've got to recognize our shared interests and work things out together—in the same way that Laura Paskus and Adrian Oglesby said in chapter 5, for example, that water settlements for an agreed-upon *reparto de aguas* are better than lawsuits that seem to last longer than Supreme Court justices. (The last are my words.)

Will we do all the things this book recommends? No. Not soon, anyway. Maybe you don't agree with some—or even all—of the things this book recommends. That's okay. But let's begin the debate. Let's talk. And then let's act.

I agree with the late John Gardner, my friend and the great U.S. secretary of health, education, and welfare when I was a U.S. senator, who said, "We're in deep trouble as a people, and history will not deal kindly with any nation which will not tax itself to cure its miseries."

New Mexico is in crisis! We know for sure that just keeping on doing the same things we've been doing isn't working. Too many New Mexicans are getting sick and dying. Too many New Mexican kids are falling by the wayside, consigned to "short lives of quiet desperation." Too many New Mexican families are losing out on the American dream. Too much of New Mexico's great natural resources is being squandered and wasted, lost to future generations.

Maybe you remember that the United States came out of World War II with a national debt that was colossal, about 140 percent of gross domestic product. Today's naysayers would have said—as some did then—"Cut the budget; we've got to have austerity." But we didn't do that. Instead, we began to invest in ourselves. Remember the GI Bill of Rights, for example? It took the unemployed returning servicemen and servicewomen and gave them first-rate education and training. It helped them buy homes, which somebody had to furnish the materials for and somebody else had to construct. This program was terribly important and uplifting for the millions of men and women who took advantage of it. And it also resulted in a huge and lasting boost for the nation's economy. What was wrong with that?

And what was wrong with President Dwight Eisenhower's massive inter-state highway program, the greatest public works project since the days of Rome? Look at all the people that great program put to work immediately. And think of what a giant and long-lasting shot in the arm it was for our economy.

What was the result of all these kinds of post–World War II investments in ourselves? The national debt overwhelmed our gross domestic product, the government's basis for its ability to pay? Is that what happened? Did the United States go bankrupt?

No, to the contrary, we proved what the English economist John Maynard Keynes had written, what my tough cowboy kind of dad said more simply, "You have to spend money to make money." The national debt as a percentage of gross domestic product, our ability to pay, shrank and shrank. Because our ability to pay, our gross domestic product, on which the government collects taxes, grew and grew.

We need more of that kind of bold action today. And of course, a lot of what needs to be done must come from the national level. But we in New Mexico should do our part, too.

We all know that. We all know that, right here in New Mexico, we need a jump start—both for our economy and for our self-confidence.

What if, for example, as recommended in this book, we immediately decided to give New Mexicans a raise by lifting the minimum wage and indexing it to the cost of living? What if, as another example, we amended the New Mexico Constitution to allow us to spend a small portion of the income each year from our massive New Mexico Land Grant Permanent Fund for early childhood education, where it would have the greatest and most lasting effect? And what if, too, we decided to invest in ourselves in another way— great new stimulus funds for infrastructure, roads and highways, school buildings, and child care, for example?

Wouldn't people say, "Something's happening in New Mexico!" Wouldn't *we* say, "We *are* New Mexico—and we're back!"

Is this going to happen? Will we begin to act? I think so—because more and more of us are coming to see that it is in our own best interest to do so. More and more of us are coming to see that we're in this thing together and that "everybody does better when everybody does better."

Can I promise that it will happen? No, but I can say one thing for sure: there is existential value in the struggle itself, and each of us must do whatever he or she can do.

We can make a start. We can do what we can.

¡Sí, se puede!

Contributors

Fred Harris, JD with distinction, is a twice-elected former U.S. senator from Oklahoma and a longtime professor—now professor emeritus—of political science at the University of New Mexico, where he is still director of the UNM Fred Harris Congressional Internship Program. An award-winning author of three novels, he has also produced nineteen nonfiction books on public policy, politics, and government, including, as coeditor, *Locked in the Poorhouse: Cities, Race, and Poverty in the United States*, and, as coauthor, a recent e-book, *These People Want to Work: Immigration Reform*.

▪ ▪ ▪ ▪

Hakim Bellamy, MA, poet laureate of Albuquerque (2012–2014), is a regional and National Poetry Slam champion and founder and president of Beyond Poetry LLC. He is also a noted musician, actor, journalist, playwright, and community organizer.

Veronica C. García, EdD, has been an outstanding New Mexico schoolteacher, principal, superintendent, and state cabinet secretary of public education. She has received numerous awards, including the National Governors' Association Award for Excellence in State Government, New Mexico Superintendent of the Year, and the Lifetime Achievement Award in Education from *Hispanic* magazine. She is presently executive director of New Mexico Voices for Children.

Pamelya Herndon, JD, attorney, CPA, and executive director of the Southwest Women's Law Center, Albuquerque, is an authority and activist in regard to the civil and human rights of women, LGBT people, African Americans, and other minorities.

Nandini Pillai Kuehn, PhD, has fifteen years of experience in health care administration and in health funding and policy. She is presently the director of New Mexico Health Services Consulting and is the founder and board president of the New Mexico health insurance cooperative New Mexico Health Connections.

Adrian Oglesby, JD, is an attorney and New Mexico water law and water management expert. He has been managing editor of the *U.S.-Mexico Law Journal*, president of the New Mexico Riparian Council, and member of the board of directors of the Middle Rio Grande Conservancy District and presently serves as director of the Utton Transboundary Resources Center, University of New Mexico.

Laura Paskus is a noted New Mexico environmental journalist and author of numerous book chapters and periodical articles. She has been managing editor of *Tribal College Journal*, assistant editor of *High Country News*, and president of the Rio Grande Chapter of the Society of Professional Journalists.

Jim Peach, PhD, an accomplished economist, is a regents professor in the Department of Economics and International Business, College of Business, New Mexico State University. He is the author of many scholarly articles and has received awards at NMSU for outstanding funded research and teaching excellence.

V. B. Price is a noted New Mexican poet and journalist—and more. He is a member of the faculty of the University of New Mexico's Honors College, former editor of the Mary Burritt Christensen Poetry Series at the University of New Mexico Press, and an adjunct associate professor at the UNM School of Architecture and Planning. He is a cofounder of the online publication

New Mexico Mercury and the author of several books, including *The Orphaned Land: New Mexico's Environment Since the Manhattan Project.*

Henry Rael, MA, after many years in the private publishing and technology sectors, worked in grassroots community and enterprise development in New Mexico, where he was the founder of a community-based economic development agency, Valle Encantado, and a cofounder of Agri-Cultura Network, a cooperative of small farms. He is presently the program officer of the McCune Foundation of New Mexico.

Lee Reynis, PhD, an accomplished economist, has served as city economist for the City of Albuquerque and chief economist for the New Mexico Department of Finance and Administration. She is the immediate past director of the University of New Mexico Bureau of Business and Economic Research, which is noted for its highly respected economic and other research, studies, and reports.

Gabriel R. Sánchez, PhD, is an associate professor of political science at the University of New Mexico, and the director of research at Latino Decisions. He is presently also executive director of the UNM Robert Wood Johnson Center for Health Policy.

Shannon Sánchez-Youngman is a doctoral student in political science at the University of New Mexico and a fellow with the UNM Robert Wood Johnson Center for Health Policy.

Aaron Sussman, MA in community planning, MA in Latin American studies, is a senior transportation planner with the New Mexico Mid-Region Council of Governments and a member of the American Institute of Certified Planners.

Veronica E. Tiller, PhD, Jicarilla Apache, is a noted authority on American Indians and the author of important books, including *Culture and Customs of Apache Indians* and *American Indian Reservations and Trust Areas*, and is the editor and publisher of an award-winning reference guide to 362 modern Indian tribes, *Tiller's Guide to Indian Country: Economic Profiles of American Indian Reservations.*

Chuck Wellborn, JD, LLM, is an attorney who, after many years of private practice in corporate transactions and startups, became the initial president and CEO of Science & Technology Corporation, University of New Mexico. He has served on the board of directors of the New Mexico Association of Commerce and Energy and of New Mexico Community Capital, and was chairman of the Albuquerque Economic Forum and president of the New Mexico State Bar Foundation. He is presently the chairman of the New Mexico Small Business Investment Company and a principal at Wellborn Strategies, LLC.

Index

Page numbers in italic text indicate tables and charts.